The Accountant's Guide to Legal Liability and Ethics

The Accountant's Guide to Legal Liability and Ethics

Marc J. Epstein, Ph.D.
Harvard Business School

Albert D. Spalding, Jr., J.D., CPA
School of Business Administration
Wayne State University

BUSINESS ONE IRWIN
Homewood, Illinois 60430

IRWIN

Homewood, IL 60430
Boston, MA 02116

© RICHARD D. IRWIN, INC., 1993

This publication is designed to provide accurate and authoritative information in regard to the subject matter covered. It is sold with the understanding that neither the author nor the publisher is engaged in rendering legal, accounting, or other professional service. If legal advice or other expert assistance is required, the services of a competent professional person should be sought.

From a Declaration of Principles jointly adopted by a Committee of the American Bar Association and a Committee of Publishers.

Sponsoring editor: Jeff Shelstad
Senior editor: Michael E. Desposito
Project editor: Stephanie M. Britt
Production manager: Diane Palmer
Designer: Jeanne M. Rivera
Typeface: 10/12 Times Roman
Printer: R. R. Donnelley & Sons Company

Library of Congress Cataloging-in-Publication Data

Epstein, Marc J.
    The accountant's guide to legal liability and ethics / Marc J.
Epstein and Albert D. Spalding, Jr.
      p.   cm.
    Includes index.
    ISBN 1-55623-993-9 ISBN 0-256-13621-1 (alk. paper)
    1. Accountants—Malpractice—United States. 2. Accountants-
-Professional ethics—United States. I. Spalding, Albert D.
II. Title.
KF2920.3.E63 1993
346.7303'3—dc20
[347.30633]   92-35236

Printed in the United States of America
1 2 3 4 5 6 7 8 9 0 DOC 0 9 8 7 6 5 4 3

About the Authors

MARC J. EPSTEIN is presently Visiting Professor on the faculty of the Graduate School of Business Administration, Harvard University in Boston, Massachusetts. He received the bachelor of arts degree from San Francisco State University and his master of business administration and Ph.D. degree in accounting from the University of Oregon. Dr. Epstein has taught at several universities, is active in numerous professional organizations, and has consulted extensively to business and governmental organizations throughout the United States. He is the author of approximately 100 professional papers and numerous books including *The Shareholders' Use of Corporate Annual Reports* (with Moses Pava) and *The Equity Funding Papers: An Anatomy of a Fraud* (with Lee Seidler and Frederick Andrews).

ALBERT D. SPALDING, JR., is on the faculty at Wayne State University School of Business Administration in Detroit, Michigan, where he teaches in the areas of taxation and legal studies, and serves as Director of the Master of Science in Taxation program. He received the bachelor of business administration degree from the University of Michigan, and both the master of business administration degree and the juris doctor degree from George Washington University, Washington, D.C. "Bert" Spalding is a certified public accountant as well as an attorney, and served for several years as a tax law specialist at the Internal Revenue Service National Office, Washington, D.C. He is the author of one other book and several articles on legal and tax subjects of interest to both attorneys and accountants.

Preface

The U.S. legal system has turned its guns onto the accounting profession. As accountants are hammered with lawsuits, judgments, and settlements, the profession is itself at risk.

If accountants perform a valuable service within the U.S. economy, they must survive the current crisis. But if lawsuits and recent legislative initiatives are any indication, accountants should not expect help from the government. They must take stock of the situation, design strategies for innovation, and move forward.

This book participates in the process of helping individual accountants find solutions. It is not intended to serve as a substitute for the engagement of legal counsel, so it is not written as a law book. Nor is it intended to summarize and restate all of the efforts of the profession (including those of the American Institute of Certified Public Accountants) to address the issues. Instead, this book proposes new ways of looking at the legal and regulatory environment, and suggests that a profession comprised of individual accountants can change, even as individual practitioners change. Much of the analysis goes to the very heart of the legal, philosophical and ethical foundation upon which the profession is built.

In 1994 a new section of the CPA exam will focus on Professional Responsibilities. In addition, the notorious white collar crimes of the 1980s have focused more attention than ever on ethics in all professions. But probably most important has been the steady increase in litigation involving accountants and auditors. The seventh largest accounting firm, Laventhol and Horwath, filed bankruptcy because of liabilities to clients and third parties. The Savings and Loan debacle has caused numerous financial institutions, investors, depositors and federal government agencies to seek compensation from accountants, and settlements have been in the hundreds of millions of dollars.

Accounting firms are being sued in record numbers, and for record amounts, and are at the center of the ongoing United States litigation explosion. Accountants are in a quandary as to their role in society, their responsibilities to their clients and other various constituencies, and their legal and ethical responsibilities. What seemed clear a decade ago is much less clear today and the potential liabilities are substantially greater.

Accountants seek guidance on how to conduct their practices in ways that minimize their potential legal liabilities. This book provides that guidance. It is intended to be an easy to read book that provides an overview of the areas of legal liability and ethical responsibility, in language that the practicing accountant can understand. It also provides case references for those accountants, lawyers or students who need further details. It is more than a reference book; it is a user-friendly companion and guide to the issues.

For the lawyers who specialize in accountants' legal liability, this book will provide an overview but will not suffice. But for the vast numbers of accountants who want to have a better understanding of the liability issues, the book is a good balance between past cases and current guidance. The book is also useful to attorneys who would like a general overview of the subject and case references for when they have such a need.

With the increased focus on ethics in the profession, the book provides the practicing accountant with discussion of the key ethical issues and some guidance on ways to resolve them. The book also discusses the areas of litigation support services and liability insurance.

Finding solutions in a changing environment is an ongoing process. We proffer not only this analysis, but our continuing involvement in the form of the supplement described on the next page. To us, the goal is not only survival, but the achievement of new levels of excellence. We believe that the profession can climb to new heights, and that this can be accomplished only when the financial and legal forces within the economy recognize such excellence.

Marc J. Epstein
Albert D. Spalding, Jr.

Notice of Supplement

As of the writing of this book, U.S. courts and legislatures continue to wrestle with the issues addressed herein. Any "balance sheet" assessment of the accounting profession will change over the months ahead.

For this reason, it is expected that this book will be supplemented by the authors when necessary. The supplement(s) will serve as interim updates pending future revisions of this work, and will include:

- Significant court decisions that impact the profession.
- Legislative developments, including movement toward tort reform and limited liability corporations.
- Promulgations of GAAS and GAAP, especially those dealing with matters that are the subject of lawsuits (and legislative and regulatory initiatives).
- Other professional developments, with particular attention to those developments reflecting an evolution of the ethics and underlying assumptions of the accounting profession.

A business reply card is provided in the back of this book. Please return it if you wish to be placed on the mailing list to be notified of supplements. There is no obligation when putting your name on the mailing list, and no invoice will be sent until a supplement has been delivered to you.

Contents in Brief

Contents

Chapter Nine
FORENSIC ACCOUNTING

Chapter Ten
OTHER SPECIAL ENGAGEMENTS AND RESPONSIBILITIES

Chapter One

Introduction

The Litigation Assault
Treating the Symptoms
Finding a Real Solution
Charting a Course
An Ongoing Process
Notes

What will happen to the U.S. accounting profession over the next decade? As juries award multimillion dollar recoveries to plaintiffs "injured" by the work of accountants, will the profession shrink out of sight? If one or more of the large, national firms join Laventhol and Horwath (and several others) in becoming insolvent,[1] what will be the effect on Wall Street and on the U.S. economy? And if smaller accounting firms are unable to purchase professional liability insurance, due to the costs associated with a recent increase in litigation and in awards against the accounting profession, and stop issuing financial statements, how will their small and medium-size businesses obtain financing?

THE LITIGATION ASSAULT

In recent years, the trend toward increased liability has been experienced by all professionals (e.g., doctors, lawyers, accountants, and engineers). The plight of the medical profession has been the most widely publicized, primarily due to developments in medical malpractice insurance. However, the irony is that doctors are subject to potentially fewer claimants in the course of any one transaction than are accountants. A doctor has to be concerned only with one possible claimant--the patient.

1

When an accountant performs an audit or assists with the preparation of financial statements, however, his or her liability may extend to both the client and such third parties as owners; creditors and suppliers; potential owners, creditors, suppliers, or investors; management; taxing or other government authorities; employees; customers; financial analysts and advisors; stock exchanges; lawyers; regulatory or registration authorities; financial press and reporting agencies; trade associations; and labor unions. All of these parties are potential plaintiffs in an accountant's liability lawsuit.[2]

The accountant must be concerned not only with his or her own legal liability, but with that of others in the profession as well. What happens to one accountant affects the entire profession. When standards that accountants have learned to depend on are rejected by the courts and the Securities and Exchange Commission (SEC), the entire profession suffers. When an insurance company must provide an expensive legal defense or settle an exorbitant claim, the entire profession pays. Remember that not every doctor had to be sued before medical malpractice premiums were raised 600 percent. And not every accountant will have to be sued. There are now thousands of claims pending against accountants, most involving insurers.

Today, we live in a very consumer-oriented society. The consumer demands to know everything necessary to avoid both economic and physical injury. Thus, the courts and SEC are placing greater burdens upon the accountants to provide more complete disclosure. The focus is shifting away from what the accounting profession perceives its standards to be and toward the reasonable expectations of the average investor or user of financial statements.

We also live in a litigious society. It seems like every time you pick up a newspaper, someone is getting sued--often an accountant. It is beginning to approach the point that every time a business becomes insolvent, the public accountant is automatically sued and the accountant is often the only "deep pocket." Often the client company has declared bankruptcy and the public accountant is the only one available to provide shareholders with money to pay for their losses. Further, some lawyers regularly check for decreases in stock prices and then proceed against the accountants in the hope of obtaining a settlement for a class action lawsuit. The thinking seems to be either that the accountant's insurer will foot the bill and pay off, or that there is nothing to lose in trying. Even when the accountant wins or settles the claim through his or her insurer, the cost of victory can be as expensive as the price of defeat.

When the "privity" rule (described in Chapter Three) was relaxed and nonclients (such as suppliers and market investors) were given permission to bring accountants to trial over the correctness and reliability of financial statements, the litigation explosion increased. Claims against accountants have multiplied, and plaintiffs are utilizing both common law negligence doctrines as well as newer statutory bases (such as the Racketeering Influenced and Corrupt Organizations, or RICO, legislation) in their efforts to recover from accountants.[3] Class action suits are common.[4] As one writer noted, accountants "are frequently the only solvent party left in the wake of corporate bankruptcy."[5] The auditor is a prime target in litigation claiming investor and creditor economic losses because it is the only available (and solvent) entity that had any direct contact with the client's business affairs.[6]

Recent Litigation. Recent litigation has been especially troublesome. One jury awarded $200 million to investors of Miniscribe Corporation, against Coopers & Lybrand, upon concluding that the accounting firm was partially at fault when the now-defunct corporation falsified its financial records.[7] Coopers is also faced with a $200 million lawsuit pertaining to the embattled Phar-Mor, Inc.[8]

The amount of the fee earned by an accountant appears to have little bearing on the amount of the judgment against the accountant if an engagement results in a lawsuit. An Arizona jury, for example, recently awarded claimants $338 million, against Price Waterhouse & Company, an amount equal to approximately 1,000 times the audit fee charged by Price Waterhouse in connection with a bank acquisition that went sour.[9] As Walter K. Olson, a senior fellow at the Manhattan Institute and author of "The Litigation Explosion: What Happened When America Unleashed the Lawsuit"[10] pointed out recently, "This extreme imbalance between the amount taken in as a fee and the amount that was going on in the transaction for which you can be sued is one of the things that drives accountants batty."[11]

Failures of thrift institutions have generated an entire body of lawsuits against accounting firms. One firm, Arthur Andersen & Company, shed many of its savings and loan clients during the mid-1980s, but it recently agreed to a $30 million settlement in the Lincoln Savings and Loan matter, and is faced with a $400 million lawsuit by the Resolution Trust Corporation pertaining to the accounting firm's involvement with the Benjamin Franklin Savings Association. Another firm, Ernst & Young, agreed to a $63 million settlement to shareholders of Lincoln Savings and Loan, and an additional $37.5 million to the Resolution Trust Corporation.[12] And it cost Coopers and Lybrand $20 million to settle a lawsuit arising from its involvement with the Silverado Banking, Savings and Loan Association.[13]

Both large and small accounting firms have been hit. In assessing a $5,000 fine against a California accounting firm whose assets are less than $100,000, the Federal Deposit Insurance Corporation accused the firm of filing false, misleading information regarding its former client, First Pacific Bancorp Inc.[14]

Ernst & Young recently reached a $400 million settlement with federal regulators, whereby the government agreed to drop several savings and loan-related lawsuits against the firm, including additional claims arising from the Lincoln Savings and Loan case.[15] $300 million of the settlement was covered by professional liability insurance, and the remaining $100 million is payable out of revenues by the 2,000 partners of the firm over four years, averaging $10,000 to $25,000 per partner per year.[16] In addition, three partners have been barred from auditing financial institutions in the future.[17]

Meanwhile, London liquidators of the Bank of Credit and Commerce International (BCCI) have initiated the filing of $8 billion of negligence suits against Price Waterhouse and Ernst & Young.[18] And Deloitte & Touche faces the prospect of hundreds of liability suits spawned by the failure of Executive Life Insurance.[19]

Liability Crisis: Statement of Position. The litigation assault is serious, and it threatens the survival of the accounting profession. If, for example, the BCCI litigation were to result in an $8 billion award against Price Waterhouse and Ernst & Young, both firms would cease to exist.[20]

In view of the peril to the profession, the six largest public accounting firms, Arthur Andersen & Co., Coopers & Lybrand, Deloitte & Touche, Ernst & Young, KPMG Peat Marwick, and Price Waterhouse, issued a joint Statement of Position expressing alarm at the litigation epidemic. The Statement of Position outlined the problem as follows:

> The present liability system has produced an epidemic of litigation that is spreading throughout the accounting profession and the business community. It is threatening the independent audit function and the financial reporting system, the strength of U.S. capital markets, and the competitiveness of the U.S. economy . . . Plaintiffs may simply be seeking to recoup losses from a poor investment decision by going after the most convenient 'deep pocket'-- the auditor.[21]

The Statement of Position also addressed the problem of joint and several liability. Accounting firms, operated as partnerships in most instances, are subject to the general theory of agency law requiring each partner to be liable for the sum total of all claims against the partnership. The Statement of Position makes the following observation:

In practical terms, this means that, even with no evidence of culpability, a company's independent auditors are almost certain to be named in any action filed against that company alleging financial fraud, for no reason other than the auditors' perceived 'deep pockets' or because they are the only potential defendant that is still solvent.[22]

TREATING THE SYMPTOMS

How should accountants deal with these pressures? The following represent some possible responses:

1. *Spend More on Legal Fees and Insurance and Settlements.* Should the accounting profession resign itself to a future of spiraling legal fees and professional liability insurance premiums? The Big Six firms spent $ 477 million on legal fees during 1991.[23] Some observations:

    a. If accountants carry on "business as usual," except for the additional "purchase" of legal services and indemnification, the profession will suffer. As has happened in many specialties within the medical profession, in certain geographical areas, the lawsuit-related costs (including malpractice insurance) can overtake the ability of professionals to generate revenue.

    b. Accounting clients, comprised of businesses, employee plans, municipalities, and other organizations, can only afford to allocate a certain portion of their budget to accounting costs. If accounting services are priced higher than these organizations can (or choose) to pay, the profession will suffer.

2. *Make More "Expectation Gap" Pronouncements.* Should accountant organizations such as the American Institute of Certified Public Accountants (AICPA) issue more pronouncements declaring that accountants are not, and never have been, and never should be, and never will be, ultimately responsible for the integrity and reliability of information provided by their clients? It is unlikely that this will accomplish anything, because:

a. Courts are not persuaded. Judges and juries tend to believe the plaintiff who claims that he or she relied upon an unqualified auditor's opinion, and understood that opinion to represent a "clean bill of health."[24]

b. Accountants themselves often lapse into statements and use language that make a similar "clean bill of health" implication.[25]

3. *Lobby for Tort Reform.* While statutory limitations on liability would certainly make it easier for the accounting profession to function and to survive, such protection will not save the profession.[26] Judges will, in appropriate circumstances, find ways to levy financial judgements against accountants, such as by imposing criminal penalties (and requirements for restitution), by finding that accountants performed wrongful acts "individually" despite the existence of a corporate structure, and by using other tactics. Since the judicial system represents a "safety valve" for redressing wrongs, it is unlikely that legislative initiatives will completely protect accountants.

4. *Hope for a Judicial Turnaround.* The ebb and flow of judicial opinion is difficult to gauge, and impossible to predict. But some recent cases have slowed, if not reversed, the trend toward increasing liability for accountants. Examples:

a. The New York Court of Appeals case of *Security Pacific Business Credit v. Peat Marwick Main & Co.*,[27] where the traditional privity rule of the *Ultramares* case (See Chapter Three) was upheld in that jurisdiction.

b. The California Supreme Court case of *Bily v. Arthur Young & Co.*,[28] which overturned prior decisions expanding the scope of auditor liability in that jurisdiction.

c. The federal court dismissal of the *Gruber v. Price Waterhouse* case[29], setting aside claims of securities law violations against the accounting firm.

    d.   The federal court dismissal of *Federal Deposit Insurance Corporation v. Ernst & Young*,[30] relieving the accounting firm of a $560 million savings and loan claim.

5. *Avoid Audits and Related Services.* This alternative is being selected by many smaller accounting firms.[31] As a result, medium and small business clients, and those clients not able or willing to hire a Big Six national accounting firm, are unable to obtain financing without audited, or at least reviewed, financial statements. Job formation and economic growth then become the consequential victims of the litigation assault on accountants.

6. *Avoid Certain Industries.* Some industries, such as those involved with high technology or banking, are already viewed as high risk.[32] When the accountants' liability risk becomes too high, auditors will be unavailable for companies in these industries.

FINDING A REAL SOLUTION

Legislative initiatives, a willingness to render a strong and stern defense in the courtroom, and the issuance of self-defining promulgations all have an important role in the accounting profession's strategy for self-preservation. But any real solution to the legal problems faced by the profession must respond to some very basic questions being asked by judges, legislators, and other representatives of our larger society, such as:

- When society licenses accountants as "certified public" accountants, what should it expect in return?
- How can the accounting profession's standards of performance be aligned with the standards imposed by courts on professions generally?
- How can accountants be made aware that their own (often self-serving) pronouncements and rules are quite properly viewed with a healthy cynicism by the courts, and are sometimes rightly overridden by judicially imposed standards?
- To what extent should society expect accountants to be the guarantors of the information they audit (and about which they render an opinion)?

CHARTING A COURSE

The problem faced by the accounting profession is not the extent to which accountants are being sued. The problem is that the courts (and, to some extent, legislators) are questioning the very assumptions upon which the profession is built.

It is time for accountants to ask questions about those assumptions, too-- and to participate in the process of resolving those questions.

This book explores the legal and ethical environment surrounding accountants. It is not merely an aggregation of information derived from court cases, statutes, and other sources. It is intended to assist accountants in analyzing that environment--and in responding to it.

The potential liability that faces the accounting profession today must be systematically approached with meaningful direction. Therefore, readers of this book are encouraged to carefully examine within these chapters the broad spectrum of the accountant's legal liability. The chapters seek to integrate theory and reality by utilizing accounting and legal concepts illustrated through significant court cases and current developments.

Chapter Two presents the common law legal liability of the public accountant to his or her client. The chapter begins with an overview of the legal relationship that exists between the accountant and the client, and based on this relationship, liability is described in terms of breach of contract and negligence. The four elements comprising negligence, the most common form of accountant liability, are discussed. The first two of these elements are analyzed from the viewpoint of duty and standard of care. This analysis covers such areas as reporting the client's financial condition, auditing and detecting fraud, and unaudited financial statements. The chapter concludes with a discussion of contributory negligence as a defense for the accountant.

In Chapter Three, the accountant's common law legal liability is further developed to include an examination of liability to third parties. The chapter explores the concept of privity and how it relates to third-party liability. The traditional view takes the position that there is no liability in the absence of privity. The modern view incorporates the *Restatement (Second) of the Law of Torts* and imposes liability on the accountant for negligence to foreseen and limited classes of persons. In addition to negligence, the chapter examines two other forms of liability--actual fraud and constructive fraud, both of which constitute the basis for third-party liability under all views.

In Chapter Four, the emphasis shifts from common law liability to statutory liability. The chapter examines federal laws relevant to the accountant's legal liability. The objectives of the Securities Act of 1933 are briefly summarized, and the specific provisions pertaining to registration misrepresentations found in Section 11 of the Act are reviewed. Included in this discussion are such topics as the due diligence defense, the S-1 review, statute of limitations, and the implications of Section 11. The chapter next examines the Securities Exchange Act of 1934, which established the SEC and provides for continuous disclosure by users listing and trading securities on stock exchanges or possessing assets over $1 million and 500 or more shareholders. The relevant sections under this Act include Section 18 (filing false documents with the SEC) and Rule 10b-5 (fraud) of Section 10(b) of the Act. The accounting provisions of the Foreign Corrupt Practices Act are also presented. The chapter concludes with an examination of the Racketeering Influenced and Corrupt Organizations Act (RICO), which has been used as a means of seeking treble damages in lawsuits against accountants.

Chapter Five examines the accountant's criminal liability based primarily upon federal statutes. Various criminal provisions of the Securities Act of 1933, the Securities and Exchange Act of 1934, the Federal Mail Fraud Statute, the Federal False Statement Statute, the Internal Revenue Code, and RICO are discussed. The analysis of four major court cases, *U.S. v. Benjamin*, *Continental Vending*, *Equity Funding*, and *National Student Marketing*, facilitates this discussion.

Chapter Six explores the extent of an accountant's obligation for the discovery of fraud and systemic weaknesses. Under the traditional approach, the accounting profession took the position that the discovery of fraud, embezzlement, and other hard-to-discover problems was not included in the services for which an accountant is usually engaged. Subsequent to the issuance of nine "expectation gap" statements on auditing standards by the AICPA, however, the profession has accepted some responsibility for the discovery of these types of problems during an audit engagement. The chapter concludes by describing the balance between expensive superaudit procedures (designed to discover fraud and systemic weaknesses) and the need for cost-effective audits of financial statements that must be sought in every auditing engagement.

Chapter Seven deals with the legal liability in reporting the findings of an audit performed by the accountant. The chapter analyzes four degrees of responsibility, one of which the accountant must choose to assume when the accountant's name is associated with audited financial statements. Emphasis is placed upon the clarity of the language being communicated and upon the relationship in disclaimers or qualifications of content versus form. The legal liability associated with the accountant's assistance with the issuance of financial statements that are merely "compiled" or "reviewed" by the accountant are also examined. The chapter concludes with a discussion of subsequently discovered facts existing at the date of the report, and a look at the unresolved accountant-attorney controversy over disclosure of pending and unasserted litigation, claims, and assessments.

In Chapter Eight, the entire subject shifts to the accountant's legal liability as a tax practitioner. The AICPA's *Statements on Responsibilities in Tax Practice* are examined in light of the guidance they provide in such areas as the accountant's responsibilities in signing a tax return as a preparer; the reasonableness to provide appropriate answers on the return; use of estimates; tax advice to clients; and other aspects of the accountant's tax assistance to clients. Also discussed are the Treasury Department's requirements in its Circular 230, which provides the rules of practice before the IRS. The chapter next examines the confidential accountant-client privilege and areas of potential criminal liability for the tax practitioner. Finally, potential liability for the unauthorized practice of law is discussed in the context of an accountant's tax practice.

Chapters Nine and Ten explore the accountant's emerging exposure to liability for his or her services rendered in the context of special engagements. In particular, the accountant's role in litigation support engagements, such as forensic accounting and service as an expert witness, is evaluated. In addition, the accountant's involvement in a review of a client's internal control procedures, as well as a fraud-detection audit, is reviewed. Probate and fiduciary accounting engagements are also discussed.

Chapter Eleven examines the accountant's professional liability insurance. The chapter points out the effect that the growing wave of litigation is having upon insurance companies and in turn, upon the accountant through higher premiums and fewer sources. The two major types of professional liability insurance being offered--occurrence and claims-made--are described. The chapter concludes with some suggestions of what to look for in a policy when purchasing professional liability insurance.

Chapters Twelve and Thirteen explore ethical issues facing accountants. First, historical catalysts for change within the profession (lawsuits, legislation, regulation) are compared to the profession's own need to develop a foundation for ethics within the profession. The roles of codes of conduct, peer review, and other self-regulatory tactics are discussed.

Second, specific ethical situations facing accountants are explored. Ethical conflicts involving confidentiality, insider information, loyalty to the client, whistle-blowing, discrimination, and other ethical concerns confront the accountant on a regular basis. These difficult situations are discussed with a view to the development of an ethical framework that will guide the accountant through these dangerous waters.

Chapter Fourteen reviews those areas that have placed the accountant in a vulnerable position, and another look is taken at third-party liability. The chapter examines the accountant's client, the engagement contract between the parties, and the documentary evidence that the accountant may need in litigation.

Those common factors that lead to litigation--suing the client for fees, client insolvency, and weak internal control--are fully developed. The chapter discusses the variety of views the courts have expressed as to the profession's standard of care and some insight is offered as to what "the" standard may be.

The authors are aware that some parts of this book tend to be somewhat technical. This is unavoidable due to the nature of the material covered. Because of this, the chapters include nontechnical summaries of concepts developed, and of cases discussed. Readers are encouraged to use these summaries and tables as references for the key points in the legal liability of the accountant. Important case references are also included so that further information can be easily obtained on specific cases.

AN ONGOING PROCESS

As of the writing of this book, U.S. courts and legislatures continue to wrestle with the issues addressed herein. Any "balance sheet" assessing the accounting profession will change over the months ahead.

For this reason, it is expected that this book will be supplemented by the authors when necessary. The supplement(s) will serve as interim updates pending future revisions of this work, and will include:

- Significant court decisions that impact the profession.
- Legislative developments, including movement toward tort reform and limited liability corporations.
- Promulgations of GAAS and GAAP, especially those dealing with matters that are the subject of lawsuits (and legislative and regulatory initiatives).
- Other professional developments, with particular attention to those developments reflecting an evolution of the ethics and underlying assumptions of the accounting profession.

A business reply card is provided in the back of this book. Please return it if you wish to be placed on the mailing list to be notified of supplements. There is no obligation when putting your name on the mailing list, and no invoice will be sent until a supplement has been delivered to you.

NOTES

1. *See* Donna K. H. Walter, "New Liability Twist Has Lawyers, Accountants Scurrying," *L.A. Times*, March 29, 1992, p. D1.
2. *See* Willis W. Hagen II, Certified Public Accountant's Liability for Malpractice: Effect of Compliance with GAAP and GAAS, 13 J.Contemp. Law 65, 66 (1987); John A. Siliciano, Negligent Accounting and the Limits of Instrumental Tort Reform, 86 Mich.L.Rev.1929, 1931 (1988).
3. Michele Gales, "Litigation Blitz Hits Accountants," *The National Law Journal*, June 16, 1986, p. 1, 26-27.
4. L. Berton, "Audit Firms Are Hit by More Investor Suits for Not Finding Fraud," *The Wall Street Journal*, January 14, 1989, p. A1, A12.
5. N. N. Minow, "Accountants' Liability and the Litigation Explosion," *Journal of Accountancy*, September 1984, pp. 70-86.
6. John A. Siliciano, Negligent Accounting and the Limits of Instrumental Tort Reform 86 Mich.L.Rev.1929, 1932-1933 (1988).
7. Kevin Moran, "Disk Maker Faces Fraud Judgment," *Houston Chronicle*, February 5, 1992, Business p. 1. The case was reportedly settled for $95 million prior to appeal. *See*, Michael Connor, "Accountants Looking for Shelter from Lawsuits," *Reuter Business Report*, November 24, 1992.
8. Emily Barker, Big Suits: Phar-Mor v. Coopers & Lybrand, *The American Lawyer*, October 1992, p.84. Coopers has filed a counter-suit against the former client, charging that its management had defrauded the accounting firm. *See* Bloomberg Business News, "Accountants Sue Phar-Mor," *New York Times*, September 12, 1992, Sec. 1; p. 35; Col. 5 (Financial Desk).
9. Philip A. Lacovara, "'Follow the Money:' Should Lawyers and Accountants Pay for the Sins of their Clients?" *The Washington Post*, July 21, 1992, p. A19.
10. New York: E.P. Dutton, 1991.
11. *See*, Jennifer E. King, "Recent Malpractice Suits Driving Up the Cost of Lawyers Liability Insurance," *Illinois Legal Times* (November 1992).
12. *See* Alison Leigh Cowan, "Big Law and Accounting Firms to Pay Millions in S.& L. Suit," *New York Times*, March 31, 1992.
13. Stewart Yerton, "Federal Help To Fight Off Fraud Suits,"*American Lawyer*, October, 1992, p. 40.
14. "Federal Reserve Imposes Fine On CPA Firm for Errant Filing: Fed Sending Signals?," *Thomson's International Bank Accountant*, Vol. 2; No. 36; p. 1 (September 28, 1992).
15. *Ibid.* Other savings and loans involved in the settlement included Western Savings Association of Phoenix; Vernon Savings and Loan Association of Dallas; and Silverado Banking Savings and Loan of Denver, where former U.S. President Bush's son Neil served as a director. *See*, Susan Schmidt, "Ernst & Young Pays $ 400 Million To Settle Thrift Regulators' Claims," *The Washington Post*, November 24, 1992, p.A1.
16. Stephen Labaton, "$400 Million Bargain for Ernst," *The New York Times*, November 25, 1992, Sec. D; p. 1; Col. 3.
17. Schmidt, *supra* note 15.
18. *See* Richard W. Stevenson, "Lawsuits to Seek Billions from B.C.C.I. Auditors," *New York Times*, October 1, 1992, Sec. D., P. 4, Col. 3 (Financial Desk).; *See also*, Gavin Souter, "BCCI Suit to Seek Billions from Auditors," *Business Insurance*, November 2, 1992, p.23.
19. M. A., "A Flood of Litigation: Liability Suits Add Up on Accountants," *Austin Business Journal*, September 28, 1992, Vol 12, No. 32, Sec. 1; p. 9.
20. *Ibid.*

21. ARTHUR ANDERSEN & CO., COOPERS & LYBRAND, DELOITTE & TOUCHE, ERNST & YOUNG, KPMG PEAT MARWICK, AND PRICE WATERHOUSE, THE LIABILITY CRISIS IN THE UNITED STATES: IMPACT ON THE ACCOUNTING PROFESSION (August 6, 1992), p.2.

22. *Ibid.*

23. *Ibid.*

24. *See, e.g.,* In re Epic Mortgage Ins. Litig., 701 F. Supp. 1192, 1212; Fed. Sec. L. Rep. ¶ 94,526 (E.D. Va., 1988) (Plaintiffs claimed that it was their understanding that an auditor's report gave the corporation a "clean bill of health.")

25. *See, e.g.,* Ahern v. Gaussoin, 611 F. Supp. 1465 (D.C. D. Oregon, 1985) (accountant made a glowing speech at shareholders' meeting, referring to the auditor's opinion as a "clean bill of health").

26. Some proposals for limitations have been developed by the Washington D.C.-based American Tort Reform Association; others have been introduced by the Coalition to Eliminate Abusive Securities Suits, a multi-industry coalition. *See* Stewart Yerton, "Federal Help To Fight Off Fraud Suits," *American Lawyer,* October 1992, p. 40 (Inside Moves).

27. 165 A.D.2d 622, 569 N.Y.S.2d 57 (N.Y.A.D., 1991).

28. 3 Cal.4th 370, 11 Cal.Rptr.2d 51, 834 P.2d 745, 61 U.S.L.W. 2145, Fed. Sec. L. Rep. ¶ 96,978 (1992), *reversing* Bily v. Arthur Young and Co., 274 Cal.Rptr. 371, 798 P.2d 1214 (1990).

29. Civ. A. No. 86-3976, 1992 WL 240572, 1992 U.S. Dist. LEXIS 14029 (E.D.Pa., Sept. 15, 1992).

30. 967 F.2d 166 (5th Cir. 1992).

31. Lee Berton, "Legal-Liability Awards Are Frightening Smaller CPA Firms Away From Audits," *Wall Street Journal,* March 3,1992, p. B1.; *See also* Mariann Caprino, "Lawsuit-Wary CPAs Screening Potential Clients to Avoid Risk," *Chicago Tribune,* November 19, 1990, p.5.

32. John W. Hill & Michael B. Metzger, Auditor Liability and the S&L Crisis: Shaping the Future of the Profession?, 1992 Ann. Rev. Banking L. 263, 329-31 (1992).

Chapter Two

Liability to Clients Generally

LIABILITY FOR BREACH OF CONTRACT

The contractual relationship that exists between the client and accountant serves as the "foundation of the accountants' responsibilities and rights."[1]

The engagement letter between the accountant and the client forms the basis of the understanding between the accountant and the client. The engagement letter describes what services are to be performed, when they are to be performed, and for whom.

15

For audit engagements, the engagement letter prescribes the exact level and type of services to be performed, and the subject matter of testing to be done.

The contract between the accountant and the client also provides an indication of the amount of fees that will be charged for the described services, and indicates the basis or formula upon which such fees will be calculated. If the accountant does not perform, and the client finds it necessary to hire a replacement accountant, the difference between the fees paid to the new firm and those that would have been paid under the old contract constitute compensatory damages for which the old accountant is liable.

Deadlines for the completion of services, as indicated or implied in the contract between the accountant and the client, are an important element of the accountant's duty. If the deadlines are not met, the accountant may be held liable for breach of contract unless circumstances not anticipated by the parties and not within the control of the accountant are involved.

Other monetary losses arising from an accountant's breach of contract may be recoverable. If, for example, a client is precluded from obtaining financing for a profitable venture or expansion due to errors in the audit of the client's financial statements, the client might be able to show a court measurable damages arising from the error. This, in turn, would add to the amount otherwise recoverable from the accountant as a result of the breach of contract.

LIABILITY FOR NEGLIGENCE

It has long been asserted that within every contract, there is a "common law duty to perform with care, skill, reasonable experience and faithfulness" that which is promised to be performed.[2] It is from this relationship that there arises a duty to exercise due care.

There are also certain classes of contracts which create a relation out of which certain duties arise as implied by law independently of the express terms of the contract, a breach of which will constitute a tort, and in such cases an injured party may sue either for breach of the contract or in tort for breach of the duty imposed by law, the rule being that, where there is a breach of duty imposed by law, an action in tort is not precluded because such duty arises out of a contract relation.[3]

Failure to conform one's conduct to the exercise of reasonable due care may be considered to be a breach of contract, but may also constitute an actionable tort in negligence.

One legal commentator explains the difference between contractual liability and tort liability by distinguishing nonfeasance, which is the complete nonperformance of a promise, and misfeasance, a defective performance.[4]

The remedy for the former would lie in contract, and the remedy for the latter would lie in either tort or contract. Another approach that has been take is that the contract induces the tort:

> Wherever there is carelessness, recklessness, want of reasonable skill, or the violation or disregard of a duty which the law implies from the conditions or attendant circumstances, and individual injury results therefrom, an action on the case lies in favor of the party injured; and if the transaction had its origin in a contract, which places the parties in such relation, as that, in performing or attempting to perform the service promised, the tort or wrong is committed, then the breach of the contract is not the gravamen of the suit. There may be no technical breach of the letter of the contract. The contract, in such case, is more inducement, and should be so stated in pleading. It induces, causes, creates the conditions or state of things which furnishes the occasion of the tort.[5]

Today, modern statutes permit the plaintiff to plead alternative causes of action. Therefore, the significance between alleging negligence and breach of contract is now mostly procedural, such as the measure of damages, venue, jurisdiction, statute of limitations, and burden of proof.

Liability for negligence, whether it be based on an action in tort or contract, represents *a departure from a uniform standard of care*.[6] This standard has been affectionately referred to as being characterized by the "reasonable person."

> This insufferable creature, who stalks through every chapter of the law of torts and is not above meddling with contracts as well, has a way of life which is all his own. He never reads a newspaper while walking along the street or steps off a pavement without looking both ways; he makes regular tests of the tire-pressures on his motorcar; he never leaves a letter unanswered for more than forty-eight hours; he always puts on goggles when working a lathe; before buying a railway ticket he reads the conditions of carriage contained in the companies' handbills; he knows the difference between felony and misdemeanor; he is always on the look out for a loose stair rod

in his house and for buttrot in the elm trees in his garden; he does not forget to turn the gas off; he pays no attention to rumor or gossip; he has never been known to make a joke; and if he has not long been divorced by his wife it can only be because she is the Reasonable Woman--a character unknown to the law. Although the Reasonable Man does not make the mistake of supposing that other people are as prudent as he is, he has strong views about what they will say or do (or at any rate what they ought to do) in any given circumstances, and these views he conveys to the legal profession.[7]

If an individual possesses special skill and knowledge, ordinary reasonable care alone is not sufficient; he must also exercise a minimum standard of that special skill, ability, and knowledge he purports to possess.[8] A well-noted excerpt from Cooley's *Tort* states:

> In all those employments where peculiar skill is requisite, if one offers his services, he is understood as holding himself out to the public as possessing the degree of skill commonly possessed by others in the same employment, and if his pretensions are unfounded, he commits a species of fraud upon every man who employs him in reliance on his public profession. But no man, whether skilled or unskilled, undertakes that the task he assumes shall be performed successfully, and without fault or error; he undertakes for good faith and integrity, but not for infallibility, and he is liable to his employer for negligence, bad faith, or dishonesty, but not for losses consequent upon mere errors of judgment.[9]

The duty, then, is to observe that degree of care that would be observed by an ordinary, prudent member of his or her profession.

This definition is broad and probably represents how negligence is most commonly viewed. However, negligence involves more than this to be actionable in a court of law. Before liability for negligence can be imposed, the following elements must be found to exist:

1. A duty to conform to a required *standard* of conduct (standard of care).
2. A failure or *breach of duty* to conform to that required standard.

3. *Causal connection* or "proximate cause" between the defendant's conduct and plaintiff's damage. Other definitions: conduct is a substantial factor in producing the damage; the damage is the natural and probable consequence of the conduct; or the damage was foreseeable.
4. Actual loss or damage incurred by the plaintiff.[10]

These requirements for proving liability are illustrated in **Figure 1.** In summary, the defendant has a duty to the plaintiff to avoid departing from that standard of conduct that will proximately cause the plaintiff damage.

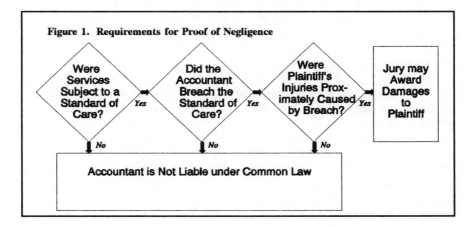

Figure 1. Requirements for Proof of Negligence

In applying this legal definition of negligence to the public accountant, a duty is owed by the accountant to the person or persons who engaged the accountant (and possibly to third parties--see Chapter Three) based on a formal written contract or an engagement letter. The public accountant's engagement most often involves either the performance of an audit or the preparation of unaudited financial statements ("write-up work"). It may also involve investigation of internal control (see Chapter Six), tax services (see Chapter Eight), bookkeeping services, or other management services.

Joint and Several Liability

If a judgment is entered against an accounting firm, each partner or owner of that firm is generally liable for the entire amount of the judgment, until it is paid in full. That is because under the common law doctrine of joint and several liability, when two or more persons' torts together cause an injury, each tortfeasor is liable to the victim for the total damages.[11]

If a successful plaintiff is able to levy against a partner in an accounting firm, and to recover a large portion of a judgment from that partner, the partner has no legal recourse under the common law for obtaining reimbursement from his or her partners, or from the firm itself. Common law does not permit mitigation of the joint and several liability rule through contribution, and courts have generally refused to entertain suits by joint tortfeasors who sought partial reimbursement from others who shared blame for their victims' injuries.[12] The rationale was that a joint tortfeasor had no one but himself or herself to blame and that courts should not be burdened by having to assess the relative fault of wrongdoers.[13]

In addition to its common law applicability, many statutes impose the doctrine of joint and several liability in certain types of legal actions, such as lawsuits involving violations of securities laws,[14] and those involving breach of fiduciary duty by pension trustees,[15] and certain penalty provisions of the Internal Revenue Code.[16]

Methods of Pro-Rating. Many jurisdictions are moving away from the common law approach to joint and several liability, toward a system that provides indemnity based on differences in relative fault.[17] This allows a tortfeasor, such as the partner in charge of an engagement, to be held responsible for most or all of a judgment pertaining to that engagement.[18] Otherwise, a minimally culpable defendant, such as a partner in another state or another country, might have to bear the burden of an entire judgment even though the actual tortfeasor was solvent. Seeing merit in this approach, many states and most legal commentators have rejected a per se bar against contribution.[19]

There are three basic methods for determining how much a judgment against a nonsettling defendant should be reduced in light of a settlement by the remaining defendants. These are the "pro rata," the "proportionate fault" and the "pro tanto" methods.[20]

The pro rata rule apportions an equal share of the liability to each defendant in a lawsuit. Relative culpability is irrelevant under this approach. When, for example, a plaintiff settles with one defendant in a two defendant case, a judgment against the nonsettling defendant is reduced by one-half, regardless of whether the settling defendant was primarily or only minimally culpable.[21] This method can deter plaintiffs from settling with fewer than all the parties.[22]

Under the proportionate fault method, the "jury assesses the relative culpability of both settling and non-settling defendants, and the non-settling defendant pays a commensurate percentage of the judgment."[23] Because the credit determination is made after a determination of liability, the proportionate method is always consistent with fault.

The problem with the proportionate method is that a holdout defendant can make settlement difficult for the plaintiffs, who bear the risk of a bad settlement.[24]   Moreover, determining the relative fault of each party imposes a considerable burden on a factfinder and "obviate[s] much of the advantage of partial settlement to the judicial system."[25]

The pro tanto rule, by contrast, reduces a nonsettling defendant's liability for a judgment against him or her in the amount paid by a settling defendant. The pro tanto method has obvious disadvantages. Like the pro rata method, it can result in judgment reduction that is inconsistent with proportionate fault. Moreover, the pro tanto method leaves "the field of settlement very much open to collusive arrangement between a plaintiff and a favored joint tortfeasor."[26]   Some jurisdictions have recognized this problem and applied a pro tanto approach that requires a showing of good faith and a hearing on culpability before approval of a settlement bar.[27] This approach is more likely to be consistent with equitable principles suggesting that damages should be apportioned in accordance with fault.[28]

Abrogating Joint and Several Liability. Some states are abolishing joint and several liability, and are allowing defendants to designate the parties who are not at fault.[29]   This reduces the attractiveness of lawsuits against larger organizations, such as large accounting firms with offices and partners in more than one jurisdiction. As noted at Chapter One, many accounting firms and organizations are actively seeking abolishment of joint and several liability, especially with regard to cases involving accounting services.

ROLE OF AUDITING STANDARDS

An "audit" is a verification of the financial statements of an entity through an examination of the underlying accounting records and supporting evidence.[30]   In an audit engagement, an accountant reviews financial statements prepared by a client and issues an opinion stating whether such statements fairly represent the financial status of the audited entity.[31] Implicit in the satisfactory performance of an audit are the more recognized procedures of confirming receivables, verification of cash, and observation of inventories.

Determining whether an audit has been conducted in accordance with generally accepted auditing standards (GAAS) depends upon the facts and circumstances of the particular audit. No two audits are identical primarily because the auditor's examination depends upon the adequacy of the client's internal control, from which such reliance the auditor determines the extent of testing and sampling necessary to formulate a sound opinion.

For example, in applying the procedure of confirming receivables with the client's debtors, the failure to use positive confirmation, which requests a reply stating whether or not the amount indicated is correct, may constitute negligence in an audit where internal control is weak. Yet, in another audit where internal control is strong, negative confirmation, which requests a reply only if the amount indicated is incorrect, may be appropriate.

The independent audit is an application of generally accepted auditing standards that have been established by the Auditing Standards Executive Committee of the AICPA as follows:

General Standards

1. The examination is to be performed by a person or persons having adequate technical training and proficiency as an auditor.
2. In all matters relating to the assignment, an independence in mental attitude is to be maintained by the auditor or auditors.
3. Due professional care is to be exercised in the performance of the examination and the preparation of the report.

Standards of Field Work

1. The work is to be adequately planned and assistants, if any, are to be properly supervised.
2. There is to be a proper study and evaluation of the existing internal control as a basis for reliance thereon and for the determination of the resultant extent of the tests to which auditing procedures are to be restricted.
3. Sufficient competent evidential matter is to be obtained through inspection, observation, inquiries, and confirmation to afford a reasonable basis for an opinion regarding the financial statements under examination.

Standards of Reporting

1. The report shall state whether the financial statements are presented in accordance with generally accepted accounting principles (GAAP).
2. The report shall state whether such principles have been consistently observed in the current period in relation to the preceding period.
3. Informative disclosures in the financial statements are to be regarded as reasonably adequate unless otherwise stated in the report.

4. The report shall either contain an expression of opinion regarding the financial statements, taken as a whole, or an assertion to the effect that an opinion cannot be expressed. When an overall opinion cannot be expressed, the reasons therefor should be stated. In all cases where an auditor's name is associated with financial statements, the report should contain a clear-cut indication of the character of the auditor's examination, if any, and the degree of responsibility he is taking.[32]

Generally accepted accounting principles, as referred to in the reporting standards, represent the technical rules and procedures by which accountants construct financial statements. "Promulgated GAAP" consist of the official publications of the American Institute of Certified Public Accountants (i.e. opinions of the Accounting Principles Board, Financial Accounting Standards Board Statements, and Accounting Research bulletins). Where there is no official publication, the consensus of the accounting profession, as manifested for example in textbooks and in the testimony of expert witnesses, determines generally accepted accounting principles.

Auditing standards are interpreted via *Statements on Auditing Standards*, which are promulgated by the Auditing Standards Board of the AICPA. According to the AICPA *Code of Professional Conduct*, every AICPA member must comply with these auditing standards and the accompanying *Statements*,[33] but compliance with other related AICPA publications, such as training materials, *Auditing Interpretations*, and *Statements on Quality Control Standards* is not mandatory. These pronouncements are referred to as "promulgated GAAS," and constitute a subset of the broader universe of "total GAAS" (i.e., the auditing practices of the profession generally).

The relationship between promulgated GAAP and GAAS, and the broader, "full" accounting principles and auditing standards, is depicted in **Figure 2**. These standards (i.e., GAAP and GAAS) constitute a proverbial two-edged sword. On the one hand, if an accountant is sued by a client or other financial statement user, the accountant will be required to justify any deviation from the above standard.[34] The courts generally give the AICPA and FASB promulgations a weight almost equal to law (the "substantive law" effect),[35] and shift the "burden of proof" against the accountant whenever a deviation occurs (the "procedural law" effect).[36]

Compliance v. Liability. On the other hand, 100 percent bonafide compliance with GAAS and GAAP is not necessarily determinative in a court of law.[37] If an accountant's compliance with GAAP and GAAS is being questioned in light of his or her common law duty of due care, the latter duty of due care takes precedence over the fact that he or she complied with the promulgated standards. And the promulgated standards

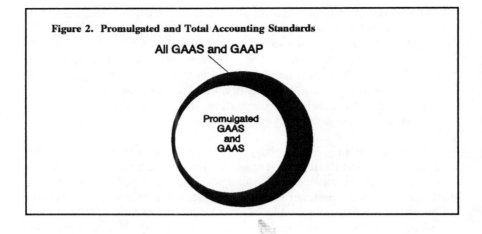

Figure 2. Promulgated and Total Accounting Standards

are meant to be flexible and broad enough that the accounting rules utilized in a particular set of financial statements, and the audit procedures rules employed in the examination of those financial statements, reflect the auditor's individual judgment.

It is this judgment that a jury must weigh in determining whether that requisite degree of care and skill prevailing in the profession was present in the audit. **Figure 3** depicts the independence with which the judicial system approaches the (often self-serving) pronouncements of professional organizations.

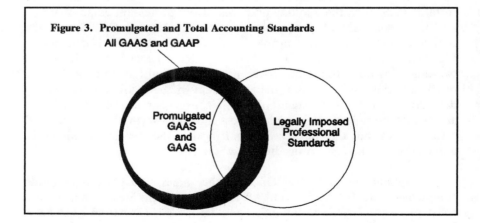

Figure 3. Promulgated and Total Accounting Standards

In addition to the common law requirement of due care, some statutes and regulations require accountants to disclose more than required by GAAS and GAAP, or to preform procedures not anticipated by those standards. For example, the securities laws require non-GAAS disclosures if an investor would have needed the information for purposes of making investment decisions.

And the Foreign Corrupt Practices Act requires disclosures of certain payments to foreign officials, even of those payments are not materials. These statutes are discussed in Chapter Four.

Subjective Materiality. Even some judges have their own ideas about the significance or materiality, for purposes of an accountant's common law duty of due care, of some items of information. In one study, researchers at the University of Arizona surveyed judges, attorneys and accountants with large accounting firm experience. They discovered that the perception of what should be considered "material," for purposes of financial statement disclosure varied widely among the three groups.[38] While very few accountants believed, for example, that a minimum dollar amount (such as $100, irrespective of the size of the audited entity) was a helpful standard for determining whether an item was material, approximately one fourth of the lawyers and judges believed that such a standard was appropriate.[39]

A second study conducted by the same researchers from the University of Arizona revealed that if accountants were to explain the standard of materiality used during the audit (such as in the report letter or in an addendum to the report letter), courts would be less willing to impose an after-the-fact standard of materiality that would render the accountants liable.[40] But the researchers also found that judges were less forgiving of accountants if an "immaterial" (under GAAS standards) defalcation was discovered but not disclosed, that if the same item was not discovered in the first place.[41]

McKesson & Robbins

Generally accepted auditing standards, as they exist today, were greatly influenced by the famous ruling of the SEC in the *McKesson & Robbins* fraud case in 1939.[42] Significant as the case was, it never went to court; instead, it was settled without litigation by the accountants who audited the company. However, *McKesson & Robbins* became the subject of an intense investigation by the Securities and Exchange Commission subsequent to the suspension of trading of McKesson stock on the New York Stock Exchange.

The main perpetrator of the fraud was Philip Musica, who had been convicted in prior years of numerous commercial frauds. Using the alias Frank Donald Coster, he began a pharmaceutical business which he incorporated in January of 1923 under the name of Girard & Co., Inc. In 1926, Coster purchased McKesson & Robbins and merged the two companies in November of that year. Coster was later joined by his three brothers who also used an alias.

Coster's fraud consisted of inflating the value of assets in order to conceal the embezzlement of profits. This overstatement was accomplished by the inclusion of fictitious inventories and accounts receivable, which was easy enough for Coster because he knew that it was not generally recognized that auditing practice required observation of inventories or confirmation of accounts receivable unless specifically requested by the client at an added expense.

In 1937, the year before the fraud was exposed, the financial statements of McKesson & Robbins, Incorporated, and its subsidiaries reported total consolidated assets in excess of $87 million of which approximately $19 million was entirely fictitious. This total represented inventory of $10 million, accounts receivable of $9 million and cash in bank of $75,000. When the end finally came in late 1938, fictitious assets had reached approximately $21 million.

The SEC concluded that even though the auditors had not failed to use procedures considered generally accepted by the profession at the time of the audit, there was a duty to discover such gross overstatements of assets as existed in this case. With immediate response, the American Institute of Accountants adopted inventory observation and confirmation of receivables as required procedures through the issuance of *Extensions of Auditing Procedures*. These procedures added greatly to the profession's auditing standards and, in time, led to the codification of generally accepted auditing procedures in 1951, and eventually the codification of *Statements on Auditing Standards*.

ROLE OF ACCOUNTING PRINCIPLES

One area of liability that is almost certain to continue to plague the accountant is the failure to correctly report information leading to an accurate representation of the client's earnings and financial condition. As long ago as 1887, a famous English decision held that the auditor's duty required more than merely verifying arithmetical accuracy of the balance sheet;[43] there should also be inquiry into its substantial accuracy in order to determine that it contained "a true and correct representation of the state of the company's affairs."[44]

The practice of accounting consists of both product and service. The "service" of the auditor is the audit itself. But the "product" is the group of financial statements, including voluminous footnotes, as certified in the auditor's report letter.

In the course of performing the audit, the auditor must, from time to time, determine whether the client's proposed financial statements comply with GAAP. Courts, in turn, are sometimes asked to review the auditor's work, including technical decisions ranging from methods of calculating interest[45] to the procedures for reporting corporate mergers.[46]

Going Concern

Accounting principles pertaining to the "going concern" assumption illustrate the dangerous grounds upon which accountants tread. The assumption that a client's operation is a "going concern" is a basic accounting principle that permeates financial accounting statements. Accounting rules for the depreciation of assets, or example, presumes that the assets will be used productively over a number of future years. And various classifications of assets, such as inventory and accumulated research and development costs, require a going concern presumption.

Despite the guidance provided by the AICPA in *SAS No. 59, The Auditor's Consideration of an Entity's Ability to Continue as a Going Concern*, auditors must use professional judgment in determining whether a troubled company qualifies as a going concern. If the company becomes insolvent after the audit, various creditors, investors, and other users of the company's audited financial statements will likely inquire as to the propriety of the auditor's decisions during the audit.[47]

The going concern presumption presents a dilemma to the accountant. If the client's operation is failing, and the accountant refuses to issue an unqualified opinion, the accountant's refusal will likely alert creditors to the seriousness of the problem, and the client will be unable to obtain (or retain) access to working capital. The accountant, in such a situation, becomes the executioner of a dying operation.

But if the weakness of the client's operation is not so serious, but the accountant nevertheless applies *SAS No. 59* (and his or her own professional judgment), an adverse auditor's report could kill an otherwise recoverable operation.

Despite the above dilemma, an auditor is generally protected during the litigation that often follows the insolvency of a client if the auditor did, in fact, express going concern qualifications in his or her report. That is because the expression of doubts about a client's ability to continue as a going concern does signal to creditors and investors the seriousness of the financial condition of the client.[48]

"The Standards are Only Evidentiary"

Courts are often asked to sift through the technical GAAP and GAAS standards in resolving claims against auditors. Courts are generally willing to accept the official pronouncements of the FASB, AICPA, and other professional standard-setting organizations as the embodiment of the "standard of care" applicable to litigants.

The judicial acceptance of promulgated standard varies, however. In part, the variance stems from different legal standards of due care in different jurisdictions. But the perceptions and attitudes of the judiciary toward the role of the accountant also cause some of the discrepancy. Some judges, for example, view the accounting discipline as an art, while others do not believe auditors should use samples. Some members of the judiciary perceive accountants as public watchdogs, while others view accountants as guarantors of the information audited. Until the judiciary can develop a narrower consensus of the accountant's role, its acceptance of promulgated GAAS and GAAP will be inconsistent.[49]

As a result of these differences, the courts sometimes require that accountants go beyond promulgated GAAP and GAAS to the larger body of standards represented by a consensus of the profession. And occasionally the courts set aside GAAS and GAAP entirely when they determine that the overall professional standards of care (without regard to of the protestations of the accounting profession) comprise the appropriate criteria for judicial review of the actions of accountants.[50] In the words of one judge, "the AICPA standards are only evidentiary."[51] **Figure 4** shows the various approaches that courts take in adjudicating claims against accountants.

UNAUDITED FINANCIAL STATEMENTS

An area of liability that has been described in terms of uncertainty is the duty owed by the public accountant when preparing unaudited financial statements or "write-up work." During the period from the late 1960s to the mid-1970s, a series of court cases brought the nonaudit services of accountants under judicial scrutiny. The first of these was *Ryan v. Kanne*,[52] in which the court acknowledged that the accountant and his client had agreed that certain financial information would be prepared by the accountant but that it would be "unaudited" (and marked "unaudited" on each page). Nevertheless, the court determined that the responsibilities of the engagement of the accountant constituted a *de facto audit*, and that the accountant was liable for inaccuracies in the financial information.

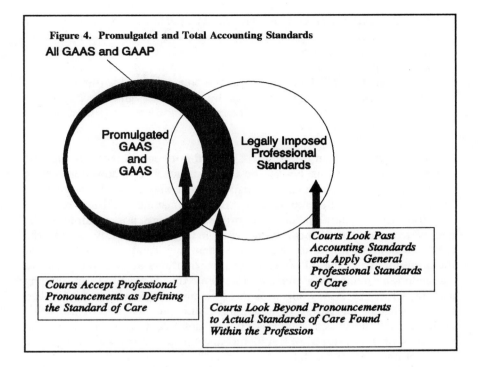

Figure 4. Promulgated and Total Accounting Standards

All GAAS and GAAP

Promulgated GAAS and GAAS

Legally Imposed Professional Standards

Courts Look Past Accounting Standards and Apply General Professional Standards of Care

Courts Accept Professional Pronouncements as Defining the Standard of Care

Courts Look Beyond Pronouncements to Actual Standards of Care Found Within the Profession

The most prominent of the new line of cases, however, was the New York case of *1136 Tenants' Corp. v. Max Rothenberg & Co.*[53] The plaintiff in that case, an unincorporated apartment cooperative, brought suit against the defendant CPAs for failure to detect a major fraud perpetrated by the plaintiff's managing agent, Riker & Co. The defendant claimed that its engagement called for only bookkeeping services and not the performance of an audit. Due to the oral nature of the engagement contract, the scope of the engagement was the primary issue. The court held that the defendant undertook to perform an audit and that since "the simplest audit procedures would have revealed Riker's defalcation," the audit was negligently performed.

If the appellate court's opinion had focused solely on the question of the scope of the engagement and no more, the *Rothenberg* decision, though strongly illustrating the importance of a written engagement contract, certainly would not have gained the prominence it has ultimately attained. However, the court went beyond the triable issues of the case in directing itself, by way of dictum, to the question of liability for unaudited statements in stating:

Moreover, *even if* defendant were hired to perform only "write-up" services, it is clear, beyond dispute, that it did become aware that material invoices purportedly paid by Riker were missing, and, accordingly, had a duty to at least inform plaintiff of this. But even this it failed to do. Defendant was not free to consider these and other suspicious circumstances as being of no significance and prepare its financial reports as if same did not exist.[54] [Emphasis in original.]

The court ruled that even if the CPA had not necessarily been engaged to audit the corporations' books, the CPA was not free to consider missing invoices and other suspicious circumstances as being of no significance, or to prepare financial statements as if those circumstances did not exist.

Prior to this opinion, auditing procedures were not required to be applied to unaudited financial statements. In fact, the only duty owed by the public accountant was to disclose to the client any fraud actually known by the accountant. It should be noted that accountants are not permitted to associate their names with financial statements they believe to be misleading and, therefore, by associating with those financial statements, it is implied that no such belief exists. It is apparent that the majority of the court believed that the missing invoices put the defendant on notice as to the possibility of the existence of fraud, and that the defendant was negligent in not informing the plaintiff.

The *1136 Tenants' Corp.* case received a great deal of attention in the accounting professional press, as well as in the briefs of plaintiffs' attorneys, and several other similar cases in other states followed in its wake. In the Minnesota case of *Bonhiver v. Graff*,[55] for example, a CPA was also held liable in a write-up engagement, and, in fact, one that was never completed. Again, the court held that the accountant's actual awareness of certain facts (that, if analyzed, would lead to the conclusion that an employee was embezzling) could not be ignored by the CPA. Instead, the court ruled that the CPA should have investigated the situation more thoroughly (even though not actually engaged to do so). And in the Nebraska case of *Seedkem, Inc., v. Safanek*,[56] a creditor, who claimed to have relied (in its decision to extend credit) upon unaudited financial statements, was allowed to proceed in a legal action against the CPA who prepared the statements.

Prior to December 1978, the only guidance offered by the AICPA in the area of unaudited financial statements was *Statement of Auditing Procedure (SAP) No. 38*, which required that a general disclaimer of an opinion attached to unaudited financial data (with the word "Unaudited" placed at the top of each page of the financial statements) was sufficient to place the user on notice that no assurance was being provided.

But, as the growing tide of court cases was making clear, the designation "certified public accountant" implied (to some users at least) a certain level of assurance despite complete compliance with *SAP No. 38*.

In December 1978, therefore, the AICPA issued *SSARS No. 1*,[57] which directed CPAs to designate their level of involvement in the preparation or review of financial statements as being either a compilation (with absolutely no assurance by the CPA) or a review (with minimal assurance). In addition, a definition for the term *financial statement* was provided, including allowable designations for various types of presentations of financial data.

Until the issuance of *SSARS No. 1*, the only promulgated standard covering nonaudit engagements was *SAP No. 38*, which simply declared that unaudited statements did not involve the expression of an opinion by the CPA. Clearly, the courts in the cases of *Ryan, 1136 Tenants' Corp.*, and their progeny were not persuaded by such a blanket disclaimer. To the extent that there is a public policy favoring the liberty of the parties to engage in a contract allowing the CPA to disclaim all responsibility for financial statements, and to ignore errors, omissions and other problems entirely and without inquiry, that public policy was set aside in favor of the other public policies noted above.

To the extent that *SSARS No. 1* is consistent with the implicit and explicit social goals advanced by the pre-SSARS court cases, compliance with *SSARS No. 1* will serve to lessen an accountant's exposure to liability. But to the extent that *SSARS No. 1*, like its predecessor, *SAP No. 38*, leads an accountant to believe that liability could be avoided by simply hiding behind disclaimers and assertions of nonliability, *SSARS No. 1* is not necessarily helpful in guiding an accountant in nonaudit situations, as some post-*SSARS No. 1* court cases have proven.

The published opinion in the *Spherex v. Alexander Grant & Co.* case,[58] for example, does not specify whether the unaudited financial statements involved were compiled or reviewed, but it does provide confirmation that the CPA was liable in either event. The liability stemmed from inaccurate financial statements prepared by the CPA from information provided by the client, on which a third party relied. The court refused to be bound by the introduction of *SSARS No. 1* standards and the designation of the financial statements as being unaudited.

The *Robert Wooler Co. v. Fidelity Bank* case[59] similarly involved a "review," rather than an audit, under the guidelines established by *SSARS No. 1*, which provide that a "review does not contemplate a study and evaluation of internal control" (AICPA *SSARS No. 1*, 1978, s. 29). The court found that the CPA was liable when internal control weaknesses triggered problems for the client, finding that *SSARS No. 1* was not determinative. The court essentially required that the CPA perform services (such as internal control testing) for which the CPA had not been hired.

Once again, even after the issuance of *SSARS No. 1*, the judicial system placed upon the accounting profession a duty of care, including a standard of inquiry and disclosure, beyond that which the profession claimed for itself and beyond that for which the individual CPA and his client had contracted.

And in a departure from a seemingly endless line of cases holding accountants liable in nonaudit circumstances, the court in the *William Iselin & Co., Inc. v. Landau* case[60] gave credence to the lower level of inquiry implemented in a "review," and shielded the CPA from liability for negligence when it turned out that the financial statements prepared by the CPA did not sufficiently warn a third party of the client's impending bankruptcy. Nevertheless, it was the testimony of expert witnesses, and not the statements or stature of *SSARS No. 1*, that persuaded the court to allow the CPA to be protected from liability.

These court decisions have left little in the way of an actual standard for preparing unaudited financial statements. There may be very little difference between performing a formal audit and preparing unaudited financial statements. However, in *Blakely v. Lisac*,[61] the court stated:

Even when performing an unaudited write-up, an accountant is under a duty to undertake at least a minimal investigation into the figures supplied to him. He is not free to disregard suspicious circumstances.[62]

The accountant's duty to investigate suspicious circumstances during nonaudit engagements is, in fact, a common requirement of many of the court cases in this area.[63] This would be required in small business circumstances as well as in connection with SEC-related (but unaudited) work.[64] Some (albeit minimal) investigation of suspicious circumstances is required even in a simple write-up engagement.[65]

TOWARD GREATER DISCLOSURE

Preference for Details of Bad News

Shareholder Preferences. Judges are not the only people asking accountants for more disclosure in financial statements. Shareholders would also prefer that accountants divulge such information as:

1. Whether the company is positioned for future growth.
2. Severe problems in product quality.
3. Likelihood of severe downturn of the company's profitability.[66]

Shareholders also want to be told about any claims against the company that could mature into lawsuits or significant settlements, even if the probability of any material effect on the financial statements is low.[67]

Risk-Based Capital Rules. The FASB, FDIC, and Federal Reserve Board have all expressed an interest in establishing rules for reporting interest-rate risk and other hazards that are faced by banks and similar organizations.[68] The FASB has already issued *Statement No. 105, Disclosure of Information about Financial Instruments with Off-Balance-Sheet Risk and Financial Instruments with Concentrations of Credit Risk*,[69] and is working on a promulgation entitled "Accounting by Creditors for Impairment of a Loan."[70]

Market Value Financial Statements

As part of the movement for greater disclosure, accountants are beginning to include market value information with historical cost financial statements. The FASB has already issued *Statement No. 107, Disclosures about Fair Value of Financial Instruments*,[71] requiring fair value reporting of certain assets and liabilities on the balance sheets of banks. This "mark-to-market" requirement, instituted in part at the urging of the Securities and Exchange Commission, is designed to avoid future collapses of banks and thrift organizations that can be blamed on unreliable historical cost financial statements.[72]

Statement No. 107 increases the level of disclosure by banks and financial institutions by requiring them to supplement their financial statements with fair value information about their assets and liabilities. "Fair value" is generally defined as "market value" except that it includes estimates for assets for which there is no market.[73]

The FASB is also developing another rule on the subject of "Investments in Debt and Equity Securities," which is expected to require financial statement reporting of fair values. And the FDICIA includes a requirement that the FDIC work with other regulatory agencies in the development of market value disclosures for the banking industry. These developments are the harbingers of future movement toward market value accounting under GAAP. To the extent that they are the result of the demands of the investing and lending public for information that can prevent mistakes like those that led to the U.S. savings and loan crisis, they are the progeny of that fiasco.

CONCLUSION

If there was ever a time when accountants could follow accounting and auditing pronouncements precisely, and thereby escape legal liability, that time is past.

Courts are unwilling to end their inquiry as to an accountant's duty after a review of standards developed primarily by the accounting profession itself. Instead, courts reflect larger concerns about the accountant's duty of care to investors, lenders, government agencies, and society itself.

As a result, more and more demands will be made upon the profession. Demands for a higher and more reliable level of accuracy and materiality. Demands for disclosure of such relevant information as market values of a client's assets and liabilities. And an insistence that accountants not conceal significant adverse information, such as pending litigation against the client.

NOTES

1. SAUL LEVY, ACCOUNTANTS' LEGAL RESPONSIBILITY (New York: American Institute of Accountants, 1954), p. 9.
2. *Accord, e.g.,* Harzfeld's v. Otis Elevator Co., 114 F. Supp. 480, 484 (W.D. Mo. 1953); Flint & Walling Mfg. Co. v. Beckett, 167 Ind. 491, 498, 79 N.E. 503, 505-506 (1906); WILLIAM L. PROSSER, SELECTED TOPICS ON THE LAW OF TORTS (1953), pp. 402-411.
3. *See* 1 C.J.S. Actions § 47, at 1104 (1987 and Supp. 1990). The term *tort* is a very complex concept and not subject to any one definition; but in the most simplistic sense, it can be defined as a civil or private wrong or injury other than breach of contract for which the essential remedy is damages, though others do exist.
4. WILLIAM L. PROSSER, LAW OF TORTS, § 92 (4th ed. 1971).
5. Dantzler Lumber & Export Co. v. Columbia Casualty, 115 Fla. 541, 156 So. 116 (1934).
6. Prosser, *supra n.4*, p. 150.
7. *See* R. W. V. DICKERSON, ACCOUNTANTS AND THE LAW OF NEGLIGENCE (Canada: T. H. Best Printing Company, 1966), p. 1.
8. Prosser, *supra note 4*, p. 161.
9. THOMAS M. COOLEY, COOLEY ON TORTS 335 (4th ed. 1932).
10. Prosser, *supra* note 4, p. 143.
11. *See* Zapico v. Bucyrus-Erie Co., 579 F.2d 714, 718 (2d Cir.1978); In re Masters Mates & Pilots Pension Plan and IRAP Litigation, 957 F.2d 1020, 1027 (2d. Cir. 1992).
12. PAGE KEETON, PROSSER & KEETON ON TORTS § 50, at 336-37 (5th L.Ed.1984).
13. *See* Zapico, 579 F.2d at 718. *See also* In re Masters Mates & Pilots Pension Plan and IRAP Litigation 957 F.2d 1020, 1027-28 (2nd Cir. 1991).
14. *See, e.g.,* § 33 F(2) of the Texas Securities Act, Tex.Rev.Civ.Stat.Ann. Article 581-33 F(2), which imposes joint and several liability on those persons who directly or indirectly, with intent to deceive or defraud or with reckless disregard for the truth or the law, materially aid a seller of securities who misrepresents material facts or omits material facts in connection with the sale. *See also* Cal.Corp.Code §§ 25401 nd 25504.1, imposing joint and several liability on those who intentionally assist in selling securities through written or oral communications which are materially untrue or omit to state material facts. *See also* 15 U.S.C.S. 78t(a), and 15 U.S.C.S. 77o (1992).

15. *See* 29 U.S.C.S. 1105(a)(2) (1992).
16. *See* IRC (26 U.S.C.S.) § 6672 (1992); Sinder v. United States, 655 F.2d 729, 732 (6th Cir.1981) (Section 6672 "imposes joint and several liability on each responsible person, and each responsible person can be held for the total amount of withholding not paid.").
17. Glus v. G.C. Murphy Co., 629 F.2d 248, 252 (3d Cir.1980), *rev'd on other grounds,* 451 U.S. 935, 101 S.Ct. 2013, 68 L.Ed.2d 321 (1981); In re Masters Mates & Pilots Pension Plan and IRAP Litigation, 957 F.2d 1020, 1028-29 (2d. Cir. 1992).
18. *See* Texas Industries, Inc. v. Radcliff Materials, Inc., 451 U.S. 630 (1981).
19. *See* Donovan v. Robbins, 75 F.2d 1170, 1178 (7th Cir.1985) ("[T]he common law's rejection of contribution among joint tortfeasors has itself been rejected by most states and most commentators.").
20. *See, e.g.,* In re Jiffy Lube Sec. Litigation, 927 F.2d 155, 160 & n. 3 (4th Cir.1991); In re Masters Mates & Pilots Pension Plan and IRAP Litigation, 957 F.2d 1020, 1028-29 (2d. Cir. 1992).
21. *See ibid. See also,* Harris, Washington's Unique Approach to Partial Tort Settlements: The Modified Pro Tanto Credit and the Reasonableness Hearing Requirement, 20 Gonzaga L.Rev. 69, 77-78 (1985).
22. See Miller v. Apartments and Homes of New Jersey, 646 F.2d 101, 109 (3d Cir.1981); In re Masters Mates & Pilots Pension Plan and IRAP Litigation, 957 F.2d 1020, 1028-29 (2d. Cir. 1992).
23. In re Jiffy Lube Sec. Litigation, 927 F.2d at 160 n. 3.
24. *Ibid* at 160-61 & n. 3.
25. In re Atlantic Fin. Mgt. Sec. Litigation, 718 F.Supp. 1012, 1018 (D.Mass.1988); In re Masters Mates & Pilots Pension Plan and IRAP Litigation, 957 F.2d 1020, 1028-29 (2d. Cir. 1992).
26. Gomes v. Brodhurst, 394 F.2d 465, 468 (3d Cir.1967).
27. *See, e.g.,* In re Jiffy Lube Sec. Litigation, 927 F.2d at 160 n. 3 ("a hearing focussing on fairness of the settlement to the non-settling defendant is required for approval").
28. *See* In re Nucorp Energy Sec. Litigation, 661 F.Supp. 1403, 1408 (S.D.Cal.1987); In re Masters Mates & Pilots Pension Plan and IRAP Litigation, 957 F.2d 1020, 1028-29 (2d. Cir. 1992).
29. *See, e.g.* Colo. Rev. Stat. Sec. 13-21-111.5.
30. *See* Willis W. Hagen II, Certified Public Accountant's Liability for Malpractice: Effect of Compliance with GAAP and GAAS, 13 J.Contemp. Law 65, 66 (1987).
31. *See* John A. Siliciano, Negligent Accounting and the Limits of Instrumental Tort Reform, 86 Mich.L.Rev.1929, 1931 (1988).
32. CODIFICATION OF AUDITING STANDARDS AND PROCEDURES.
33. AICPA, CODE OF PROFESSIONAL CONDUCT, RULE 202.
34. See ROLAND F. SALMONSON, AUDITING STANDARDS, THE LAW AND THIRD PARTIES 181 (Ph.D. dissertation, University of Michigan, 1956).
35. *See* Rhode Island Hospital National Bank v. Swartz, Bresenoff, Yavner & Jacobs, 455 F. 2d 847 (4th Cir. 1972), where an AICPA-issued *Statement on Auditing Procedure* was applied in a manner analogous to the way courts would apply Treasury Regulations to a tax return filed by a taxpayer. *See also* Hagen, *supra* note 30, at p. 82.
36. *See* Goss v. Crossley (In Re Hawaii Corp.), 587 F. Supp 609 (D. Hawaii 1983); SEC v. Arthur Young & Co., 590 F.2d 785 (9th Cir. 1979); Rhode Island Hospital Trust Nat'l Bank v. Swartz, Bresenoff, Yavner & Jacobs, 455 F.2d 847 (4th Cir. 1972); United States v. Simon, 425 F.2d 796 (2d Cir. 1969), *cert. denied,* 397 U.S. 1006 (1970).
37. Maryland Casualty Co. v. Cook, 35 F. Supp 160 (D.C., Mich., 1940).
38. *See* Marianne M. Jennings, Phillip M.J. Reckers, & Daniel C. Kneer, The Auditor's dilemma: The Incongruous Judicial Notions of the Auditing Profession and Actual Auditor Practice, 29 Am. Bus. Law J. 101, 115 (1991).

39. *Ibid* at 107.
40. *Ibid* at 113.
41. *Ibid* at 113.
42. "In Re McKesson & Robbins, Inc.," *SEC Accounting Series Release No. 19* [1937-82 Transfer Binder], FED. SEC. CODE. (CCH) ¶ 72020 (1940).
43. Leeds Estate, Building & Investment Co. v. Shepherd, 36 Ch.D. 787 (188).
44. *Ibid.* at 802.
45. *See, e.g.,* Fairview Hospital and Healthcare Services v. Bowen, 1988 WL 235563, Medicare & Medicaid Guide ¶ 37,063 (D. Minn., 1988).
46. Hawaii Corporation v. Crossley, 567 F. Supp. 609 (D. Hawaii, 1983).
47. *See* Siliciano, *supra* note 31, at p. 1932.
48. *See* Drabkin v. Alexander Grant & Co., 905 F.2d 453 (U.S.App.D.C, 1990) (even though the auditor failed to disclose significant problems, the auditor was not liable because auditor had expressed going concern doubts).
49. *See* Jennings, Reckers, & Kneer, *supra* note 38, at 115.
50. *E.g.,* U.S. v. Simon, 425 F.2d 796 (2nd Cir. 1969). *See* James W. Zisa, *Guarding the Guardians: Expanding Auditor Negligence Liability to Third-Party Users of Financial Information,* 11 Campbell L. Rev. 123 (1989); and James L. Costello, *The Auditor's Responsibilities for Fraud Detection and Disclosure: Do the Auditing Standards Provide a Safe Harbor?* 43 Maine L. Rev. 265 (1991).
51. Maduff Mortg. Corp. v. Deloitte Haskins & Sells, 779 P.2d 1083, 1086 (Or. App., 1989).
52. Ryan v. Kanne, 170 N.W. 2d 395 (Iowa 1969).
53. 1136 Tenants' Corp. v. Max Rothenberg & Co., 36 A.D. 2d 804, 319 N.Y.S.2d 1007 (N.Y. App. Div. 1971), *aff'd without opinion*, 30 N.Y.2d 585, 281 N.E.2d 846, 330 N.Y.S.2d 800 (1972).
54. *Ibid.* 319 N.Y.S. 2d at 1008.
55. Bonhiver v. Graff, 311 Minn. 111, 248 N.W. 2d 291 (1976).
56. Seedkem, Inc. v. Safanek, 466 F. Supp. 340 (D.Neb. 1979).
57. AICPA, *Statement on Standards for Accounting and Review Services No. 1,* (1978).
58. Spherex v. Alexander Grant & Co., 122 N.H. 898, 451 A.2d 1308 (1982).
59. Robert Wooler Co. v. Fidelity Bank, 330 Pa. Super. 523, 479 A.2d 1027 (1984).
60. William Iselin & Co., Inc., v. Landau, 128 A.D.2d 453, 513 N.Y.S.2d 3 (1987).
61. Blakely v. Lisac, 357 F. Supp. 255, 266 (D. Ore. 1972).
62. *Ibid.* 357 F. Supp. at 266.
63. *Supra* note 57.
64. U.S. v. Natelli, 527 F.2d 311 (1975).
65. Blakely v. Lisac, 357 F. Supp 255 (Ore. 1972).
66. Marc J. Epstein, "Annual Reports and Shareholders," *Corporate Board: Journal of Corporate Governance,* Vol. XII, No. 69, p.10 (July/August 1991).
67. *See* Marc. J. Epstein, "Corporate Governance and the Shareholders' Revolt," *Management Accounting,* August 1992, p.32.
68. *See* 57 F.R. 52346 (FDIC Semiannual Agenda of Regulations, November 3, 1992); *See also,* Steve Cocheo, "Market Value Debate Grinds On," *ABA Banking Journal,* p. 12 (November 1992).
69. Financial Accounting Standards Board.
70. *See,* "Small Banks Voice Concerns about Changes in Accounting for Impaired Loans," *BNA's Banking Report,* Vol. 59, No. 12; p. 469 (October 5, 1992).
71. Financial Accounting Standards Board.
72. *See* Donald G. Simonson, "Marking-To-Market: Is It Any Way to Run a Bank," *U.S. Banker,* November 1992, p. 63.
73. *See* Martha L. Ellett, "Disclosure Deadline Nears for Market Value Accounting," *Magazine of Bank Management,* October, 1992, p. 16.

Chapter Three

Third Party Liability

PRIVITY OF CONTRACT

I n the preceding chapter, the examination of the public accountant's legal liability focused on the concept of negligence. Negligence was described as the breach of duty owed to certain persons to conform to a required standard of conduct, that standard being to exercise reasonable care and to perform with that degree of knowledge, judgment, and skill employed by other members of the profession.

When one of these "certain persons" claiming that such a "duty" has been breached happens to be the accountant's client, no particular problem arises because the accountant's duty owed to the client exists by virtue of the contract between the two parties. In other words, it is implicit in the contractual relationship that each party owes the other a duty to perform the terms of the contract with reasonable care. For example, if *Y* contracts with *X* to perform services for *X* but in so doing fails to exercise reasonable care, *Y* has breached his duty owed to *X*, and *X* will have a cause of action for negligence, assuming that all of the elements of negligence exist.

The duty exists because of the relationship between the parties created by the contract, and no duty is owed to any other person not a party to the contract. In essence, this is the concept of *privity of contract.*

Privity of contract means that the rights or obligations that exist under a contract are between the original parties to that contract, and failure to perform with due care results in a breach of that duty to only those parties. Thus, in the example above, if a third party is damaged as a result of *Y*'s negligence to *X* and attempts to recover against *Y*, this adds an entirely new dimension of complexity.[1]

In early common law, the public accountant's legal liability to third parties for ordinary negligence was based primarily on the concept of *privity.* Lack of privity was treated almost as a conclusive defense. Unless the parties to the civil litigation were in privity by some legal relationship, no liability was imposed for ordinary negligence.[2]

The *Glanzer* Case. Although courts through the years have tended to be less insistent upon privity in cases resulting in physical harm, one of the first successful attacks against the privity requirement for a purely economic loss was the 1922 case of *Glanzer v. Shepard.*[3] In that case, a public weigher was employed by a merchant seller to weigh bags of beans being sold to the plaintiff buyer. The public weigher was instructed to furnish weight certificate copies to both the plaintiff buyer and the merchant of the beans. The weigher negligently overstated the weight of the beans and was held liable to the third-party buyer for the overpayment made to the merchant. In his opinion, Judge Cardozo stated in pertinent part:

> We think the law imposes a duty toward buyer as well as seller in the situation here disclosed. The plaintiff's use of the certificates was not an indirect or collateral consequence of the action of the weighers. It was a consequence which, to the weighers' knowledge, was the end and aim of the transaction.

* * * * *

> The defendants held themselves out to the public as skilled and careful in their calling. They knew that the beans had been sold, and that on the faith of their certificate payment would be made. They sent a copy to the plaintiffs for the very purpose of inducing action. All this they admit. In such circumstances, assumption of the task of weighing was the assumption of a duty to weigh carefully for the benefit of all whose conduct was to be governed. We do not need to state the duty in terms of contract or of privity. Growing out of a contract, it has nonetheless an origin not exclusively

contractual. Given the contract and the relation, the duty is imposed by law.[4]

Thus, the lack of privity was not fatal because the intended use of the certificate, known to the weigher, was the "end and aim" of the employment, and the duty of due care was "for the benefit of all those whose conduct was to be governed" or foreseen.

As a result of the *Glanzer* approach, courts began to hold licensed professionals, including certified public accountants, accountable to nonclients. **Figure 5** depicts the applicability of the *Glanzer* approach.

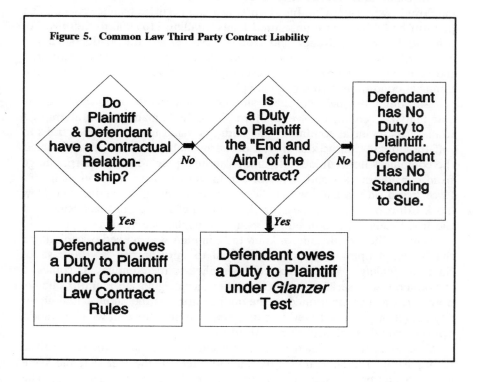

Figure 5. Common Law Third Party Contract Liability

The concepts developed in *Glanzer* were to be revived in later years, much to the chagrin of the accounting profession, in a series of successful attacks against the doctrine of privity, which had so effectively served to shield accountants from third-party liability.

NEGLIGENCE

Traditional View: No Liability to Third Parties

The *Ultramares* Case. Nine years after *Glanzer*, the same court handed down the landmark decision of *Ultramares Corporation v. Touche*[5] in which Judge Cardozo refused to extend the scope of liability to the full limits of foreseeability for negligence resulting in purely economic damage to third parties not in privity.

In *Ultramares*, the defendant firm of certified public accountants was employed by Stern & Co., Inc., to prepare and certify a balance sheet. The plaintiff had made three unsecured loans totalling $165,000 to Stern & Co. prior to Stern's insolvency and bankruptcy. When the lender sued the company's auditors, the lender claimed reliance on their audit opinion that the company's balance sheet "present[ed] a true and correct view of the financial condition of [the company]."[6]

Although the balance sheet showed a net worth of $1 million, the company was actually insolvent. Stern & Co., Inc.'s management attempted to mask its financial condition; the auditors failed to follow paper trails to "off-the-books" transactions that, if properly analyzed, would have revealed the company's impecunious situation. The jury, precluded by the trial judge from considering a fraud cause of action, returned a verdict in plaintiff's favor based on the auditor's negligence in conducting the audit. The New York Court of Appeals, speaking through Chief Judge Cardozo, reinstated the fraud cause of action but set aside the negligence verdict.

The auditor in Ultramares knew the company was in need of capital and that its audit opinion would be displayed to third parties "as the basis of financial dealings."[7] In this regard, it supplied to the company 32 copies of the opinion "with serial numbers as counterpart originals."[8] Plaintiff's name, however, was not mentioned to the auditor nor was the auditor told about any actual or proposed credit or investment transactions in which its audit opinion would be presented to a third party.[9]

The auditors had failed to verify certain fictitious accounts receivables, to inquire into inflated inventory, and to question the fact that the same accounts had been assigned to more than one bank at the same time. The Court of Appeals agreed with the trial court's findings that the accountants' conduct was negligent; nevertheless, it declined to find the defendant liable to a third-party plaintiff. Cardozo explained:

> If liability for negligence exists, a thoughtless slip or blunder, the failure to detect a theft or forgery beneath the cover of deceptive entries, may expose accountants to a liability in an indeterminate amount for an indeterminate time to an indeterminate class. The

hazards of a business conducted on these terms are so extreme as to enkindle doubt whether a flaw may not exist in the implication of a duty that exposes to these consequences.[10]

With respect to the negligence claim, the court found the auditor owed no duty to the third party creditor for an "erroneous opinion." In an often-quoted passage, it observed: "If liability for negligence exists, a thoughtless slip or blunder, the failure to detect a theft or forgery beneath the cover of deceptive entries, may expose accountants to a liability in an indeterminate amount for an indeterminate time to an indeterminate class. The hazards of a business conducted on these terms are so extreme as to enkindle doubt whether a flaw may not exist in the implication of a duty that exposes to these consequences."[11]

Although acknowledging the demise of privity of contract as a limitation on tort liability in the context of personal injury and property damage, the court distinguished between liability arising from a "physical force" and "the circulation of a thought or the release of the explosive power resident in words."[12] It also distinguished its own prior decision in *Glanzer*, in which a seller of beans requested the operator of a public scale to give a certificate of weight to the buyer. When the certificate proved inaccurate and the buyer sued, the court held the operator liable for negligence. As the court explained, the difference between the cases was that "the transmission of the certificate [in *Glanzer*] was not merely one possibility among many, but the 'end and aim of the transaction,' as certain and immediate and deliberately willed as if a husband were to order a gown to be delivered to his wife, or a telegraph company, contracting with the sender of a message, were to telegraph it wrongly to the damage of the person expected to receive it."[13]

Instead of overruling *Glanzer*, Cardozo simply chose to distinguish it by stating that "the service rendered by the defendant in *Glanzer v. Shepard* was primarily for the information of a third person, in effect, if not in name, a party to the contract, and only incidentally for that of the formal promise. In the case at hand, the service was primarily for the benefit of the Stern Company. . . and only incidentally or collaterally for use of those to whom Stern and his associates might exhibit it thereafter."[14]

This became known as the *primary benefit rule*. "It was based on the premise that a company ordinarily needs audited financial statements for many purposes--for management guidance, taxes, debt and equity investors, lenders, suppliers, customers--no single purpose alone being a decisive reason for obtaining audited financial statements."[15] And therefore, the fact that a client engaged an accountant to perform an audit was not conclusive proof that the primary beneficiary was always the client; sometimes it might be a third party.

In summarizing its holding, the *Ultramares* court emphasized that it was not releasing auditors from liability to third parties for fraud but merely for "honest blunder."[16]   It questioned "whether the average business man receiving a certificate without paying for it, and receiving it as one of a multitude of possible investors, would look for anything more."[17]

The *Credit Alliance* Case. The "privity rule" established in New York by *Ultramares*, and followed by many other jurisdictions, has not served to prevent nonclients from recovering from accountants. The New York Court of Appeals, for example, has not required privity of contract as a universal prerequisite to third party suits against auditors; rather, on occasion, it has found an equivalent privity of relationship between the auditor and the plaintiff.[18]

For example, in *White v. Guarente*,[19] one of 40 limited partners sued the partnership's auditor for professional negligence in failing to disclose in an audit report that the general partners had withdrawn funds from the partnership in violation of the partnership agreement. The court observed that the limited partnership agreement contained an express provision requiring an annual audit by an accountant, and that the accountant had also prepared the partnership's tax returns on which the limited partners relied in preparing their personal returns. The court determined that the accountant had a duty to exercise due care for the benefit of the limited partners, even though the accountant's client was the partnership itself.

Distinguishing *Ultramares*, the court commented that the "services of the accountant were not extended to a faceless or unresolved class of persons, but rather to a known group possessed of vested rights, marked by a definable limit and made up of certain components."[20]   Following the rationale of the *Glanzer* case, the *Guarente* court ruled that the furnishing of the audit and tax return information to be "one of the ends and aims" of the accountant's engagement and "within the contemplation of the parties to the accounting retainer."[21]

The New York Court of Appeals restated privity rule in light of *Ultramares*, *Guarente*, and other cases in the 1985 case of *Credit Alliance v. Arthur Andersen & Co.*[22]   *Credit Alliance* involved two separate cases, combined into one lawsuit, with different fact situations: in the first case, the plaintiff alleged that it had loaned funds to the auditor's client in reliance on audited financial statements overstating the client's assets and net worth; in the second, the same scenario occurred, but the plaintiff also alleged that the auditor knew plaintiff was the client's principal lender and communicated directly and frequently with plaintiff regarding its continuing audit reports. The court dismissed the plaintiff's negligence claim in the first case, but sustained the claim in the second.[23]

The *Credit Alliance* court rendered the following rule for determining auditor liability to third parties for negligence: "Before accountants may be held liable in negligence to noncontractual parties who rely to their detriment on inaccurate financial reports, certain prerequisites must be satisfied: (1) the accountant must have been aware that the financial reports were to be used for a particular purpose or purposes; (2) in the furtherance of which a known party or parties was intended to rely; and (3) there must have been some conduct on the part of the accountants linking them to that party or parties, which evinces the accountants' understanding of that party or parties' reliance."[24]

Discussing the application of its rule to the cases at hand, the *Credit Alliance* court observed the primary, if not exclusive, "end and aim" of the audits in the second case was to satisfy the lender. The auditor's "direct communications and personal meetings [with the lender] result[ed] in a nexus between them sufficiently approaching privity."[25] In contrast, in the first case, although the complaint did allege the auditor knew or should have known of the lender's reliance on its reports: "There was no allegation of either a particular purpose for the reports' preparation or the prerequisite conduct on the part of the accountants ... [nor] any allegation [the auditor] had any direct dealings with plaintiffs, had agreed with [the client] to prepare the report for plaintiffs' use or according to plaintiffs' requirements, or had specifically agreed with [the client] to provide plaintiffs with a copy [of the report] or actually did so."[26]

The *Security Pacific* Case. The New York Court of Appeals has upheld the *Ultramares*-through-*Credit Alliance* series of cases in the recent case of *Security Pacific Business Credit, Inc. v. Peat Marwick Main & Co.*[27] In that case, a creditor sued an accounting firm, asserting it had issued credit to a debtor in reliance on the accounting firm's "valuation" of the debtor's accounts receivable and inventory. It asserted that its reliance was based on one telephone call from its vice-president, to the predecessor accounting firm's audit partner during and with respect only to the 1984 audit process and audit work papers supplied to it by the debtor. The creditor claimed losses on the loans of at least $8 million.[28]

In ruling in favor of the accounting firm, the *Security Pacific* court observed that the New York privity rule cases, such as *Credit Alliance*, permit some flexibility in the application of the doctrine of privity to accountants' liability. They do not, however, a departure from the principles articulated in *Ultramares*, *Glanzer*, or *Guarente*. Instead, the privity rule cases are intended to preserve the wisdom and policy set forth in *Ultramares* and its progeny.[29]

Conduct Linking Accountant to Plaintiff. As a result of the post-*Ultramares* cases, the privity rule evolved from a requirement that a plaintiff have privity of contract (i.e., an engagement agreement, written or oral) with an accountant before the accountant can be held liable by the plaintiff, to a requirement that there be "privity of relationship." Under the *Credit Alliance* test, the auditor may have liability to a third party if there is distinct conduct "linking" the auditor to the third party in a manner that "evinces [auditor] understanding" of third party reliance.[30]

The "linking conduct" element appears to require that the existence of the third person be known to the auditor, and that the auditor either directly convey the audit report to the third person or otherwise act in some manner specifically calculated to induce reliance on the report.[31] In this regard, a mere "unsolicited phone call" by the third party to the auditor is insufficient. The auditor must be aware of a "particular purpose" for the audit engagement and must act to further that purpose.[32]

Privity Rule Jurisdictions. The highest courts in some states, such as Alabama, Idaho, Nebraska, and Pennsylvania, have adopted the privity rule by rendering state court decisions following *Ultramares* and *Credit Alliance*.[33] In other states, such as Delaware, Colorado, and Indiana, courts other than the highest court have ruled likewise.[34] In others, such as Arkansas, Illinois, Kansas and Utah, legislatures have enacted the rule by statutory law.[35]

Restatement Second of the Law of Torts

In 1968, a federal district court sitting in Rhode Island rendered a decision that began the development of a new trend in accountants' third-party liability through a series of major cases.[36] This decision represented a broad departure from the traditional requirement of privity. Instrumental to this case and those that followed was the revival of *Glanzer v. Shepard* and the application of Section 552 of the *Restatment (Second) of the Law of Torts*.

The Restatement Second Approach. The *Restatement (Second) of the Law of Torts*, published in 1977, represents a very persuasive compendium of the common law as developed and analyzed by some of the foremost legal scholars. Section 552 contains the following language:

1. One who, in the course of his business, profession or employment, or in a transaction in which he has a pecuniary interest, supplies false information for the guidance of others in their business transactions, is subject

to liability for pecuniary loss caused to them by their justifiable reliance upon the information, if he fails to exercise reasonable care or competence in obtaining or communicating the information.

2. Except as stated in subsection (3), the liability stated in subsection (1) is limited to loss suffered (a) by the person or one of the persons for whose benefit and guidance he intends to supply the information, or knows that the recipient intends to supply it; and (b) through reliance upon it in a transaction which he intends the information to influence, or knows that the recipient so intends, or in a substantially similar transaction.

3. The liability of one who is under a public duty to give the information extends to loss suffered by any of the class of persons for whose benefit the duty is created, in any of the transactions in which it is intended to protect them.[37]

The *Restatement (Second)* forms an alternative to the traditional *Ultramares* rule. This modern approach examines two aspects: (1) the individual person for whose guidance the information is supplied, and (2) the use or transaction for which guidance the information is supplied.

The *Restatement (Second)* takes the position that the third-party plaintiff need not be identified or known at the time that the information is supplied.

It is enough that the maker of the representation intends it to reach and influence either a particular person or persons, known to him, or a group or class of persons, distinct from the much larger class who might reasonably be expected sooner or later to have access to the information, and foreseeability to take some action in reliance upon it. It is enough, likewise, that the maker of the representation knows that the recipient intends to transmit the information to a similar person, persons, or group. It is sufficient, in other words, that the maker knows that the information is intended for repetition to a certain group or class of persons, and that the plaintiff proves to be one of them, even though the maker never had heard of him when the information was given. It is not enough that the maker merely knows of the ever-present possibility of repetition to anyone, and the possibility of action in reliance upon it, on the part of anyone to whom it might be repeated.[38]

Even when the maker is informed of the identity of a definite person to whom the recipient intends to transmit the information, the circumstances may justify a finding that the name and identity of that person was regarded by the maker, and by the recipient, as important only because the person in question was one of a group whom the information was intended to reach, and for whose guidance it was being supplied. In many situations the identity of the person for whose guidance the information is supplied is of no moment to the person who supplies it, although the number and character of the persons to be reached and influenced, and the nature and extent of the transaction for which guidance is furnished, may be vitally important. This is true because the risk of liability to which the supplier subjects himself by undertaking to give the information, while not affected by the identity of the person for whose guidance the information is given, is vitally affected by the number and character of such persons, and the nature and extent of the proposed transaction. On the other hand, the circumstances may occasionally show that the identity of the person for whose guidance the information is given is regarded by the person supplying it, and by the recipient, as important and material; and therefore the person supplying the information understands that his liability is to be restricted to the named person, and to him only. Thus where the information is procured for transmission to a named or otherwise described person, whether the maker is liable to another to whom in substitution the information is transmitted in order to influence his conduct in an otherwise identical transaction, depends upon whether it is understood between the person giving the information and the person procuring its transmission that it is to be transmitted to the named individual and to him only.[39]

The drafters of the *Restatement (Second)* provided the following hypothetical illustrations to help clarify the above language:

2. *A* is negotiating with the X Bank for a credit of $50,000. The Bank requires an audit by certified public accountants. *A* employs B & Company, a firm of accountants, to make the audit, telling them that it is to meet the requirements of the X Bank. B & Company agree to make the audit, with the express understanding that it is for transmission to X Bank only. The X Bank fails, and *A* without any further communication with B & Company submits their certification to the Y Bank, which in reliance upon it extends a credit of $50,000 to *A*. The audit is so carelessly made as greatly to overstate the financial resources of *A*, so Y Bank suffers pecuniary loss through its extension of credit. B & Company is not liable to Y Bank.

3. The same facts as in Illustration 2, except that nothing is said about supplying the information for the guidance of X Bank only, and *A* merely informs B & Company that he expects to negotiate a bank loan, and has the X Bank in mind. B & Company is subject to liability to Y Bank.

4. The same facts as in Illustration 2, except that *A* informs B & Company he expects to negotiate a bank loan, but does not mention the name of any bank. B & Company is subject to liability to Y Bank.

* * * * *

7. *A*, a certified public accountant, is employed by B Company to prepare and certify a balance sheet for the corporation. *A* is not informed of any intended use of the balance sheet, but *A* knows that such certificates are customarily used in a wide variety of financial transactions with the corporation, and that it may be relied upon by lenders, investors, shareholders, creditors, purchasers, and the like, in numerous possible kinds of transactions. In fact, B Company uses the certified balance sheet to obtain a loan from X Bank. Because of *A*'s negligence the balance sheet presents an inaccurate picture of the finances of B Company, and through reliance upon it X Bank suffers pecuniary loss. *A* is not liable to X Bank.[40]

The *Restatement (Second)* also takes the position that the maker of a misrepresentation is liable for those transactions or substantially similar transactions which he intends to influence or knows that the recipient intends to influence.

> Thus accountants who negligently make an audit of the books of the A Corporation, which they are told is to be used only for the purpose of obtaining a particular line of banking credit, are not subject to liability to a wholesale merchant whom the corporation induces to supply it with goods on credit by showing him the audit and the certification. On the other hand, it is not necessary that the transaction in which the negligent audit is relied on shall be identical in all of its minutest details with the one intended. It is enough that it is substantially the same transaction, or one substantially similar. Thus, in the situation above stated, if the corporation, finding that at the moment it does not need the credit to obtain which the audit was procured, uses it a month later to obtain the same credit from the same bank, the accountants will remain subject to liability to the bank for the loss resulting from its

extension of credit, unless the financial condition of the corporation has materially changed in the interim, or so much time has elapsed that the bank cannot justifiably rely upon the audit.

There may be many minor differences which do not affect the essential character of the transaction. The question may be one of the extent of the departure which the maker of the representation understands is to be expected. If he is informed that the information which he supplies is to be used in applying to a particular bank for a loan of $10,000, the fact that the loan is made by that bank for $15,000 will not necessarily mean that the transaction is a different one. But if the loan is for $500,000, and secured by an issue of bonds, the very difference in amount, with the type of security not usually contemplated on a loan, would lead the ordinary borrower or lender to regard it as a different kind of loan. The ordinary practices and attitudes of the business world are to be taken into account; and the question becomes one of whether the departure from the contemplated transaction is so major, and so significant, that it cannot be regarded as essentially the same transaction. It is also possible, of course, that more than one kind of transaction may be understood as intended.[41]

The following hypothetical illustrations are also provided:

9. *A*, a certified public accountant, negligently certifies a balance sheet for B Corporation, which shows it to be in a favorable financial condition although it is in fact insolvent. *A* knows that B Corporation intends to exhibit the balance sheet to C Corporation as a basis for applying for credit for the purchase of goods. In reliance upon the balance sheet, C Corporation buys the controlling interest in the stock of B Corporation, and as a result suffers pecuniary loss. *A* is not to liable to C Corporation.

10. The same facts as in Illustration 9, except that *A* expects that C Corporation will be asked to extend credit for the purchase of washing machines, and credit is extended instead for the purchase of electric refrigerators. *A* is subject to liability to C Corporation.[42]

The *Rusch Factors* Case. The judicial acceptance of the *Restatement (Second)* theory developed throughout a series of cases starting with *Rusch Factors*, in which the court ultimately concluded that *Ultramares* was an "unwarranted inroad upon the principle that 'the risk reasonable to be perceived defines the duty to be obeyed.'"[43] In the *Rusch Factors* case, a

Rhode Island corporation engaged the defendant public accountant to prepare certified financial statements for the purpose of obtaining financing from the plaintiff. The statements represented the corporation to be stable and financially solvent. In reliance, the plaintiff made a large loan to the corporation but never recovered the full amount because of the subsequent insolvency of the corporation. In finding the defendant liable for negligence and completely rejecting the privity requirement, the court relied heavily upon the *Glanzer v. Shepard* case and Section 552 of the *Restatement (Second) of the Laws of Torts*.

The court pointed out the similarity of the *Rusch* case to *Glanzer*. The plaintiff in each case was a "single party whose reliance was actually foreseen by the defendant" whereas the plaintiff in *Ultramares* "was a member of an undefined, unlimited class of remote lenders and potential equity holders not actually foreseen but only foreseeable."[44]

A foreseen person has been defined as "one or more specifically identified persons or entities who are known by the auditor to be intended recipients, directly or indirectly, of his audit opinion for the purpose of reliance in a particular business transaction known to the auditor"; and foreseeable persons as "the potentially very large number of persons, not identified to the auditor by specific persons. . . in a specific transaction, who may foreseeably be expected to receive his audit report when distributed by the client, and in some way to act or forbear to act in reliance upon it."[45]

The *Ryan v. Kanne* Case. The next in this series of cases was *Ryan v. Kanne*.[46] Kanne, the owner of certain lumber companies, was in need of financing and, at the advice of a creditor, employed certified public accountants to prepare an unaudited balance sheet for the purposes of determining the feasibility of incorporating Kanne's businesses. The creditor directed the CPAs to pay particular attention to Accounts Payable-Trade, known by all parties to be the critical part of the undertaking. The CPAs guaranteed the accuracy of that item to be correct to within $5,000. In reliance, the lumber businesses were incorporated and its assets and liabilities were taken over by the corporation. Later it was discovered by re-audit that Accounts Payable-Trade was incorrectly stated by $22,689.22. The plaintiff CPAs brought suit and recovered their fee while the defendant corporation counterclaimed and recovered for plaintiffs' negligence.

The court rejected both the privity requirement and the primary benefit test and adopted the formula that the accountant owes a duty of care to a third party who "is actually foreseen and a member of a limited class of persons." The court was not ready to extend liability to all foreseeable persons but only to "those who were actually known to the author as prospective users of the report and take into consideration the end aim of the transaction."

The court also lent support to the *Restatement (Second)* position "to the extent that it extends the right to recover for negligence to persons for whose benefit and guidance the accountant *knows* the information is intended especially when the party to be benefitted is identified before the statement or report is submitted by the accountant."[47] [Emphasis in the original.] The court was not impressed by the lack of certification of the statement, but instead focused on the substance of the agreement and the representation made therein.

The *Shatterproof Glass* Case. Next came the 1971 Texas decision of *Shatterproof Glass Corporation v. James,*[48] which chose to adopt the approach of Section 552 of the *Restatement (Second) of the Law of Torts.* The defendant accounting firm in that case was engaged by Paschal to prepare certified audits of the Paschal Enterprises for the purpose of obtaining bank credit. In addition, Paschal authorized the defendants to also make this information available to the plaintiff, Shatterproof Glass Corporation, which was considering making Paschal a distributor. The defendant was informed of this fact and also that the plaintiff acted as bankers for its distributors. The plaintiff, relying on the audit that represented Paschal as having a substantial net worth, made a sizable loan to Paschal. Paschal turned out to have a deficit net worth and the loan was not repaid. The court held that the accountants were under a duty to exercise due care toward the third-party plaintiff, and granted relief to the plaintiff despite the absence of privity.[49] The court stated:

> As is evident from recent decisions involving investors and other persons who extend credit to corporations, the Courts have replaced "privity" and "primary benefit" with the concepts of "good faith" and "common honesty."[50]

The *Rhode Island Hospital* Case. In *Rhode Island Hospital Trust National Bank v. Swartz, Bresenoff, Yavner & Jacobs,*[51] the court specifically relied upon *Rusch Factors.* In this case, International Trading Corporation, an importer of cement, obtained loans from plaintiff bank under the pretense of making leasehold improvements to its facilities, when in fact the capital was used for operating expenses. The loan agreement required International to furnish yearly financial statements to the bank. The defendant public accountants failed to discover the fictitious leaseholds. Despite a disclaimer to the fairness of the certified financial statements, the Fourth Circuit Court of Appeals reversed the lower District Court's dismissal of the complaint.

The case was remanded for further proceedings to determine the extent of the bank's reliance on the financial statements, but the Fourth Circuit held that "an accountant should be liable in negligence for careless financial misrepresentations relied upon by actually foreseen and limited classes of persons."

The *Raritan* Case. In *Raritan River Steel Company v. Cherry, Bekaert & Holland*,[52] Intercontinental Metals Corporation (IMC) retained the defendants, a firm of certified public accountants and individual partners working for the firm, to provide an audit report on IMC's financial status. The plaintiffs, Raritan River Steel Company (Raritan) and Sidbec-Dosco, extended credit to IMC on the basis of what they contended was an incorrect overstatement of IMC's net worth contained in the audit report prepared by the defendants. The plaintiffs sought to hold the defendants liable for losses resulting from the extension of credit to IMC.

In assessing the scope of an accountant's liability for negligent misrepresentation to persons other than the client for whom the financial audit was prepared, the North Carolina Supreme Court adopted the *Restatement (Second)* approach. The Court held that the plaintiffs had stated a legally sufficient claim against the defendants for negligent misrepresentation by alleging that at the time that the defendants prepared the audited financial statements for IMC, they knew: (1) the statements would be used by IMC to represent its financial condition to creditors who would extend credit on the basis of them; and (2) Sidbec-Dosco and other creditors would rely on those statements.[53]

A "No-Particular-Reason" Audit? Under the *Restatement* rule, an auditor retained to conduct an annual audit and to furnish an opinion for no particular purpose generally undertakes no duty to third parties. Such an auditor is not informed "of any intended use of the financial statements; but . . . knows that the financial statements, accompanied by an auditor's opinion, are customarily used in a wide variety of financial transactions by the [client] corporation and that they may be relied upon by lenders, investors, shareholders, creditors, purchasers and the like, in numerous possible kinds of transactions. [The client corporation] uses the financial statements and accompanying auditor's opinion to obtain a loan from [a particular] bank. Because of [the auditor's] negligence, he issues an unqualifiedly favorable opinion upon a balance sheet that materially misstates the financial position of [the corporation] and through reliance upon it [the bank] suffers pecuniary loss."[54] Consistent with the text of section 552, the authors conclude: "[The auditor] is not liable to [the bank]."[55]

How credible is such an approach? In the above example, does not the accountant understand or realize that future borrowing by the client will depend, in part if not entirely, upon the information conveyed by the financial statements? The *Restatement* asks courts (including juries in many accountant liability cases) to determine whether the accountant knew whether a particular report letter would be relied upon by a particular creditor, instead of being generally relied upon by all creditors in the normal course of business, as a prerequisite for finding liability on the part of an accountant. And yet the client's the list of creditors is routinely reviewed as part of the accountant's examination of a client's liabilities.

Restatement Second Jurisdictions. The *Restatement (Second)* approach is quickly replacing the *Ultramares* approach in many states, both by statute and by case law, and is now considered the majority view. Despite the theoretical and practical difficulties, including those described above, courts in many jurisdictions, including Florida, Georgia, Iowa, Kentucky, Louisiana, Michigan, Minnesota, Missouri, Montana, New Hampshire, North Carolina, North Dakota, Ohio, Rhode Island, Tennessee, Texas, Washington, and West Virginia, have followed the *Restatement (Second)* approach or a variation of that approach.[56]

Liability to Reasonably Foreseeable Users

A third approach to third-party liability, gaining acceptance in a growing minority of states, is the *reasonably foreseeable users* approach. This doctrine expands the accountant's liability to include not only clients and other primary beneficiaries of the engagement (the *Ultramares* approach), and not only users who were actually known to the accountant, or members of a class of users known to the accountant (the *Restatement (Second)* approach), but also any other foreseeable third parties. To recover against a negligent accountant under this reasonably foreseeable users test, a nonclient need only prove that the accountant should have expected the nonclient to make use of the accountant's work product. This third approach represents a further broadening of the class of the allowable group of claimants who may target accountants in their quest for solvent defendants.

The *Rosenblum* Case. The New Jersey case of *H. Rosenblum, Inc. v. Adler*[57] illustrates this third approach. In that case, the Rosenblum family agreed to sell its retail catalog showroom business to Giant Stores in exchange for Giant common stock. In so doing, the Rosenblums relied upon the 1971 and 1972 fiscal year financial statements audited by Touche Ross & Company.

In early 1973, after the Rosenblum agreement had been reached, it was revealed that the financial statements of Giant Stores had reported assets that were not owned and had omitted substantial amounts of accounts payable. Trading of Giant Stores stock on the American Stock Exchange was stopped in April 1973 and never resumed. By September 1973, Giant Stores had filed a petition for bankruptcy, and the stock held by the Rosenblums was worthless. The Rosenblums sued Touche Ross for negligence, even though the Touche auditors had not known the Rosenblums during the 1971 and 1972 audits, and even though Touche Ross had no knowledge that the financial statements would be relied upon during merger and acquisition negotiations.

The lower courts in the *Rosenblum* case did not allow the Rosenblums to pursue their claims against Touche Ross for both years, on the grounds that the Rosenblums met neither the *Ultramares* privity test or the *Restatement (Second)* foreseen class of users test. The state supreme court overturned the lower courts, however, holding that the reasonable consequences of negligence should govern the extent to which the negligence is actionable. That is, the defendant should be liable for all foreseeable consequences of his or her negligence.

Justice Schreiber in the *Rosenblum* case noted that:

When the defendants prepared the Giant case, they knew or should have known that Giant would probably use the audited figures for many proper business purposes. They knew that it was to be incorporated into Giant's annual report, a report that would be transmitted to each Giant stockholder, and would be filed with the SEC in conjunction with Giant's proxy solicitation material for its annual shareholder meeting. The defendants also know or should have known that the audited financial statements would be available and useful for other proper business purposes, such as public offerings or securities, credit, and corporate acquisitions. These were clearly foreseeable potential uses of the audited financials at the time of their preparation.[58]

The state supreme court held that a negligent independent auditor is responsible for damages incurred by all reasonably foreseeable third parties who rely on the financial statements. The only limitation on this standard is the requirement that the plaintiffs may only go forward against the accountant-defendants when the plaintiffs can prove that the financial statements were originally obtained for a proper business purpose.[59]

In reaching its decision, the *Rosenblum* court found no reason to distinguish accountants from other suppliers of products or services to the public and no reason to deny to third party users of financial statements recovery for economic loss resulting from negligent misrepresentation.[60] From its review of the purpose and history of the audit function, it concluded: "The auditor's function has expanded from that of a watchdog for management to an independent evaluator of the adequacy and fairness of financial statements issued by management to stockholders, creditors, and others."[61] Noting the apparent ability of accounting firms to obtain insurance against third party claims under the federal securities laws, the court posited the same or similar protection would be available for common law negligent misrepresentation claims.[62]

When the New Jersey court formulated a rule of liability it restricted the auditor's duty to "all those whom that auditor should reasonably foresee as recipients from the company of the statements for its proper business purposes, provided that the recipients rely on the statements pursuant to those business purposes."[63] According to the court, its rule would preclude auditor liability to "an institutional investor or portfolio manager who does not obtain audited statements from the company" or to "stockholders who purchased the stock after a negligent audit" unless they could demonstrate "the necessary conditions precedent."[64]

The New Jersey court offered no principled basis for its "conditions precedent" requirement. Institutional investors, portfolio managers, or prospective stock purchasers who may pick up an audit report from a stockbroker, friend, or acquaintance or otherwise acquire it indirectly are no less "foreseeable" users. In view of the lack of any effective limits on access to audit reports once they reach the client, an auditor can foresee its reports coming into the hands of practically anyone. Thus, the court's approach evinces an Ultramares-like concern about the prospect of unlimited auditor liability, but offers no reasoned explanation of its decision to establish a limit based solely on the company's distribution, a factor over which the auditor has no control.

The *Timm Schmidt* Case. Within a month after the *Rosenblum* decision, the *Citizens State Bank v. Timm, Schmidt & Company* decision was published in Wisconsin.[65] There, Citizens State Bank sued the accounting firm of Timm, Schmidt after one of the bank's business debtors went bankrupt.

In deciding for the bank, the court refused to impose the *Restatement (Second)* limitations on third-party actions against accountants. Instead of limiting recovery to those parties who were actually known to have been potential financial statement users (or were in a class of known users), the court in *Timm Schmidt* extended the scope of plaintiffs to include all reasonably foreseeable financial statement users.[66]

And instead of limiting this extension to situations involving plaintiffs who obtained the financial statements for a proper business purpose, as did the *Rosenblum* court, the court in the *Timm Schmidt* case limited this extension only in those situations dictated by strong public policy reasons.

The *Timm Schmidt* court relied on compensation, risk-spreading, and deterrence rationales, noting that "[u]nless liability is imposed, third parties who rely on the accuracy of financial statements will not be protected. Unless an accountant can be held liable to a relying third party, this negligence will go undeterred. ... If relying third parties, such as creditors, are not allowed to recover, the cost of credit to the general public will increase because creditors will either have to absorb the cost of bad loans made in reliance on faulty information or hire independent accountants to verify the information received. Accountants may spread the risk through the use of liability insurance."[67]

Criticism of the Reasonably Foreseeable Users Approach. The reasonably foreseeable users doctrine has been criticized by some courts as being too broad.[68] Typical of such criticism is the following observation by the court in the *Raritan* case, as follows:

> An accountant performs an audit pursuant to a contract with an individual client. The client may or may not intend to use the report for other than internal purposes. It does not benefit the accountant if his client distributes the audit opinion to others. Instead, it merely exposes his work to many who he may have no idea would scrutinize his works. We believe that in fairness accountants should not be liable in circumstances where they are unaware of the use to which their opinions will be put. Instead their liability should be commensurate with those persons or classes of persons whom they know will rely on their work. With such knowledge the auditor can, through purchase of liability insurance, setting fees, and adopting other protective measures, appropriate to the risk, prepare accordingly.[69]

Summary of Third Party Liability for Negligence. The access of third parties, such as lenders and investors, to the accountant-defendant in a negligence lawsuit is generally dependent upon the jurisdiction in which the accountant has worked. But sometimes the jurisdiction of a lawsuit is determined by other factors, such as the residence of the plaintiff or a place of business of a multistate (or multinational) client.

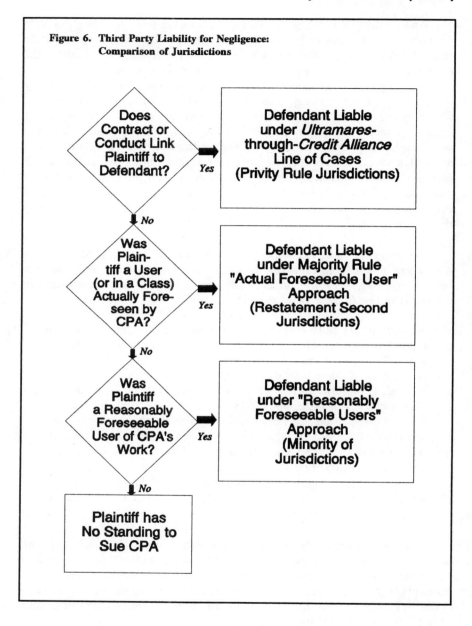

Figure 6. Third Party Liability for Negligence:
           Comparison of Jurisdictions

In privity rule jurisdictions, such as New York, that access is relatively limited. In "reasonably foreseeable users" jurisdictions like New Jersey, the access is almost unlimited. **Figure 6** shows the widening exposure of the accountant as states drift from the common law approach of *Ultramares*, toward the reasonably foreseeable approach of some states.

As in the case of New York and New Jersey, nothing more than a geographical border such as the Hudson River (or a state boundary line) determines the extent of an accountant's liability to third parties.

It is unlikely that a uniform rule will emerge in the near future. For that reason, each accountant should be aware of the rule in his or her home state, and also be aware of the rule in states into which the accountant's work product might stray.

FRAUD

Recovery by third parties against public accountants has consistently been allowed for common law fraud despite the lack of privity. Actual fraud, as opposed to constructive fraud, has less frequently been the basis for accountant liability in reported cases, and this is fortunate for the profession. Those fraud actions which do succeed in civil suits are also often subject to criminal fraud proceedings (see Chapter Five).

Common law fraud or deceit requires the presence of the following elements in order to be actionable:

1. False representation of a material fact.
2. Knowledge or belief by the defendant that the representation is false. This is often referred to as "scienter."
3. Intent to deceive and induce ("to act or refrain from action") plaintiff to reply upon the representation.
4. Justifiable reliance by the plaintiff.
5. Damages suffered by the plaintiff as a result of the reliance.[70]

It was stated in the *Rusch Factors* case that "[a]n intentionally misrepresenting accountant is liable to all those persons whom he should reasonably have foreseen would be injured by his misrepresentation."[71] The court also expressed the opinion that "[n]either actual knowledge by the accountant of the third person's reliance nor quantitative limitation of the class of reliant persons is requisite to recovery for fraud."[72]

GROSS NEGLIGENCE: INFERENCE OF FRAUD

As has previously been indicated, Judge Cardozo took the position in *Ultramares Corp. v. Touche* that a third party not primarily benefitted could not recover against a public accountant for simple negligence. However, in so doing, Cardozo explained that "[o]ur holding does not emancipate accountants from the consequences of fraud. It does not relieve them if their audit has been so negligent as to justify a finding that they had no genuine belief in its adequacy, for this again is fraud."[73]

In *Ultramares*, the concept was developed that gross negligence raised an inference of fraud. Cardozo stated that "negligence or blindness, even when not equivalent to fraud, is nonetheless evidence to sustain an inference of fraud. At least this is so if the negligence is gross" especially when the gross negligence is "so flimsy, as to lead to the conclusion that there was no genuine belief back of it."[74]

This concept was carried one step further in *State Street Trust Co. v. Ernst*[75] where the court seemingly reached its decisions solely on the basis of gross negligence,[76] thereby giving rise to a subtle departure from *Ultramares* where the basis of liability had been fraud, with gross negligence merely giving rise to an inference of fraud. In *State Street Trust*, the defendant auditors rendered an unqualified certified report to the client company with knowledge that the plaintiff was making the client a loan based on the strength of the certified balance sheet. A month later, defendants sent a letter to the client stating that the provision for uncollectible accounts was inadequate, thereby overstating the receivables, but failed to convey this information which was known at the time of the certification, to the plaintiff. Subsequently, the client went into bankruptcy. Whereas the accountants in *Ultramares* failed to verify the receivables, the accountants in the present case did not act upon their findings as to the state of the receivables either because of bad judgment or oversight. Whatever the reason, the court stated that "[a] refusal to see the obvious, a failure to investigate the doubtful, if sufficiently gross, may furnish evidence leading to an inference of fraud so as to impose liability for losses suffered by those who rely on the balance sheet. In other words, heedlessness and reckless disregard of consequence may take the place of deliberate intention."[77]

If the actions of the accountant appear to the jury to be grossly negligent, or if the accountant appears to have been reckless, it is very likely that the court will allow both clients and nonclients to recover from the accountant and his or her accounting firm. This exception to the *Ultramares* privity rule is a dangerous trap for accountants when negligence is quite obvious to a judge or to the laypersons on a jury.

CONCLUSION

Only if an accountant has been negligent (or fraudulent, or in breach of contract) does an accountant have significant exposure from a lawsuit based on common law claims. The various rules regarding third party liability do not determine the extent of an accountant's duty--they only determine the size of the group of plaintiffs having access to the accountant in court.

For that reason, an accountant's grasp of the legal rules regarding third party liability has little to do with the governance of his or her work.

In fact, an accountant can best avoid the entire issue of third party liability if the accountant conducts his practice **as if** his or her work would always be subject to the "reasonably foreseeable users" test. Nothing can be gained (except exposure to lawsuits) from an accountant's effort to hide behind privity rules (or even *Restatement* rules) in the hope that some users of the accountant's work product will be kept out of the courtroom on the basis of a jurisdictional technicality.

NOTES

1. *See* William H. Volz, Accountant's Liability to Third Persons: Resistance in Negligence, 4 Barrister 31 (Fall 1982).
2. Landell v. Lybrand, 264 Pa. 406, 107 A. 783 (1919).
3. Glanzer v. Shepard, 233 N.Y. 236, 135 N.E. 275 (1922).
4. *Ibid.* 135 N.E. at 275-76.
5. Ultramares Corporation v. Touche, 255 N.Y. 170, 174 N.E. 441 (1931).
6. *Ibid.* 174 N.E. at 442.
7. *Ibid,* 174 N.E. at 442.
8. *Ibid.*
9. *Ibid. See also* Bily v. Arthur Young & Co., 11 Cal.Rptr.2d 51, 89; 834 P.2D 745, 753 (1992).
10. *Ibid.* 174 N.E. at 444.
11. *Ibid,* 174 N.E. at 442.
12. *Ibid,* 174 N.E. at 445.
13. *Ibid,* 174 N.E. at 445.
14. *Ibid.* 174 N.E. at 446.
15. R. James Gormley, Accountants' Professional Liability--A Ten-Year Review, 29 Bus. Law. 1207 (1974).
16. *Ibid,* 174 N.E. at 448.
17. *Ibid.*
18. *See Bily, supra* note 9, 11 Cal.Rpt.2d at 60, 834 P.2d at 754.
19. 43 N.Y.2d 356, 401 N.Y.S.2d 474, 372 N.E.2d 315 (1977).
20. *Ibid,* 401 N.Y.S.2d at 477, 372 N.E.2d at 318.
21. *Ibid,* 401 N.Y.S.2d at 478, 372 N.E.2d at 319.
22. 65 N.Y.2d 536, 493 N.Y.S.2d 435, 483 N.E.2d 110 (1985).
23. *See Bily, supra* note 9, 11 Cal.Rpt.2d at 60, 834 P.2d at 754.
24. *Ibid,* 493 N.Y.S.2d at 443, 483 N.E.2d at 118.
25. *Ibid,* 493 N.Y.S.2d at 445, 483 N.E.2d at 120.

26. *Ibid*, 493 N.Y.S.2d at 444, 483 N.E.2d at 119.
27. 79 N.Y.2d 695, 586 N.Y.S.2d 87, 597 N.E.2d 1080 (1992).
28. *Ibid.*, 79 N.Y.2d at 699; 586 N.Y.S.2d at 88, 597 N.E.2D 1081.
29. *Ibid*, 79 N.Y.2d at 702, 586 N.Y.S.2d at 90, 597 N.E.2d at 1083.
30. *Ibid*, 493 N.Y.S.2d at 443, 483 N.E.2d at 118.
31. *See* Haddon View Inv. Co. v. Coopers & Lybrand, 436 N.E.2d 212, 214-215; 70 Ohio St.2d 154 (1982); First Nat. Bank of Commerce v. Monco Agency Inc., 911 F.2d 1053, 1060 (5th Cir.1990).
32. Security Pacific Business Credit, Inc. v. Peat Marwick Main & Co., 79 N.Y.2d 695, 700; 586 N.Y.S.2d 87, 89; 597 N.E.2d 1080, 1082 (Ct.App.N.Y. 1992).
33. *See* Colonial Bank of Alabama v. Ridley & Schweigert, 551 So.2d 390 (Ala.1989); Idaho Bank & Trust Co. v. First Bancorp of Idaho, 115 Idaho 1082, 772 P.2d 720 (1989); Citizens National Bank v. Kennedy & Coe, 232 Neb. 477, 441 N.W.2d 180 (1989); Landell v. Lybrand 264 Pa. 406, 107 A. 783 (1919).
34. McLean v. Alexander, 599 F.2d 1190, 122 (3d Cir.1979) [Delaware law]; Stephens Indus. Inc. v. Haskins & Sells, 438 F.2d 357 (10th Cir.1971) [Colorado law]; Ackerman v. Schwartz, 947 F.2d 841 (7th Cir.1991) [Indiana law].
35. Ark.Stat.Ann. § 16-114-302 (Supp.1990); Ill.Rev.Stat. ch. 111, ¶ 5535.1 (Supp.1990); Kan.Stat.Ann. § 1-402(b); Utah Code Ann. § 58-26-12 (Supp.1990).
36. Rusch Factors, Inc. v. Levin, 284 F. Supp. 85 (1968).
37. Restatement (Second) of Torts, Section 552 (Tentative Draft No. 12, 1966).
38. *Ibid*.
39. *Ibid*.
40. *Ibid*.
41. *Ibid*.
42. *Ibid*.
43. *Rusch Factors*, 284 F. Supp. at 91.
44. *Ibid*.
45. Gormley, *supra* note 15, 29 Bus. Law. at 1209-10.
46. Ryan v. Kanne, 170 N.W. 2d 395 (Iowa, 1969).
47. *Ibid*. 170 N.W. 2d at 403.
48. Shatterproof Glass Corp. v. James, 466 S.W. 2d 873 (Texas, 1971).
49. The court stated at 880: "We find and hold that within the scope defined in *Restatement, Second, Torts*, Section 552 (Tent, Draft No. 12, 1966), an accountant may be held liable to third parties who rely upon financial standards, audits, etc., prepared by the accountant in cases where the latter fails to exercise ordinary care in the preparation of such statements, audits, etc., and the third party because of such reliance suffers financial loss or damage."
50. 366 S.W. 2d at 887.
51. Rhode Island Hospital Trust National Bank v. Swartz, Bresenoff, Yavner & Jacobs, 455 F.2d 847 (4th Cir. 1972).
52. Raritan River Steel v. Cherry, Bekaert & Holland, 367 S.E. 2d 609 (N.C. 1988); *reversed on other grounds*, 329 N.C. 646 (N.C. 1991).
53. *Ibid*, 322 N.C.App at 216, 367 S.E.2d at 618.
54. Rest.2d Torts, § 552, com. (h), illus. 10.
55. *Ibid*.
56. Bethlehem Steel Corporation v. Ernst & Whinney, 822 S.W.2D 592 (Tenn.1991) (modified Restatement test adopted); First Fla. Bank N.A. v. Max Mitchell & Co., 558 So.2d 9 (Fla. 1990; Badische Corp. v. Caylor 257 Ga. 131, 356 S.E.2d 198 (1987); Pahre v. Auditor of State, 422 N.W.2d 178 (Iowa 1988); Law Offices of Lawrence J. Stockler, P.C. v. Rose 174 Mich.App. 14, 436 N.W.2d 70, 81-82 (1989), leave to appeal denied, 434 Mich. 862 (1990); Bonhiver v. Graff, 311 Minn. 111, 248 N.W.2d 291 (1976); Aluma Kraft Mfg. Co. v. Elmer

Fox & Co., 493 S.W.2d 378 (Mo.Ct.App.1973); Thayer v. Hicks, 243 Mont. 138, 793 P.2d 784 (1990); Spherex Inc. v. Alexander Grant & Co., 122 N.H. 898, 451 A.2d 1308 (1982); Raritan River Steel Co. v. Cherry, 367 S.E.2d 609 (N.C., 1988), *reversed on other grounds*, 329 N.C. 646 (N.C. 1991); Haddon View Inv. Co. v. Coopers & Lybrand, 70 Ohio St.2d 154, 436 N.E.2d 212 (1982); Shatterproof Glass Corp. . James, 466 S.W.2d 873 (Tex.Civ.App.1971); Haberman v. Pub. Power Supply Sys., 744 P.2d 1032 (Wash., 1987); First Nat'l Bank v. Crawford, 386 S.E.2d 310 (W.Va. 1989); First Nat. Bank of Commerce v. Monco Agency Inc., 911 F.2d 1053 (5th Cir. 1990) (Louisiana law); Ingram Indus., Inc. v. Nowicki 527 F.Supp. 683 (E.D.Ky.1981) (Kentucky law); Bunge v. Eide 372 F.Supp. 1058 (D.N.D.1974); Rusch Factors, Inc. v. Levin (D.R.I.1968) 284 F.Supp. 85 (Rhode Island law).

57. 93 N.J. 324, 461 A.2d 138 (1983).
58. *Ibid.* at 352, 461 A.2d at 153.
59. *Ibid.*
60. *Ibid*, 461 A.2d at 142-146.
61. *Ibid*, 461 A.2d at p. 149.
62. *Ibid.*
63. *Ibid*, 461 A.2d at 153.
64. *Ibid.*
65. Citizens State Bank v. Timm, Schmidt & Co., 113 Wisc. 376, 335 N.W. 2d 361 (1983).
66. *Ibid.* at 386, 335 N.W. 2d at 366.
67. *Ibid.* 335 N.W.2d at 365.
68. First Florida Bank, N.A. v. Max Mitchell & Co., 558 So.2d 9, 12-15 (Fla.1990) (rejecting "expansive reasonably foreseeable approach" in favor of Restatement rule); First Nat'l Bank v. Crawford, 182 W.Va. 107, 386 S.E.2d 310, 311-312 (1989) (rejecting foreseeability and privity rules in favor of "middle ground" offered by Restatement rule); Raritan River Steel Co. v. Cherry, Bekaert & Holland, 322 N.C. 200, 367 S.E.2d 609, 617 (1988); Haberman v. Pub. Power Supply Sys., 109 Wash.2d 107, 744 P.2d 1032, 1067-1068 (1987), *modified* 750 P.2d 254 (1988) (adopting Restatement rule and rejecting expansive rule of liability "[i]n deference to legitimate fears of indeterminate liability to third persons").
69. Raritan River Steel v. Cherry, Bekaert & Holland, 367 S.E. 2d 609, 616 (N.C. 1988). S.E.2d at 616
70. WILLIAM L. PROSSER, LAW OF TORTS (4th ed. 1971), pp. 685-86.
71. *Rusch Factors*, 284 F. Supp. at 90.
72. *Ibid.*
73. *Ultramares*, 174 N.E. at 448.
74. *Ultramares*, 174 N.E. at 447 and 448.
75. State Street Trust Co. v. Ernst, 278 N.Y. 104, 15 N.E. 2d 416 (1938).
76. *See* dissenting opinion of Lehman, J., *Ibid.* 15 N.E. 2d at 424.
77. *Ibid.* 15 N.E. 2d at 419.

Chapter Four

Statutory Liability (Civil)

FEDERAL SECURITIES LAWS

The common law protection against the negligent work of accountants and other professionals is not the only source of recovery by injured clients and third parties. The passage of the Securities Act of 1933 and the Securities Exchange Act of 1934 ushered in a significant and potentially greater source of liability to public accountants than had existed under the common law.

Securities Act of 1933

Full and fair disclosure of a material nature in the public offer of securities and the prevention of misrepresentation and fraudulent practices in their sale were the basic objectives of the Securities Act of 1933.

More specifically, the statute regulates the disclosure of material facts in the registration statement and prospectus as part of a new offering of securities to the public. A registration statement contains information and documents that must be filed with the SEC, such as capital structure, description of management and the business enterprise, and financial statements certified by independent public accountants.[1] A prospectus is a document created by the issuer "setting forth the nature and objects" of an issue of securities and "inviting the public to subscribe to the issue."[2]

Section 11. Section 11 permits purchasers of a registered security to sue certain parties, including accountants, in a registered offering when false or misleading information is included in a registration statement filed with the SEC.[3] Under this Section plaintiffs need only show a material misstatement or omission to establish their case.[4] The applicable portion of the section reads:

(a) *Persons possessing cause of action; persons liable.* In case any part of the registration statement, when such part became effective, contained an untrue statement of a material fact or omitted to state a material fact required to be stated therein or necessary to make the statements therein not misleading, any person acquiring such security (unless it is proved that at the time of such acquisition he knew of such untruth or omission) may, either at law or in equity, in any court of competent jurisdiction, sue--

* * *

(4) every accountant. . . or any person whose profession gives authority to a statement made by him, who has with his consent been named as having prepared or certified any part of the registration statement, or as having prepared or certified any report or valuation which is used in connection with the registration statement, with respect to the statement, in such registration statement, report, or valuation, which purports to have been prepared or certified by him. . .[5]

Section 11 of the 1933 Act allows purchasers of a registered security to sue certain enumerated parties in a registered offering when false or misleading information is included in a registration statement. The section was designed to assure compliance with the disclosure provisions of the Act by imposing a stringent standard of liability on the parties who play a direct role in a registered offering. If a plaintiff purchased a security issued pursuant to a registration statement, he need only show a material misstatement or omission to establish a prima facie case. Liability against the issuer of a security is virtually absolute, even for innocent misstatements. Other defendants, including accountant, bear the burden of demonstrating due diligence.[6]

The misrepresentation or statement can be the result of "ordinary" negligence.[7] In stating a Section 11 claim against an accountant, a plaintiff need not prove fraud, gross negligence, privity, reliance, causation or scienter in order to recover.[8]

As a result of Section 11, an accountant may be held liable by purchasers of stock for statements attributed to the accountant on the face of an SEC registration statement.[9] Certified financial statements attached to an SEC registration create exposure for the accountant except to the extent that the accountant can successfully assert affirmative defenses.[10]

Section 11 requires a "reasonable" investigation by accountants.[11] This means that accountants are expected to investigate, to various degrees, facts supporting and contradicting inclusions in registration statements. They must undertake that investigation which a reasonably prudent person in that position would conduct.[12]

Whether an auditor performs a reasonable investigation is inextricably tied to compliance with professional standards, including generally accepted auditing standards ("GAAS"), and generally accepted accounting principles ("GAAP"), and the common law requirement of ordinary care.[13] Failure to comply with GAAS, GAAP and ordinary care may result in Section 11 liability.[14]

"Ordinary care," for purposes of Section 11, can result in a more rigorous standard of care than that prescribed by GAAP and GAAS. If, for example, it item of information would not be disclosed on financial statements because it is not "material" for purposes of GAAP and GAAS, disclosure might still be required under Section 11. That is because fact which has been omitted from a registration statement is "material" for purposes of Section 11 "if there is a substantial likelihood that a reasonable shareholder would consider it important. . . under all the circumstances."[15] For example, if a client changes to a new auditor, GAAP and GAAS do not require the new auditor to disclose all of the possible reasons for the change in the client's next set of financial statements.

Under Section 11, however, such a disclosure might be mandated, because it might appear to a jury in an accountant's liability lawsuit that such a disclosure would be important under all the circumstances.[16]

Section 12. Section 12 of the Securities Act of 1933 consists of two parts, Section 12(1) and Section 12(2). Section 12(1) imposes civil liability on anyone who violates the registration requirements of the SEC.

Section 12(2) applies to any person who offers or sells securities by means of any prospectus containing an untrue statement of a material fact. It also applies to the omission of a material fact necessary in order to make a prospectus, in the light of the circumstances under which the prospectus os provided, not misleading. The statute provides that such a person shall be liable to the person purchasing a security described in the prospectus for rescission or, if the plaintiff has sold the security, for damages.[17]

Section 12 covers the same kind of misleading information as does Section 11, but looks to the offending prospectus, rather than the offending registration statement, for its application.

The language of Section 12(2) technically applies to "offerors"or "sellers" of the securities liable to the persons purchasing "from" them.[18] However, some courts have observed that accountants can be held responsible for "aiding and abetting" such offerors and sellers. Such aiding and abetting liability can apply to accountants under the securities laws if there is (1) a securities violation by a primary wrongdoer, (2) knowledge of the wrongdoing by the accountant, and (3) substantial assistance in the primary wrongdoing by the accountant.[19]

In *Sandusky Land, Ltd. v. Uniplan Groups, Inc.*,[20] the Court ruled that an accounting firm could be held liable as an aider-abettor of violations of section 12(2) of the 1933 Securities Act. The accounting firm in *Uniplan* had allegedly issued a misleading written opinion to investors concerning the tax benefits of a recommended investment. Even though the accounting firm was not the actual seller of the offending securities, the Court found no use in " 'attempting to delineate a legally cognizable distinction between. . . persons . . . exposed to liability under section 12(2) and those persons charged with aiding and abetting and conspiring in the violation of [that section]."[21]

The "substantial assistance" triggering an accountant's liability under Section 12(2) can occur intentionally, or because of sheer recklessness on the part of the accountant.[22] That is because the courts have determined that an accountant charged with the specific responsibility of a competent professional audit cannot relieve himself or herself of liability by shutting his or her eyes to what was plainly to be seen.[23]

Section 15. Section 15 of the Securities Act of 1933 gives teeth to the bite of Sections 11 and 12 by making those who control, through stock ownership, agency, or otherwise, persons that have violated sections 11 or 12 of the Securities Act jointly and severally liable with the controlled persons.[24]

The purpose of Section 15 is to impose liability on those persons (and their aiders and abettors) who control or influence corporations or other organizations or persons ("controlled persons") and who are in some meaningful sense culpable participants in the fraud perpetrated by those controlled entities.[25] The statute imposes liability on persons who might attempt to evade liability under common law principles utilizing "dummies" that would act in their place and under their control.[26] A controlling person covered by Section 15 is liable for the acts of another if the controlling person acted in bad faith and directly or indirectly induced the conduct which violates the securities law.[27]

The *Crazy Eddie* Case. The case of *Bernstein v. Crazy Eddie, Inc.*[28] provides an example of a situation leading to an accountant's liability under Sections 11, 12(2) and 15. In that case, Crazy Eddie, Inc., made several public offerings of its securities. Its founder, president, and primary owner sold millions of shares of stock, and then suddenly resigned his position as president of the company. Successor management discovered that the financial statements of the corporation immediately prior to and during the public offerings were fraudulent. Those financial statements had been included in, and referred to, both the SEC registration statements and the prospectuses of Crazy Eddie, Inc.

The financial picture of Crazy Eddie, Inc., had been misstated in several ways. Management had inflated Crazy Eddie's net income, inventory figures, and per store sales figures through a series of improper financial reporting practices. For example, they treated wholesale transactions as retail sales, creating the impression that per store sales were materially higher than they actually were. They treated as inventory merchandise that Crazy Eddie intended to return to manufacturers, nicknaming this merchandise "reeps." Transactions that were really consignments they treated as sales. In pursuit of these schemes, they altered and destroyed documents, including invoices, inventory count sheets, debit memos, sales-incentive-related materials, and accounting records. And they conducted a mass shredding of corporate documents days or weeks before new management assumed control.

In addition, the founder of the corporation and his family sold approximately five to ten million dollars' worth of inventory to themselves and other related parties in unrecorded cash transactions for eventual resale to others.

The family termed these sales "nehkdi," an Arabic slang word for under-the-table transactions. One of the motives for inflation of Crazy Eddie's inventory was to offset and conceal the "nehkdi" sales.

The plaintiffs in the *Crazy Eddie's* case, purchasers of stock prior to disclosure of the faulty financial statements, sued the accounting firm along with the board of directors and other defendants. The plaintiffs alleged that the accounting firm violated several generally accepted auditing standards and accounting principles in failing to look behind the corporation's irregular books and fabricated records and, and that it made patently false explanations for the "loss" of destroyed records. As a result, the plaintiffs were able to show that the certified financial statements and projections in the registration statements and prospectuses were false and misleading in violation of Sections 11 and 12 because they gave an unduly optimistic impression of the financial health of Crazy Eddie's, Inc.

In ruling against the accounting firm, the court held that in order to bring Section 11 and 12 claims against an auditor, a plaintiff need not plead or prove fraud or gross negligence.[29] Nor must a claimant prove that each instance of misinformation is material.[30] Instead, a plaintiff need only identify any material misstatements in the registration statements that, taken as a whole, are misleading.[31]

The *Jiffy Lube* Case. In another case, *Jiffy Lube Securities Litigation*,[32] the prospectus and registration statements of Jiffy Lube International included an unqualified opinion letter prepared as the result of an audit by an accounting firm. The SEC brought an action against the accounting firm under Sections 11 and 12 as a result of several problems, including the following:

1. Accounts designated "loans receivable" were deceptive and materially false and misleading when made because the accounting firm knew that JLI had lent certain of its franchisees large amounts of capital, without which the franchisees could not survive. In return, these franchisees gave Jiffy Lube substantial area development fees and initial franchise fees which Jiffy Lube booked as revenues. Because the accounting firm knew that these undercapitalized franchises were experiencing serious operational and financial difficulties, it was aware that the substantial monies loaned by Jiffy Lube to them were improperly recorded on the client's books and records as assets without an adequate allowance for doubtful accounts. As a result, assets were overstated, and the financial statements did not conform to GAAP.

2. Similarly, the fact that the area franchise fees and initial franchise fees would probably never be collected meant that they should never have been recorded as revenues in the first place, due to the operational and financial difficulties of the franchisees. Therefore, Jiffy Lube's reported revenues and net income figures were inflated, again in breach of GAAP.

3. One particular franchisee had been indirectly owned by Jiffy Lube. However, Jiffy Lube, allegedly upon the advice of the accounting firm, brought in a third party to own larger percentage of the stock of the franchisee so that Jiffy Lube would not be required under the equity method of accounting for investments to record losses incurred by the franchisee.[33] Jiffy Lube also purchased several quick lube centers and resold them to the same franchisee, reporting a significant profit from the purchase and sale. That profit, as well as franchise fees from the "unaffiliated" franchisee (which equalled all of Jiffy Lube's net income for one quarter and 24 percent of its income for one year) could be recorded without a disclosure that the franchisee was a related party.

The court in the *Jiffy Lube* case concluded that the Sections 11 and 12 claims against the accounting firm were properly stated, and resulted in the types of misleading registration statements and prospectuses that those provisions of the securities laws are designed to prevent.[34]

The *BarChris* Case. Another case establishing liability for accountants under Sections 11 and 12 was *Escott v. BarChris Construction Corporation*.[35] BarChris was a fast-growing, unusually successful construction company primarily engaged in building bowling centers. In order to meet its continual need for working capital to finance the expanding operations, BarChris sought to sell debentures. The required registration statement of the debentures was filed with the Securities and Exchange Commission, and BarChris obtained the necessary financing. However, the industry became overbuilt and the corporation eventually defaulted in interest payments on the debentures and filed for bankruptcy. Plaintiffs brought suit under Section 11 of the Securities Act of 1933 against, among others, the public accountants, who audited the financial statements contained in the registration statement. They alleged that the statement contained material false statements and material omissions. In finding the defendant public accountants liable, the court examined and discussed some of the following issues relevant to Section 11:

1. *Due Diligence Defense.* The liability that is imposed upon the public accountant under Section 11 for material misstatements or omissions can be avoided by the "due diligence" defense which provides that the burden of proof placed upon the public accountant shall be sustained upon a showing that "he had, after reasonable investigation, reasonable ground to believe and did believe, at the time such part of the registration statements became effective, that the statements therein were true and that there was no omission to state a material fact required to be stated therein or necessary to make the statements therein not misleading."[36]

2. *Reasonableness.* The standard use to determine "reasonableness" of the investigation and grounds for belief is that "required of a prudent man in the management of his own property."[37]

3. *Materiality.* The *BarChris* court defined materiality as "matters which an average prudent investor needs to know before he can make an intelligent informed decision whether or not to but the security."[38]

4. *S-1 Review--Due Diligence Review.* For purposes of determining whether there are false or misleading statements in the certified balance sheet as of the *effective date,*[39] subsequent events to the balance sheet date should be reviewed to ascertain any material changes that require disclosure. This is accomplished through an S-1 review, which indicates whether there was a reasonable belief in the year-end figures.

The *BarChris* court concluded that the defendant public accountants had not satisfied their burden of proof by establishing the due diligence defense. The S-1 review was determined to be useless because the review had not measured up to the standards of either the profession or the firm. The review program conformed to generally accepted auditing standards, but the execution was totally inadequate. Approximately only 20½ hours were devoted to the review. Glib answers to questions that were asked were considered satisfactory without any verification. What were thought to be valid contracts were in fact intercompany sales to subsidiaries and fictitious contracts that could have been detected by examining the contract documents. An increase in notes payable was explained in the review as merely a tight cash position when in fact payment checks were being held up because there was no money in BarChris's bank account to cover them. The court concluded:

This is not to say that he should have made a complete audit. But there were enough danger signals in the materials which he did examine to require some further investigation on his part. Generally accepted accounting standards required such further investigation under the circumstances. It is not always sufficient merely to ask questions.[40]

5. *Standard of Care.* The *BarChris* court did not specifically define the required standard of conduct to be exercised by the public accountant. By not deferring to accounting experts, the court appears to have decided that something other than *professional standards* should be determinative.
6. *Statute of Limitations.* A plaintiff must bring action within one year of discovery of the misstatement or omission and within three years of the date offered to the public.

Securities Exchange Act of 1934

The Securities and Exchange Commission was established by the Securities Exchange Act of 1934 for the express purpose of administering the Acts of 1933 and 1934. The 1934 Act is primarily concerned with *continuous disclosure* by issuers listing and trading securities on a stock exchange or possessing assets over $1 million and equity securities of any class held by 500 or more persons. The 1933 Act requires disclosures on new security issues by means of a registration statement and prospectus up to the effective date of the issue, which may require inquiry and examination beyond completion of the audit; the 1934 Act requires financial data only up to the close of the last fiscal year in the initial registration and the annual filing of 10-K reports 120 days after the end of every fiscal year.[41]

Section 18. This section deals specifically with documents filed with the SEC and imposes liability on any person who makes a material false or misleading statement in the document. The relevant portion reads:

Any person who shall make or cause to be made any statement in any application, report, or document filed pursuant to this title or any rule or regulation thereunder. . . , which statement was at the time and in the light of the circumstances under which it was made false or misleading with respect to any material fact, shall be liable to any person (not knowing that such statement was false or misleading) who, in reliance upon such statement, shall have purchased or sold a security at a price which was affected by such statement, for damages caused by such reliance, unless the person sued shall prove that he acted in good faith and had no knowledge that such statement was false or misleading.[42]

Section 18 of the 1934 Act creates a private cause of action against persons, such as accountants, who 'make or cause to be made' materially misleading statements in reports or other documents filed with the Securities and Exchange Commission. Under section 18 liability extends to persons who, in reliance on such statements, purchased or sold a security whose price was affected by the statements. To recover from an accountant, the plaintiff need not show that the accountant acted fraudulently (or with gross negligence). Liability is limited, however, in the important respect that the defendant is accorded the defense that he acted in good faith and had no knowledge that such statement was false or misleading.[43]

Despite the good faith defense, accountants have been brought under the purview of section 18. In *Fischer v. Kletz*,[44] for example, the court found that failure of public accountants to disclose information acquired subsequent to filing a form 10-K report, which made the financial statements materially false and misleading, stated a cause of action for liability to third parties under Section 18. And in *Re Equity Funding Corporation of America Securities Litigation*,[45] it was held that an accountant prepared and certified false and misleading financial statements in connection with filings required under the statutes and rules to which section 18 applies, and thus fall within the class of persons who can be held liable under that section of the securities laws.[46] As a result of these and other cases, the good faith defense has not been eliminated, but it is limited to the extent that an accountant is not entitled to the good faith defense if he or she has been extremely negligent (i.e., the accountant engaged in gross negligence) or has otherwise fraudulently breached his or her duties.[47]

Section 10(b) and Rule 10b-5. The scope of Section 10(b) of the Securities Exchange Act of 1934 is as broad and expansive as Section 18 is narrow and limited. Section 10(b) is the primary antifraud provision of the Exchange Act, and makes it unlawful for any person to "use or employ" a "manipulative or deceptive device or contrivance" in connection with the purchase or sale of any security.

Section 10(b), and Rule 10b-5 adopted thereunder, are intended to protect the ordinary investor against insufficient information by deceptive practices. The application of Section 10(b) and Rule 10b-5 have been expanded in recent years to include accountants. It should be noted that Rule 10b-5 has served as a substitute basis for liability when other sections of the securities laws proved to be inadequate[48] and sometimes even when they proved adequate.[49]

Rule 10b-5 provides that it is unlawful for any person, directly or indirectly, by the use of any means or instrumentality of interstate commerce, or of the mails:

1. To employ any device, scheme or artifice to defraud.
2. To make any untrue statement of a material fact or to omit to state a material fact necessary in order to make the statement made, in the light of the circumstances under which they were made, not misleading, or
3. To engage in any act, practice or course of business which operates or would operate as a fraud or deceit upon any person, in connection with the purchase or sale of any security.[50]

As a result of Rule 10b-5, have held that depending on the circumstances, accountants may have a duty to disclose information to investors when they make affirmative statements on which they know the investors will rely.[51]

There are three routes by which an accountant may be held liable under the Rule. First, an accountant is directly liable for intentional or reckless misrepresentations if the accountant knows his or her statements will be communicated to third parties.[52] The Rule interprets Section 10(b) of the securities exchange statute by prohibiting any person from making false or misleading statements "in connection with" the purchase or sale of a security, even if the person plays an auxiliary role in the transaction.

Second, an accountant may be held liable for knowingly joining and substantially assisting in the misrepresentations of another, regardless of whether he makes any false statements of his own. Although the Supreme Court has twice reserved decision on liability for aiding and abetting a violation of Rule 10b-5,[53] several courts of appeals, have consistently recognized the validity of such a theory.[54] Like any conspiracy to defraud, this route generally requires knowledge of the fraud and intent to join in it.

Third, an accountant may be held liable for recklessly aiding and abetting a primary violation regardless of whether he or she has made misrepresentations of his or her own, when the accountant's assistance in the fraud is particularly substantial and unusual or when he or she owes some special duty of disclosure.[55] This third path differs from conspiracy and the usual principles of aiding and abetting insofar as it allows liability for reckless disregard of facts indicating a client's fraud and the accountant's assistance in it.[56]

The "in connection with" requirement of Rule 10b-5 seems to necessitate the existence of privity in the purchase or sale of the security. However, this requirement has been dispelled, as noted above,[57] and privity need not exist for accountants' liability to third parties under Rule 10b-5. To be held liable under Rule 10b-5, an accountant must simply be aware that his or her statements are to be communicated to investors. This concept was firmly enunciated in a nonaccountant case, *SEC v. Texas Gulf Sulphur Co.*,[58] in which the court interpreted Congressional intent as considering the "in connection with" requirement satisfied, so that Rule 10b-5 is violated, whenever assertions are made, as here, in a manner reasonably calculated to influence the investing public.[59]

The *Herzfeld* Case. The full thrust of Section 10(b) and Rule 10b-5 was felt in *Herzfeld v. Laventhol, Krekstein, Horwath & Horwath*[60] in which the U.S. District Court for the Southern District of New York permitted recovery against accountants under Rule 10b-5 notwithstanding compliance with generally accepted accounting principles. The plaintiff investor had purchased securities of the client corporation prior to an audit prepared by the defendant in connection with a private offering of the client's securities. Subsequent to the audit, the client corporation offered to refund all investments to the private offering prior to the audit. In reliance upon the audited financial statements, the plaintiff declined the refund and kept the securities. The plaintiff, who lost most of his investment due to bankruptcy of the corporation, claimed that the financial statements were false and misleading because profits from the sale of nursing home properties were reported in the income statement on a deferred basis, which transformed the corporation into a profitable position. Due to the defendant's concern as to the collectibility of the balance receivable on the contracts, the audit opinion was qualified by indicating:

> . . . subject to the collectibility of the balance receivable on the contract of sale (see Note 4 of Notes to Financial Statements).

The court, in holding that the disclosure in the qualification note was inadequate and that the absence of essential details about the noncollectibility made the statement misleading, stated that the note, "absent disclosure of the reasoning and facts which prompted it, would not alert potential investors to the uncertainties." Though the qualification was explicit as required, it was still considered insufficient.

The elements of proof to maintain a 10b-5 action seem to require the following:

1. Material representation.
2. Reliance by the plaintiff.
3. Damages suffered as a result of the reliance.
4. Scienter.

The first element, material representation, can include the omission of material information, or the inclusion of misleading information. Overstatement of sales revenues as the result of "prebilling" (recording sales prior to the occurrence of such sales) is an example of such material representation.[61]

The last element, scienter, can be defined as a mental state of mind embracing an intent to deceive, manipulate, or defraud as defined by the courts. Many courts have recognized that reckless conduct on the part of the accountant can satisfy the scienter requirements for a primary violation under Rule 10b-5.[62] This applies even if the accountant is accused of merely aiding and abetting the primary offender.[63] Reckless conduct can be defined as conduct which is highly unreasonable and which represents an extreme departure from the standards of ordinary care, to the extent that the danger was either known to the defendant or so obvious that the accountant must have been aware of it.[64]

Courts have also ruled that scienter on the part of an accountant can occur when the accountant is grossly negligent, if the plaintiffs are third parties whose reliance upon the accountant's audit or opinion letter is reasonably foreseeable.[65] Gross negligence is established by such plaintiffs when they are able to show that the accountant exhibited an egregious refusal to "see the obvious or to investigate the doubtful.[66]

It should be observed that the reliance by plaintiff in the *Herzfeld* case involved two unusual aspects. First, the securities were not purchased in reliance upon the audited financial statements; rather, they were retained in reliance. Second, the plaintiff never bothered to read the part of the report containing the explanatory note, yet the court still found that the plaintiff justifiably relied upon the income statement.

The question was raised as to whether compliance with generally accepted accounting principles in treating the doubtful collectibility of the receivables shielded the accountants from liability. The court responded by stating that the requisite duty owed to investors was full and complete disclosure by fair presentation of the company's financial condition, which compliance with generally accepted accounting principles did not conclusively guarantee.

Rule 2(e) Proceedings

Rule 2(e) of the Rules of Practice before the SEC gives the Commission the power to temporarily or permanently "disbar" any person by denying her or him the privilege of appearing and practicing before it if that person:

1. Does not possess the requisite qualifications to represent others;
2. Lacks character or integrity.
3. Engages in unethical or improper professional conduct;
4. Has willfully violated any provision of the federal security laws, or has willfully aided and abetted such violation.

The Commission also has the power to suspend any person from appearing or practicing before it if that person:

1. Has been convicted of a misdemeanor involving moral turpitude;
2. Has been convicted of a felony;
3. Has had his license to practice as an accountant suspended or revoked;
4. Has been permanently enjoined from violating provisions of the federal securities laws;
5. Has been found by the Commission in an administrative proceeding or by a court of competent jurisdiction to have violated provisions of federal securities laws.[67]

These sanctions of disbarment and suspension are not only applicable to individual accountants, but also to an entire accounting firm. Practice before the Commission is defined as "(1) transacting any business with the Commission, and (2) the preparation of any statement, opinion or other paper by any. . . accountant, filed with the Commission in any registration statement, notification, application, report or other document with the consent of such. . . accountant."

Thus, if the Commission refused to accept an accountant's audit opinion because of that accountant's disbarment or suspension, the resulting impact can be catastrophic. If clients are unable to obtain timely filings with the SEC through their accounting firm, they are not likely to remain clients very long.

It is no wonder, then, that firms placed in such a position are more than willing to consent to alternative sanctions in order to avoid the more severe ones, not to mention the expense of litigation and unfavorable publicity. In a consent decree, the consenting party, in essence, does not admit guilt, but promises never to do it again. Various alternative sanctions have been imposed upon accounting firms, such as:

1. Prohibition against taking on new clients likely to result in SEC filings for a specified period;
2. Reviews and inspections of adoption and compliance with professional auditing standards and procedures;
3. Continuing education programs.

Review of Accounting Firm Procedures. In 1975, Peat, Marwick, Mitchell & Company agreed to the institution of a Rule 2(e) proceeding as part of a settlement offer arising out of PMM's examination of the financial statements of several companies, including National Student Marketing Corporation. The settlement required a review of certain audit and accounting procedures used by the firm. This "review and report" type of sanction should not be thought of as punitive, but as a constructive means of preventing similar problems in the future.

The provisions of the settlement offer contained the following:

Ordered

1. This proceeding under Rule 2(e) of the Commission's Rules of Practice is instituted. PMM's offer of settlement, dated June 1975, is hereby accepted.
2. An investigation will be made of the manner in which the audit practice of PMM is conducted with respect to audit clients whose financial statements reported upon by PMM are filed with the Commission.
   a. That examination will be carried out by a committee (the "Committee") whose compensation and expenses will be borne by PMM. The members of the Committee will be chosen by PMM from a list of persons acceptable to the staff of the Commission.
   b. The joint understanding of the Commission and of PMM concerning the examination is outlined in a memorandum addressed to the Committee. The memorandum is Annex B to PMM's offer of settlement.
   c. It is contemplated by the Commission and by PMM that the examination can be completed and the report of the Committee submitted within six months.
   d. PMM will promptly take all steps reasonably necessary and appropriate to adopt and implement any reasonable recommendations the Committee

may make with respect to the manner in which such audit practice is conducted, provided, however, that if PMM demonstrates to the satisfaction of the Commission that a recommendation of the Committee is not reasonable or need not be implemented either in the form recommended or with reasonable modifications, such recommendation need not be adopted.

e. The contents of the investigation, the working papers, and other documents (except the Committee's report) and the deliberations of the Committee will be held confidential except from PMM and the Commission.

3. PMM will promptly take all steps reasonably necessary and appropriate to adopt and implement the procedures contained in Annex C to PMM's offer of settlement. PMM will notify the Chief Accountant of the Commission prior to any amendment of such procedures within the next five years.

4. PMM will conduct a study of the use of the percentage of completion method of accounting and establish guidelines in this area for its audit practice, which will be applied in the conduct of its audits for fiscal years beginning on or after December 27, 1975.

5. For the six-month period from May 1, 1975, through October 31, 1975, PMM has not accepted and will not accept audit engagements from new audit clients which contemplate the issuance by PMM of an auditor's opinion, in respect of financial statements which it is expected by PMM will be filed with the Commission within the next succeeding twelve-month period. Such limitation shall not induce an audit client (i) in which a significant equity or debt interest is held or acquired by a present client of PMM; (ii) for which PMM has provided professional services since January 1, 1974, and prior to May 1, 1975; (iii) which is controlled by a foreign entity provided the financial statements of the client are not separately filed with the Commission; (iv) which is a client or a subsidiary or a division of a client of a foreign affiliated firm of PMM; (v) which since July 1, 1974, and prior to May 1, 1975, has communicated with PMM concerning the possible

engagement of PMM as its auditor (the Commission having been advised of the number of such instances); or (vi) if its acceptance by PMM as an audit client is approved in the particular circumstances by the Chief Accountant of the Commission.

6. A review will be conducted in 1976 and in 1977 at PMM's expense of the matters considered under the AICPA program for the review of quality control procedures of multi-office firms and to determine whether PMM has taken all steps reasonably necessary and appropriate to adopt and implement the procedures described in Annex C to PMM's offer of settlement and any recommendation of the Committee (subject to the proviso stated in Paragraph 2.d).

   a. Each review will be conducted by a panel operating under the AICPA program, or (if such a panel is not prepared to act) by the Committee of not less than three accountant members thereof, or (if the Committee or three of its members are not prepared to act) by a group of not less than three certified public accountants chosen by PMM from a list of persons acceptable to the staff of the Commission.

   b. The results of each review will be reported to the Commission and to PMM.

   c. The contents of each review, the working papers, other documentation (except the report of its results), and deliberations of the reviewers will be held confidential except from PMM and the Commission.

7. The Commission retains jurisdiction of this proceeding.[68]

Suspension or Disbarment. Rule 2(e) proceedings might also result in the temporary or permanent denial of the privilege of practicing before the SEC. In a recent case involving the misrepresentation by accountants in violation of Rule 10b-5, for example, one of the accountant was disbarred in a Rule 2(e) proceeding from practicing before the SEC.

That case involved an SEC action against an accountant whose actions, in the view of the SEC, aided and abetted a negligent representation that led to the bankruptcy of ZZZZ Best Company, Inc.[69] ZZZZ Best was a Nevada corporation organized in December 1985.

ZZZZ Best was in the business of providing residential and commercial carpet, upholstery and drapery cleaning services. In December 1986, ZZZZ Best raised $ 15 million in a public offering registered pursuant to a Form S-1 registration statement filed on October 23, 1986, and effective on December 9, 1986. On January 31, 1987, ZZZZ Best's securities were registered with the Securities and Exchange Commission. The company's securities were traded in the over-the-counter market and, from December 1986 until July 1987, certain of the company's securities were quoted on the National Association of Securities Dealers, Inc., Automated Quotation System ("NASDAQ").

ZZZZ Best filed for bankruptcy protection in July 1987. A trustee was appointed, and all of ZZZZ Best's remaining assets were subsequently liquidated.

In September 1986, the accountant, Larry G. Baker, had been retained by ZZZZ Best to audit ZZZZ Best's financial statements for its fiscal years ended April 30, 1984, and April 30, 1985. Baker issued an unqualified report as of September 29, 1986. The audit report was included in ZZZZ Best's registration statements with the explicit written consent of Baker.

Contrary to Baker's representation in his audit report, however, Baker had apparently failed to audit ZZZZ Best's fiscal 1984 and 1985 financial statements in accordance with GAAS. Specifically, in the performance of his audit of ZZZZ Best's financial statements, Baker failed to comply with several major GAAS provisions, in that he:

1. Failed to obtain sufficient competent evidential matter, in that he obtained all of his underlying accounting data from ZZZZ Best's management and gathered no corroborating evidential matter from third parties. In fact, the accounting data that Baker received from ZZZZ Best was entirely fabricated. He also
   a. failed to obtain evidence corroborating ZZZZ Best's bank statements; and
   b. failed to communicate with and review the work of ZZZZ Best's predecessor auditor.
2. Failed to disclaim an opinion despite the evidentiary deficiencies.
3. Failed to adequately plan the audit and to consider audit risk.

The SEC determined that Baker's representation in his audit report letter that his examinations were made in accordance with GAAS was materially false and misleading.

The SEC and Baker entered into a consent order, pursuant to Rule 2(e), whereby the accountant is permanently denied the privilege of appearing or practicing before the Commission.[70]

FOREIGN CORRUPT PRACTICES ACT

Many provisions of the Foreign Corrupt Practices Act (FCPA), an antibribery law originally enacted in 1977 and most recently amended in 1988, are dependant upon the existence and effectiveness of internal accounting controls of U.S. businesses.   The audit committee of the corporate board of directors is often the most logical group already in place in U.S. corporations that has the capacity to the develop, implement, and ascertain compliance with corporate codes of ethics.[71]   Such codes are critical to the firm's compliance with the FCPA because they establish corporate policy with regard to bribes, "grease payments," and disbursements of similar character.   This article discusses the existing and potential involvement of the audit committee in the process of compliance with the FCPA by U.S. businesses. Based on a study of audit committee operations, this article examines their oversight role with respect to the FCPA.

The enactment of the FCPA represented a response by Congress to the discovery that bribery of foreign officials and other forms of unsavory conduct were often used by American companies to secure business abroad. So widespread was the appearance of corruption, that Securities and Exchange Commission investigations led some to conclude that over 300 American companies had made questionable payments to foreign officials.

Despite accusations of attempting to export American puritanical values to cultures and countries where such values are not necessarily present, Congress enacted the 1977 FCPA with the understanding that bribery by business officials was *per se* unethical and detrimental to American business. Bribery is simply a way of doing business in many countries. Nevertheless, Congress voted to require that U.S. corporations not participate in such business tactics, with the practical result that companies from other countries with less concern about the morality of bribes would often be provided with export incentives and an opportunity to edge out American companies in many situations. In so doing, Congress set in motion its renewed effort to eradicate bribery by American corporations, since, as was indicated at hearings on the original FCPA, it believed that bribery: (a) tainted the credibility of American business operations and the principles of free enterprise in general; (b) caused embarrassment with allies and foes alike; (c) created foreign policy difficulties; and (d) generally tarnished the world's image of our nation.

Accounting and Antibribery Provisions

The FCPA consists of two parts. One part deals with the prohibitions against bribery, and those prohibitions are inserted both as an amendment to the Securities and Exchange Act, as applied to publicly held companies considered "issuers" of securities,[72] as well as an identical stand-alone provision directed at all other American businesses.[73] Generally, the FCPA prohibits corporate officers from knowingly participating in bribes or offers of bribes to foreign officials in order to obtain or retain business. "Grease payments," or payments to essentially clerical or low-level employees for purposes of facilitating performance of routine administrative functions such as clerical processing or procurement of licenses, are treated as an exception under the FCPA.[74]

The second part of the FCPA contains record-keeping requirements, imposing a duty upon U.S.corporations to keep books, records and accounts in reasonable detail, and in a manner that accurately and fairly reflects and transactions involving dispositions of assets[75] In addition, companies were required to develop and maintain adequate systems of internal control. Congress intended that these accounting standards would lead to greater credibility of corporate records and less likelihood of concealment of bribes by American corporations.

Penalties

Violators of both the anti-bribery and the accounting provisions of the FCPA face civil liabilities, and violators of the anti-bribery provisions also face criminal liabilities.[76] The SEC has jurisdiction to investigate companies who may have violated the anti-bribery and accounting provisions, and may bring a civil injunction action against an issuer. The SEC may also refer a bribery case to the Department of Justice for prosecution.[77] The Department of Justice has authority to investigate American companies other than issuers, and handles all criminal prosecutions.[78] In addition, the Criminal Division of the Department of Justice has offered to respond to written requests for an advance indication of its position in light of specific circumstances under its "Opinion Procedure."[79]

Violation of the FCPA can result in a fine for a corporation of up to $2 million, and a fine for an individual of up to $100 thousand. In addition to these fines, civil penalties of $10 thousand per violation can be imposed on individuals or corporation by either the SEC or the Department of Justice. Criminal violations can also result in imprisonment of up to five years. Individual corporate employees may be convicted even if his or her employer has not been found to have violated the FCPA.

Imposition of civil and criminal penalties can be precluded if a U.S. corporation can demonstrate that sufficient safeguards have been established to ensure that there can be no implicitly or explicitly "authorized" violation of the FCPA.

Monitoring Compliance of Written Antibribery Policies

While management is responsible for establishing the companies' control structure, including internal accounting controls, most violations of the FCPA occur when management overrides these controls.[80] Consequently, the certified public accountant cannot necessarily accept management's assurances of such compliance without considering the adequacy of the evidence presented in support of its claim. As part of their audits, independent auditors obtain management's representations to confirm oral or implicit representations and to remind management of its primary responsibilities for the financial statements. Likewise, audit committees should obtain management's written assurances that existing requirements of the FCPA have been met.

Audit Committee Review of Management Compliance Procedures. Written assurances alone, of course, do not relieve the audit committee of the responsibility of overseeing compliance with the FCPA. They complement, rather than replace, other procedures. To exercise due care in monitoring internal accounting controls and to ascertain that compliance with the FCPA is based on objective and competent evidence, the audit committee should review management's evaluation of the adequacy of corporate internal control procedures and request that both internal and external auditors corroborate these conclusions. In addition to stating that the company has complied with the FCPA, management should respond formally to pertinent comments found in the independent auditor's management letter and in internal audit reports. These responses should contain management's statements of agreement or disagreement with the auditors' findings and a description of the resolution of the problem or deficiency in order to provide an indication of the strength of compliance to internal controls.

Client's Reliance upon Independent Auditors. If significant internal control weaknesses come to the attention of a corporation's independent auditors during a financial audit, the auditors are required under *Statements on Auditing Standards (SAS) No. 30, Required Communication of Material Weaknesses in Internal Accounting Control*, to communicate such weaknesses to the board of directors or its audit committee. A company may voluntarily engage the CPA to specifically review its system of internal accounting controls and to express an opinion on that system. Pursuant to *SAS No. 30, Reporting on Internal Accounting Control*, however, the accountant is not called upon to express an opinion *per se* as to whether the company is in compliance with the accounting control provisions of the FCPA.

Several authoritative pronouncements do implicitly require CPAs to monitor corporate compliance with the FCPA. Four of nine recently promulgated "Expectation Gap" *Statements on Auditing Standards* (*SAS's*) involve the role of the corporate audit committees as well as the responsibilities of CPAs and other related matters. *SAS No. 53, The Auditor's Responsibility to Detect and Report Errors and Irregularities* (which supersedes *SAS No. 16*), and *SAS No. 54, Illegal Acts by Clients* (which supersedes *SAS No. 17*), respectively require auditors to notify the audit committee (or its equivalent) of any suspected fraud or illegal acts. *SAS No. 60, Communication of Internal Control Structure and Related Matters in an Audit*, requires auditors to report a broader set of internal control deficiencies to the audit committee (or its equivalent) of any suspected fraud or illegal acts. *SAS No. 61, Communications with Audit Committees*, requires the auditors to disclose certain potential and resolved matters pertaining to the audit committee or to those responsible for overseeing the financial reporting process (e.g., the owner of a small proprietorship).

In light of these developments, the FCPA will inevitably add significance to the CPAs' study and evaluation of internal accounting control. CPAs currently evaluate those controls and ascertain the reliability of accounting data to determine the nature, timing and extent of other audit tests, not to form an opinion on management's representations as to the adequacy of all internal accounting controls. Yet clients will undoubtedly request (or otherwise expect) CPAs to expand their scope to help the client measure compliance with the FCPA.

DECEPTIVE TRADE PRACTICE LEGISLATION

Most states have consumer legislation that includes a private right of action against businesses and professionals who engage in deceptive trade practices.[81] These statutes often include provisions for recovery of a plaintiff's attorney fees and costs, as well as treble damages or punitive damages.

The deceptive trade practice laws often have a longer statute of limitations than is allowed for malpractice lawsuits, so plaintiffs who do not file their lawsuits in time to make a malpractice claim are given a "second chance" under these statutes. The statutes of limitations are not triggered, in addition, until the plaintiff discovers a deceptive trade practice. A two-year statute of limitations, for example, would allow a plaintiff to sue an accountant any time within two years of his or her discovery of an accountant's deceptive trade practice. Few states would exclude the services of accountants from accountability under their deceptive trade practice legislation.[82]

CIVIL RICO LIABILITY

The Racketeer-Influenced and Corrupt Organizations (RICO) statute, enacted in 1970, has become a widely used weapon against accountants.[83] RICO provides both civil (treble damages) and criminal sanctions for certain types of illegal activities. Although RICO was intended to serve as an important tool in the efforts of U.S. federal prosecutors in their efforts against organized crime, its "plain reading" is not so limited.

Accountants have been the target of numerous RICO actions. Despite the highly technical nature of the statue, accountants have been accused of using the U.S. mail, and the telephone wires, while "conspiring" to cause injury to investors, stockholders, lenders, and other plaintiffs. Accountants are frequently the targets of plaintiffs seeking deep pockets for purposes of obtaining such litigation advantages as treble damages, statutory attorney fees and costs, and a civil "preponderance of the evidence" standard of proof (rather than a criminal "beyond a reasonable doubt" standard).

It is impossible to take sufficient steps so as to be assured that an accountant or other professional would not be named as a RICO defendant. A general understanding of the nature of the RICO statute can, however, provide insight as to the types of activities that could result in a RICO judgment. The following explanation, therefore, serves to summarize the more relevant sections of RICO in view of an accountant's potential liability.

Technical Provisions of RICO

Under RICO, "any person" is prohibited from acquiring or maintaining "any interest in . . . any enterprise which is engaged in, or the activities of which affect, interstate or foreign commerce" through a "pattern of racketeering activity."[84] In addition, if a "pattern of racketeering" is proven to exist, and if the income from that activity is used to acquire or operate an enterprise affecting interstate commerce or to conduct an "enterprise's affairs through a pattern of racketeering activity or collection of unlawful debt," or to conspire to do any of these activities, RICO can trigger a forfeiture of such income. RICO also prohibits conducting an enterprise through a pattern of racketeering activity or the collection of unlawful debts. A "pattern" of racketeering activity requires at least two acts of racketeering activity within a few years. "Racketeering activity" is defined as any of a number of "predicate acts" included in a list of major state felonies and federal crimes.[85] It is not necessary to prove that a business is involved in organized crime, or even "illegitimate," since even legitimate businesses can find themselves involved in criminal activity.[86]

To establish a RICO violation, plaintiffs must prove all the elements of one of three subsections of the RICO statute. Under subsection 1962(a), proof of (1) injury (2) caused by the acquisition, establishment, or operation of an enterprise (3) through money acquired (4) through a pattern of racketeering or unlawful debt collection, must be established. Under subsection 1962(b), the plaintiff asserts that the defendant caused (1) injury, which in turn was (2) caused by acquisition or control of an enterprise (3) through a pattern of racketeering or unlawful debt collection. Under subsection 1962(c), finally, proof that (1) a person (2) conducts an enterprise (3) through a pattern of racketeering or unlawful debt collection involving (4) predicate acts that (5) cause injury to the plaintiff's business or property, is required.

Predicate Acts

As indicated above, any number of possible predicate acts, such as common law fraud, conspiracy, or embezzlement, can trigger a RICO action. The most common predicate acts alleged by plaintiffs against accountants and other defendants, in an effort to establish a pattern of racketeering activity, have been the federal crimes of mail fraud and wire fraud. The federal mail fraud statute provides:

> Whoever, having devised or intending to devise any scheme or artifice to defraud, or for obtaining money or property by means of false or fraudulent pretenses, representations, or promises ... for the purpose of executing such scheme or artifice or attempting so to do, places in any post office or authorized depository for mail matter, any matter or thing whatever to be sent or delivered by the Postal Service, or takes or receives therefrom, any such matter or thing, or knowingly causes to be delivered by mail according to the direction thereon, or at the place at which it is directed to be delivered by the person to whom it is addressed, any such matter or thing, shall be fined not more than $1,000 or imprisoned not more than five years, or both.[87]

The wire fraud statute, in turn, provides:

> Whoever, having devised or intending to devise any scheme or artifice to defraud, or for obtaining money or property by means of

false or fraudulent pretenses, representations, or promises, transmits or causes to be transmitted by means of wire, radio, or television communication in interstate or foreign commerce, any writings, signs, signals, pictures, or sounds for the purpose of executing such scheme or artifice, shall be fined not more than $1,000 or imprisoned not more than five years, or both.[88]

A plaintiff attempting to secure a RICO judgment by proving acts of mail fraud or wire fraud must show that the defendant was involved in (1) a scheme to defraud or obtain money or property by false pretenses, while (2) using the mail or telephone in furtherance of such scheme, and (3) having specific intent to defraud or deceive. These factors must be pleaded and proved with care and technical accuracy, but the plaintiff's standard of proof is a "preponderance of the evidence" rather than, as in criminal cases, "beyond a reasonable doubt."

To prove "fraud" under the federal mail and wire fraud statutes, it is sufficient to prove a "scheme" consisting of "omissions of material facts," breach of fiduciary duty, or other deceptive conduct. In addition, fraudulent intent, as evidenced by (1) an obvious motive for the fraud (coupled with an opportunity to pursue such motive), or (2) behavior which patently indicates fraudulent intent, must be proven. Accountants are most often "caught" by these statutory provisions when it can be shown that the accountant was involved in a conflict of interest with respect to financial statements, or was grossly negligent (or worse) in omitting the disclosure of adverse information on a client's financial statements.

Until Congress changes the RICO statute in order to limit its application to "legitimate" business enterprises, RICO will continue create problems for accountants. RICO's treble-damages provision is an attractive feature for plaintiffs (including disgruntled investors and creditors). And as more and more RICO cases are decided, the plaintiff's pathway through the maze of procedural hurdles will become clearer.[89] The accountant's best defenses are probably as follows:

1. Avoid omissions of adverse financial statement information and disclosures;
2. Avoid conflicts of interest and the appearance of being too closely aligned with the management of client firms;
3. Avoid any other relationships that could be construed as constituting a "conspiracy" or as an "enterprise" designed to profit at the expense of clients or third party users of financial statements.

CONCLUSION

Accounting principles in the U.S. are established primarily by the accounting profession, and reflected in statements issued by the nongovernmental Financial Accounting Standards Board. In some countries of Europe, and in other countries elsewhere in the world, accounting rules are dictated by the government, and are often the result of political considerations. The closest U.S. analog to this latter approach is the U.S. Internal Revenue Code.

A growing body of laws and regulations, however, are encroaching upon the independence of the U.S. accounting profession. Some of the laws, like the original securities statutes of 1933 and 1934, reflect an effort by the government to address problems that have resulted in nationwide financial disasters. Others, like Rule 10b-5 (and its enforcement by the SEC) were not originally intended to regulate the accounting profession, but are used in that manner today. Few, if any, were initiated specifically to overstep the accounting profession's traditional domain. And yet, as has been seen in this Chapter, the accountant's domain is being invaded under cover of a variety of laws and regulations.

How should the accounting profession respond? One approach is to react to the changes. To wait until Congress, and agencies like the SEC, begin to make demands upon the profession, and then to attempt to meet those demands.

Another approach is to stay ahead of the process. The trends are not obscure. There is growing conviction among regulators, legislators, courts and the public at large that accountants should be held accountable to investors and others who rely upon financial information. And there is a growing expectation that information with which accountants are associated is reliable and verifiable. Finally, there is widening acceptance of a "social contract" view of the accounting profession: a view that sees certification of public accountants as a privilege granted by the state. The privilege calls for loyalty to the public (especially the investing and lending public), rather than solely to one's self or one's client, in return.

NOTES

1.   15 U.S.C.S. § 77(g) (1992).
2.   15 U.S.C.S. § 77(j) (1992).
3.   Herman & MacLean v. Huddleston, 459 U.S. 375, 381 (1983).
4.   *Ibid* at 382.
5.   15 U.S.C. § 77k (1992).
6.   Herman & MacLean v. Huddleston, 459 U.S. 375, 381-382 (1983).

7. Newcome v. Esrey 862 F.2d 1099, 1106 (4th Cir.1988); Steiner v. Southmark Corp., 734 F.Supp. 269, 278 (N.D.Tex.1990); Bernstein v. Crazy Eddie, Inc., 702 F.Supp. 962, 973 (E.D.N.Y.1988), *vacated in part on other grounds*, 714 F.Supp. 1285 (E.D.N.Y.1989).
8. In re Gap Stores Securities Litigation, 79 F.R.D. 283, 297 (N.D.Ca.1978).
9. McFarland v. Memorex Corp., 493 F.Supp. 631, 643 (N.D.Cal.1980), *modified on other grounds*, 581 F.Supp. 878 (N.D.Cal.1984). *Cf.* Ahern v. Gaussoin, 611 F.Supp. 1465, 1483 (D.Or.1985) (subsequent events up to effective date of registration statement are relevant to show that financial statement was false or that it had become misleading).
10. Herman & MacLean v. Huddleston, 459 U.S. 375, 382 (1983).
11. 15 U.S.C.S. § 77k(b)(3) (1992).
12. *See* Feit v. Leasco Data Processing Equipment Corp., 332 F.Supp. 544 (E.D.N.Y.1971); *See also* Escott v. Barchris Construction Corp., 283 F.Supp. 643, 703 (S.D.N.Y.1968) (Accountants held to GAAS).
13. *See* Escott v. Barchris Construction Cor., 283 F.Supp. 643, 703 (S.D.N.Y.1968).
14. *See* Straus v. Holiday Inns, Inc., 460 F.Supp. 729, 732 (S.D.N.Y.1978) (Section 11 liability "may lie for wholly negligent conduct.").
15. TSC Industries, Inc. v. Northway, Inc., 426 U.S. 438, 449 (1976).
16. *See* Avant-Garde Computing Inc. Securities Litigation (Civil NO. 85-4149-AET), 1989 WL 103625, 1989 U.S. Dist. LEXIS 10483 (D.N.J. Sept. 5, 1989).
17. 15 U.S.C.S. § 77l (1992).
18. 15 U.S.C.S. § 77l(2) (1992).
19. *See* Armstrong v. McAlpin, 699 F.2d 79, 91 (2d Cir.1983); *Cf.* In re Elscint, Ltd. Securities Litigation, 674 F.Supp. 374 (D.Mass.1987).
20. 400 F.Supp. 440, 444 (N.D.Ohio 1975).
21. *Ibid*. at 444, *citing* In re Caesars Palace Securities Litigation, 360 F.Supp. 366, 380-81 (S.D.N.Y.1973).
22. *See* Rolf v. Blyth, Eastman Dillon & Co., 570 F.2d 38, 44 (2d Cir.), *cert. denied*, 439 U.S. 1039 (1978).
23. *See* Mishkin v Peat, Marwick, Mitchell & Co., 658 F.Supp. 271, 273 (S.D.N.Y.1987), and cases cited; Admiralty Fund v. Hugh Johnson & Co., 677 F.2d 1301, 1312 (9th Cir.1982).
24. *See* 15 U.S.C.S 77o (1992); *see also* 15 U.S.C.S. 78t(a) (1992) (similar provision at §20 of the Securities and Exchange Act of 1934).
25. Lanza v. Drexel & Co., 479 F.2d 1277, 1299 (2d Cir.1973).
26. *See* Paul F. Newton & Co. v. Texas Commerce Bank, 630 F.2d 1111, 1115-16 (5th Cir. 1980).
27. Strong v. France, 474 F.2d 747, 752 (9th Cir.1973).
28. Bertstein v. Crazy Eddie, Inc., 702 F.Supp. 962, 971 (E.D. New York, 1988), *vacated in part by* In re Crazy Eddie Securities Litigation, 714 F.Supp. 1285 (E.D.N.Y., 1989).
29. *See*, In re Lilco Sec. Litig., 625 F.Supp. 1500, 1502-03 (E.D.N.Y.1986); Schoenfeld v. Giant Stores Corp., 62 F.R.D. 348, 350-51 (S.D.N.Y.1974).
30. *See* Quantum Overseas, N.V. v. Touche Ross & Co., 663 F.Supp. 658, 664 (S.D.N.Y.1987); cf. Isquith v. Middle S. Utils., Inc., 847 F.2d 186 (5th Cir.), *cert. denied*, 488 U.S. 926 (1988) (test for determining adequacy of disclosure is whether disclosure is materially false and misleading as a whole).
31. *See* Herman & MacLean v. Huddleston, 459 U.S. 375, 381-82 (1983).
32. 772 F.Supp. 258 (D. Md. 1991).
33. *See* AICPA, *Accounting Principles Board Opinion No. 18, The Equity Method of Accounting for Investments in Common Stock* (New York:AICPA); AICPA, *FASB Interpretation No. 35, Criteria for Applying the Equity Method of Accounting for Investments in Common Stock*, (New York, AICPA).
34. 772 F.Supp at 267.
35. Escott v. BarChris Construction Corporation, 283 F. Supp. 643 (S.D.N.Y. 1968).

36. 15 U.S.C.S. § 77(k)(b) (1992).

37. 15 U.S.C.S. § 77k (1992).

38. 17 C.F.R. Section 230.405(1) (1992).

39. 15 U.S.C.S. § 77(h)(a) (1992).

40. 283 F. Supp. at 703.

41. 15 U.S.C.S. § 78(m) (1992).

42. 15 U.S.C.S. § 78(r) (1992).

43. Ernst & Ernst v. Hochfelder, 425 U.S. 185, 211 n.31 (1976); Rich v. Touche Ross & Co., 415 F.Supp. 95, 103 (S.D.N.Y. 1976).

44. 266 F. Supp. 180 (S.D.N.Y. 1967).

45. Re Equity Funding Corp. of America Securities Litigation, 416 F.Supp. 161, 191 (C.D. Calif. 1977).

46. *See*, Lee J. Seidler, Frederick Andrews, & Marc J. Epstein, THE EQUITY FUNDING PAPERS (John Wiley: 1977).

47. *See also* Jacobson v. Peat, Marwick, Mitchell & Co., 445 F. Supp. 518 (S.D.N.Y. 1977) (fraudulent failure to audit a client's financial statements in accordance with GAAS can result in § 18 liability).

48. Heit v. Weitzen, 402 F. 2d 909 (2d Cir. 1968), *cert. denied*, 395 U.S. 903 (1969).

49. Drake v. Thor Power Tool Co., 282 F. Supp. 94 (N.D.Ill 1967).

50. 17 C.F.R. § 240.10b-5 (1992).

51. *Cf.* Arthur Young & Co. v. Reves, 937 F.2d 1310, 1330-31 (8th Cir.1991); Roberts v. Peat Marwick, Mitchell & Co., 857 F.2d 646, 653 (9th Cir.1988); Rudolph v. Arthur Andersen & Co., 800 F.2d 1040, 1045 (11th Cir.1986); Sharp v. Coopers & Lybrand, 649 F.2d 175, 180-84 (3rd Cir.1981) (circumstances may support duty of disclosure) with Schatz v. Rosenberg, 943 F.2d 485, 496-97 (4th Cir.1991); Zoelsch v. Arthur Andersen & Co., 824 F.2d 27, 35-36 (D.C.Cir.1987); Barker v. Henderson, Franklin, Starnes & Holt, 797 F.2d 490, 496-97 (7th Cir.1986); Windon Third Oil & Gas Drilling Partnership v. FDIC 805 F.2d 342, 347 (10th Cir.1986).

52. *See, e.g.*, Fine v. American Solar King Corp., 919 F.2d 290, 298 (5th Cir.1990); Admiralty Fund v. Hugh Johnson & Co., 677 F.2D 1301, 1312 (9th Cir.1982); Chemical Bank v. Arthur Andersen & Co., 552 F.Supp. 439, 454-55 (S.D.N.Y.1982), *rev'd on other grounds,* 726 F.2d 930 (2d Cir.1984).

53. *See* Herman & MacLean v. Huddleston, 459 U.S. 375, 379 n. 5 (1983); Ernst & Ernst v. Hochfelder, 425 U.S. 185 191-92 n. 7 (1976).

54. Abell v. Potomac Insurance Co., 858 F.2d 1104, 1115 (5th Cir.1988), *vacated in part on other grounds sub nom.* Abell v. Wright, Lindsey & Jennings, 492 U.S. 918 (1989); Bane v. Sigmund Exploration Corp., 848 F.2d 579 (5th Cir.1988); Woodward v. Metro Bank, 522 F.2d 84 (5th Cir.1975).

55. Woodward v. Metro Bank of Dallas, 522 F.2d 84, 97 (5th Cir. 1975); Abell v. Potomac Ins. Co., 858 F.2d 1104, 1127 (5th Cir. 1988); *see also* Rolf v. Blyth, Eastman Dillon & Co., 570 F.2d 38, 44-47 (2d Cir. 1978), *cert. denied,* 439 U.S. 1039 (1978); Woods v. Barnett Bank, 765 F.2d 1004, 1010, 1011 (11th Cir.1985); Cleary v. Perfectune, Inc., 700 F.2d 774, 777 (1st Cir.1983).

56. Akin v. Q-L Investments, Inc., 959 F.2d 521 (5th Cir. 1992).

57. See Heit v. Weitzen, 402 F. 2d 909 (2d Cir. 1968); Fischer v. Kletz, 266 F. Supp. 180, 189-94 (S.D.N.Y. 1967); and Drake v. Thor Power Tool Co., 282 F. Supp. 94, 104 (N.D.Ill. 1967).

58. 401 F. 2d 833 (2d Cir. 1968).

59. *Ibid,* 401 F. 2d at 862.

60. Herzfeld v. Laventhol, Krekstein, Horwath & Horwath, 378 F. Supp. 112 (S.D.N.Y. 1974).

61. *See* S.E.C. v. Burns, 816 F.2d 471 (9th Cir. 1987).

62. Broad v. Rockwell Int'l Corp., 642 F.2d 929, 961-62 (5th Cir.) (*en banc*), *cert. denied*, 454 U.S. 965 (1981); *see also* Shivangi v. Dean Witter Reynolds, Inc., 825 F.2d 885, 889 (5th Cir.1987); Rolf v. Blyth, Eastman Dillon & Co., Inc., 570 F.2d 38, 44 (2d Cir), *cert. denied*, 439 U.S. 1039 (1978).

63. S.E.C. v. Seaboard Corp., 677 F.2D 1301, 1312 (9th Cir.1982).

64. *Rolf, supra* note 62, 570 F.2d at 47.

65. Mishkin v. Peat, Marwick, Mitchell & Co., 658 F.Supp. 271, 273 (S.D.N.Y.1987). *See* Goldman v. McMahan, Brafman, Morgan & Co., 706 F.Supp. 256, 259 (S.D.N.Y.1989). *See also* See Basic, Inc. v. Levinson, 485 U.S. 224 (1988).

66. *Ibid. See also* Jordan v. Madison Leasing Co., 596 F.Supp. 707, 710 (S.D.N.Y.1984) ("negligence, if gross, or blindness, although not equivalent to fraud, is sufficient to sustain an inference of fraud").

67. 17 C.F.R. § 201.2(e).

68. In Re Peat, Marwick, Mitchell & Co., SEC ACCOUNTING SERIES RELEASE No. 173 [1937-1982 Transfer Binder] FED. SEC. L. REP. (CCH) ¶72,195 (June 27, 1979).

69. *See* In re ZZZZ Best Securities Litigation, [1991 Transfer Binder] Fed.Sec.L.Rep. ¶ 95,416, at 97,075 (C.D. Cal. 1991).

70. In the Matter of Larry G. Baler, CPA, Admin. Proc. File No. 3-7850, 1992 SEC LEXIS 2317 (Sept. 16, 1992).

71. *See,* Alan Reinstein, Joe Callaghan, & Louis Braiotta, Jr., Corporate Audit Committees: Reducing Directors' Legal Liabilities, 61 J. Urb. Law 375 (1984).

72. 15 U.S.C.S. § 78dd-1 (1992).

73. 15 U.S.C.S. § 78dd-2 (1992).

74. 15 U.S.C.S. §§ 78dd-1(b), 78dd-2(b), 78dd-1(f)(3), and 78dd-2(h)(4) (1992).

75. 15 U.S.C.S. § 78m(b)(1)-(3) (1992).

76. 15 U.S.C.S. §§ 78m(b)(6), 78dd-1(a), 78dd-2(a)-(c), 78ff (1992).

77. 15 U.S.C.S. § 78u(d) (1992).

78. 15 U.S.C.S. § 78dd-2(c) (1992).

79. 28 C.F.R. 50.80 (1992).

80. Neumann, Frederick L., "Corporate Audit Committees and the Foreign Corrupt Practices Act," *Journal of Accountancy*, March 1981, p.79.

81. *See generally* Annot., Right to Private Action Under State Consumer Protection Acts. 62 A.L.R.3d 169 (1975); Comment, Consumer Protection Act Private Right of Action: A Re-evaluation, 19 Gonz. L. Rev. 673 (1983/84).

82. Maryland is an exception to the rule. *See,* MD. COM. LAW. CODE ANN. §16-104 (1990) (exempting the services of certified public accountants). *See generally,* Annot., Scope and Exemptions of State Deceptive Trade Practice and Consumer Protection Acts, 89 A.L.R. 3d 399 (1979).

83. Organized Crime Control Act of 1970, Title IX, Pub. L. No. 91-452, 84 Stat. 941 (1970), codified at 18 U.S.C.S. §§ 1961-1938 (1992)./

84. 18 U.S.C.S. § 1962(b) (1992).

85. 18 U.S.CS. § 1961 (1992).

86. 473 U.S. 479, 495 (1985).

87. 18 U.S.C.S. § 1341 (1992).

88. 18 U.S.C.S. § 1343 (1992).

89. *See,* Albert D. Spalding, "How to Start a Civil RICO Lawsuit (Part 1: Introduction to RICO)," *The Practical Lawyer* Volume 38, No. 6, Sept. 1992, pp.15-23; and Albert D. Spalding, "How to Start a Civil RICO Lawsuit (Part 2: Specific Pleading Requirements)," *The Practical Lawyer*, Vol. 38, No. 7 (October 1992), pp. 75-84.

Chapter Five

Statutory Liability (Criminal)

A ccountants are being indicted under an increasing array of criminal statutes and proceedings. All criminal prosecutions require some form or element of criminal intent. Intent, however, is as hard to disprove as it is to prove. And in situations where the accountant's work product reflects some form of negligence or poor work, it is often difficult to avoid being accused of making an intentional effort to defraud or cause harm.

In previous chapters, several statutes have been discussed with respect to their civil liability implications. Many of these same statutes also have additional provisions for criminal penalties if the wrongdoer's actions rise to the level of criminal intent. This chapter discusses these criminal provisions and their implications for accountants.

FEDERAL SECURITIES LAWS

For the most part, state law has been essentially ineffective on the criminal level in regulating inadequate financial disclosure by public accountants, and issuance of false and misleading certified financial statements, in connection with publicly traded entities. Though many states have adopted the Uniform Securities Act, Section 101, which is patterned after Rule 10b-5, the continuing difficulty stems from obstacles involving complex interstate control which result from the nature of the activity.

Thus, it is the federal government which has thrust upon it the main burden of enforcing the federal securities and criminal statutes. Many of the SEC regulations discussed in the last chapter have criminal counterparts.

Section 24

Under the Securities Act of 1933, Section 24 deals with untrue statements or omission of material facts in a registration statement, and provides:

> Any person who willfully violates any of the provisions of this title, or the rules and regulations promulgated by the Commission under authority thereof, or any person who willfully, in a registration statement filed under this title, makes any untrue statement of a material fact or omits to state any material fact required to be stated therein or necessary to make the statements therein not misleading, shall upon conviction be fined not more than $5000 or imprisoned not more than five years, or both.[1]

The *Benjamin* Case. In *United States v. Benjamin,*[2] the criminal convictions of a certified public accountant, a lawyer, and promoter for willfully conspiring by use of interstate commerce to sell unregistered securities and to defraud in the sale of securities in violation of Section 24 of the Securities Act of 1933 were affirmed.

The facts of the case began when Mende, the principal promoter, purchased the holdings of an old corporation shell because of a registration exemption for securities sold, disposed of or bona fide offered to the public prior to 1933. This corporation had been authorized to issue 1,500,000 shares with a par value of 10 cents per share, and currently had approximately 964,000 shares outstanding. There were no assets and the purchase price for nearly of the outstanding shares was $5,000 plus a $1,500 fee. The name was changed to American Equities Corporation and the par value was raised to $1 per share. Benjamin, Mende's lawyer, interested an inactive financially troubled securities firm into selling shares of the corporation.

Howard, the certified public accountant, was engaged to prepare a report which included a pro forma balance sheet for American Equities Corporation. Without examining the corporation's books and records, but based on a false listing of real estate holdings in Detroit and balance sheets of corporations purportedly owned or controlled by American Equities Corporation, all of which were provided for Howard; the pro forma balance sheet showed total assets of $7,769,657.11 and net worth of $3,681,049.70. A few months later, Howard rendered a second "Auditor's Report." Some of the corporations included in the first audit report did not appear in the second, while newly added corporations were included without any investigation by Howard as to their acquisition.

The accountant claimed that he had protected himself with the label "pro forma" and that he thought the reports were for management's purposes and was unaware that they were being used to peddle stock. However, the evidence, including his own testimony, contradicted this claim. "[H]e admitted knowing that the promoters intended to use the stock as collateral for the purchase price in various acquisitions and that his statements were shown to prospective lenders or sellers."

As to the accountant's argument that the statements were "pro forma," the court stated:

> It would be insulting an honorable profession to suppose that a certified public accountant may take the representations of a corporation official as to companies it proposes to acquire, combine their balance sheets without any investigation as to the arrangements for their acquisition or suitable provision reflecting payment of the purchase price, and justify the meaningless result simply by an applique of two Latin words.[3]

The reports, which represented American Equities as owning properties and companies which "it neither owned nor had any firm arrangements to acquire," were nonetheless found to be *false* despite being "pro forma." The court made reference to Montgomery's *Auditing Theory and Practice* by citing the following:

> Although pro forma statements "purport to give effect to transactions actually consummated or expected to be consummated at a date subsequent to that of the date of the statements, auditors consider it proper to submit their report and opinion on such statements only when the nature of the transactions effected is clearly described in the statements, and when satisfactory evidence of their bona fides is available, such as actual subsequent consummation or signed firm contracts."[4]

Having established the falsity of the statements, the Government set out to prove beyond a reasonable doubt the accountant's culpable state of mind. The court found the following circumstances sufficient to show that the accountant "had actual knowledge of the falsity of his reports and deliberately conspired to defraud investors."

1. The accountant admitted seeing deeds to real estate purportedly owned by American Equities which did not name American Equities as grantee.
2. The accountant's failure to examine the books prior to rendering the first report, when such an inspection would have revealed that there was nothing paid at the time the capital stock account was written up from par of 10 cents to par of $1 per share.
3. Including as an asset over $700,000 of "unrecovered Development Costs" of a dormant mining company known by the accountant to have been through insolvency proceedings.
4. The accountant asserting in a profit and loss statement that six companies were "acquired within the last few months," when in fact he knew that some had not been acquired at all.
5. Other factors such as the accountant being unable to obtain a $200 advance from American Equities, and the fact that the hotel where he and Benjamin were staying at the time he delivered the second report "extolling the prospects of this $87 million company" had turned off their food and telephone service for nonpayment of bills and had threatened to hold their baggage.

The court noted that the Government was not required to go as far as it had in proving the accountant's willfulness. The belief was expressed that "the Government can meet its burden by proving that a defendant deliberately closed his eyes to facts he had a duty to see. . . or recklessly stated as facts things of which he was ignorant."[5] The court also referred to other circuits which had held the willfulness requirement satisfied by mere "proof of representations which due diligence would have shown to be untrue."[6] In concluding its remarks on the accountant's state of mind, the court observed:

In our complex society the accountant's certificate and the lawyer's opinion can be instruments for inflicting pecuniary loss more potent than the chisel or the crowbar. Of course, Congress did not mean that any mistake of law or misstatement of fact should subject an attorney or an accountant to criminal liability simply because more skillful practitioners would not have made them. But Congress equally could not have intended that men holding themselves out as members of these ancient professions should be able to escape criminal liability on a plea of ignorance when they have shut their eyes to what was plainly to be seen or have represented a knowledge they knew they did not possess.[7]

Section 32(a) and Section 1001

Under the Securities Exchange Act of 1934, Section 32(a) deals with false or misleading statements required to be filed and provides:

Any person who willfully violates any provisions of this title, or any rule or regulation thereunder the violation of which is made unlawful or the observance of which is required under the terms of this title, or any person who willfully and knowingly makes, or causes to be made, any statement in any application, report, or document required to be filed under this title or any rule or regulation thereunder or any undertaking contained in a registration statement. . . which statement was false or misleading with respect to any material fact, shall upon conviction be fined not more than $10,000, or imprisoned not more than two years, or both. . . . but no person shall be subject to imprisonment under this section for the violation of any rule or regulation if he proves that he had no knowledge of such rule or regulation.[8]

The Federal False Statements Statutes, Section 1001, imposes criminal sanctions for false statements made in matters within a federal department jurisdiction such as the SEC and provides:

Whoever, in any matter within the jurisdiction of any department or agency of the United States knowingly and willingly falsifies, conceals or covers up by any trick, scheme, or device a material fact, or makes any false, fictitious or fraudulent statements or representation, or makes or uses any false writing or document knowing the same to contain any false, fictitious or fraudulent statement or entry, shall be fined not more than $10,000 or imprisoned not more than five years, or both.[9]

The *Simon* Case. By far, the leading case in the area of accountant criminal liability is *United States v. Simon*,[10] also referred to as the *Continental Vending* case. The defendant public accountants were convicted of conspiracy to violate Section 1001 of the federal false statements statute and section 32 of the Securities Exchange Act of 1934, and for violation of the mail fraud statutes (discussed below). The defendant accountants were fined, but no prison sentences were imposed. The verdicts were affirmed on appeal.

Harold Roth was the president of Continental Vending Machine Corporation--the company audited--and also supervised Valley Commercial Corporation, an affiliate of Continental. Roth also owned 25 percent of the stock of each company. It was alleged that Continental made loans to Valley and that Roth borrowed money from Valey to finance his stock market transactions. When it became evident that Valley could not repay its debt to Continental, Roth posted collateral, of which 80 percent consisted of securities in Continental, to secure his debt to Valley and Valley's debt to Continental.

The indictments charged that the auditors failed to disclose that the loans outstanding from Valley to Roth were approximately equal to the loans outstanding from Continental to Valley, and that a substantial part of Roth's collateral was Continental common stock. The financial statements which defendants certified contained the following footnote which did not provide full disclosure:

> The amount receivable from Valley Commercial Corp. (an affiliated company of which Mr. Harold Roth is an officer, director and stockholder) bears interest at 12 percent a year. Such amount, less the balance of the notes payable to that company, is secured by the assignment to the Company of Valley's equity in certain marketable securities. As of February 15, 1963, the amount of such equity at current market quotations exceeded the net amount receivable.[11]

The government contended that if the footnote had included all that the defendants knew, at the very least it should have read:

> The amount receivable from Valley Commercial Corp. (an affiliated company of which Mr. Harold Roth is an officer, director and stockholder), which bears interest at 12 percent a year, was uncollectible at September 30, 1962, since Valley had loaned approximately the same amount to Mr. Roth who was unable to pay. Since that date Mr. Roth and others have pledged as security for the repayment of his obligation to Valley and its obligation to Continental (now $3,900,000, against which Continental's liability to

Valey cannot be offset) securities which, as of February 15, 1963, had a market value of $2,978,000. Approximately 80 percent of such securities are stock and convertible debentures of the Company.[12]

Continental's annual report containing the financial statements was mailed to shareholders, which provided the basis for applying the federal mail fraud statute. At about this time, the market value of the collateral began declining drastically. A subsequent bad check by Continental to the IRS eventually led to a government padlock on Continental's plant, suspension of trading in Continental stock by the American Stock Exchange, an SEC investigation, and ultimate bankruptcy.

Simon established two significant concepts in accountant criminal liability:

1. An accountant has a duty "to disclose what he knows when he has reason to believe that, to a material extent, a corporation [or client's business] is being operated not to carry out its business in the interest of all the stockholders but for the private benefit" of its officers or management.[13] The defendants failed to investigate their suspicions that "Continental's loans to Valley were not for a proper business purpose but to assist Roth in his personal financial problems."[14]

2. Compliance with generally accepted accounting principles is not a conclusive defense to criminal liability. The appellate court approved of the trial court's instructions to the jury which it summarized in pertinent part as follows:

   [T]he 'critical test' was whether the financial statements as a whole 'fairly presented the financial position of Continental as of September 30, 1962, and whether it accurately reported the operations for fiscal 1962.' If they did not, the basic issue became whether defendants acted in good faith. Proof of compliance with generally accepted standards was 'evidence which may be very persuasive but not necessarily conclusive that he acted in good faith, and that the facts as certified were not materially false or misleading.'[15]

Eight expert independent accountants on behalf of the defendants testified that the disclosure in the footnote was not inconsistent with generally accepted principles or generally accepted auditing standards. And the court noted that that neither generally accepted accounting principles nor generally accepted auditing standards required disclosure of the make-up of the collateral or of the increase of the receivable after the closing date of the balance sheet. Despite these observations, the court found that the disclosure should have been made, and held the accountants liable.[16]

Equity Funding--The Weiner Case

In May of 1975, three independent auditors were convicted in Federal court on thirty out of thirty-two counts charging such criminal offenses as securities fraud and filing false documents. This case, *United States v. Weiner*,[17] centered around the audits performed for the now infamous Equity Funding Corp. of America (EFCA). Julian Weiner, the partner in charge of the Equity Funding account, was found guilty on six counts of securities fraud, three counts of filing false statements, and one count of filing a false 10-K report with the SEC. Marvin Lichtig, the former audit manager before he became a vice president with Equity Funding, was found guilty on six counts of securities fraud, five counts of filing false registration statements, one count of filing a false listing application with the New York Stock Exchange and the SEC, and one count of filing a false 10-K report with the SEC. Solomon Block, who succeeded Lichtig as audit manager, was found guilty on five counts of securities fraud, one count of filing false statements, and one count of filing a false 10-K report with the SEC.

The actual facts of the Equity Funding fraud represent the most fascinating aspect of this case.[18] These facts are presently described. However, two points should be made clear. First, it will be noted that the *Weiner* case is one of the only trial court decisions discussed in this book. The others are appellate decisions handed down by a court of appeals. This is significant because case law and statutory interpretations receive their real weight of authority from appellate decisions. Trial court decisions are rarely as persuasive as appellate decisions other than for the parties involved or as establishing the facts and grounds for appeal. However, the *Weiner* verdict was one of those exceptional cases where the developments at the trial level were exceedingly noteworthy, though not so noteworthy that a court of appeals couldn't change the outcome. Second, Equity Funding was not an insurance fraud or an elaborate computer fraud. EFCA was essentially a securities fraud. "[T]he insurance activity was merely one particular phase of a much larger stock fraud that began at or before the time of EFCA's first public offering in 1964. The fraud was designed to pump up the value of the Company's stock by systematically inflating EFCA's reported earnings through every means available to the conspirators."[19]

In the *Report of the Trustee of Equity Funding Corporation of America* dated October 31, 1974, the fraud is described in terms of three distinct phases: the Funding Phase, the Foreign Phase, and the Insurance Phase.

Funding Phase. EFCA derived most of its real income from the commissions earned through sales of "Equity Funding Programs." Such funding programs consisted of selling mutual fund shares to program participants. These, in turn, were used by the participants to secure a one-year note for a loan made by EFCA equal to the amount of the first year premium on an insurance policy. Each year, for a ten-year term, the participant would purchase additional mutual fund shares sufficient to secure a new loan equal to the annual insurance premium. Thus, if the income and appreciation of the mutual fund shares exceeded the interest owed on the loans, the program would result in the payment of a portion of the insurance premiums for the participant.

Sometime in 1964, EFCA began to inflate its reported earnings by recording fictitious commission income from the sale of the programs. From 1964 to 1973, this scheme alone resulted in $85 million of bogus income. The inflated commissions also led to inflation of the asset Funded Loans Receivable, which represented the amounts loaned to participants of the programs. The inflated income and assets served the desired purpose of favorably influencing the value of EFCA stock. However, this scheme was not bringing in needed case flow. In addition, the increasing funded loans receivable asset had reached its limit because it was becoming too excessive to explain. These problems, though, were temporarily alleviated by the foreign phase of the fraud.

Foreign Phase. In 1968, a new scheme was developed to obtain needed cash and at the same time reduce the funded loans receivable asset. Funds were borrowed from various sources, usually foreign, without recording these amounts as liabilities. The funds were then either recorded as income or applied the federal loans receivable as though participants were repaying their loans. As the funded loans asset was being reduced, more fictitious income was able to be reported through the inflated commissions. The cash flow was important, of course, but the goal of the fraud was to maintain high reported income so as to keep pushing the value of EFCA stock up. So, besides the unrecorded loans, income was kept inflated by such devices as selling fictitious assets (valuable future commissions) to controlled foreign shells. This alone accounted for $17.2 million of bogus income in 1969. During this period, events were transpiring which required greater amounts of cash and income than the foreign phase could supply. This led to the last phase of the fraud.

Insurance Phase. EFCA had a contract with Pennsylvania Life Insurance Company whereby Penn Life agreed not to go into the funding business in return for an exclusive sales agreement with EFCA to sell Penn Life policies. However, in 1968, EFCA wanted to be released from the agreement so that it could sell insurance policies underwritten by its subsidiary, Equity Funding Life Insurance Company (EFLIC). The release required EFCA to coinsure (reinsure) $250 million in face amount of insurance over a three-year period. The first year, 1968, called for $125 million to be reinsured with Penn Life. The act of reinsurance consists of the resale of insurance policies to a second insurance company. In this agreement, EFCA was permitted to retain the first year's premiums and, in addition, was to be paid by Penn Life 80 percent of the first year's premiums on the reinsured policies. Thus, cash flow needs and increased earnings would be provided.

It became evident to EFCA by the middle of the first year that not enough insurance could be sold to meet its commitment. If this had become known to the industry, the prospects for favorable reinsurance agreements with other companies would have been diminished. To solve this problem and meets its quote for 1968, EFCA offered "special class" insurance policies to its employees and agents in which the first year premium was paid by the company. In turn, these policies were reinsured with Penn Life.

To meet the 1969 quota, a new scheme was devised whereby pending business (applied-for insurance policies not yet approved or paid for by the applicant) was counted as sold and so recorded. These policies were then reinsured with Penn Life. This ultimately led to an added drain on cash flow due to the fact that EFCA found it necessary to pay renewal premiums on those policies that never became effective in order to avoid an unusually high lapse rate on reinsured policies. However, the cash flow problem was only just beginning.

In 1970, the fraud entered into the final stage of the insurance phase. From 1970 through March of 1973, when the fraud was uncovered, EFCA created and recorded wholly fictitious insurance policies which were then reinsured. This scheme resulted in substantial cash payments from the reinsurers during the first year the bogus policies were reinsured. But the next year, renewal premiums had to be paid to the reinsurers by EFCA. In order to obtain the necessary cash to pay the premiums, more and more fictitious policies had to be reinsured. As each year passed, it became necessary to increase the magnitude of fictitious insurance in order to keep the reinsured policies in force and avoid discovery. By 1972, this scheme had created a negative cash flow of $1.7 million. In time, this operation would have reached an unmanageable level.

Up to the very moment of the EFCA collapse, new schemes were being developed to solve the cash flow problem. For example, one such scheme, which began in 1971, involved filing claims for death benefits on the fictitious policies with the reinsurers. Originally, the object of the false death claims was to maintain the expected percentage of claims. However, when members of the conspiracy discovered during 1972 that some EFLIC officers had been filing false death claims for their own purposes, their talents were immediately put to use supervising the fraudulent activity on a large-scale operation, this time for the company. If the Equity Funding fraud had gone undetected, the goal for false death claims in 1973 was set at between $3 and $5 million.

Eventually, the total fraud was exposed by an employee who had been terminated purportedly due to overstaffing.

Report of the Special Committee on Equity Funding. A special committee of the American Institute of Certified Public Accountants was appointed to investigate the audits performed for Equity Funding in order to determine whether auditing standards needed changing. In a report issued by the committee, it was found that generally accepted auditing standards, as they presently exist, could not be blamed for the failure to discover the fraud. The report concluded:

> [E]xcept for certain observations relating to confirmation of insurance in force and auditing related party transactions, generally accepted auditing standards are adequate and that no changes are called for in the procedures commonly used by the auditors. In reaching this conclusion, the committee is aware that it is possible to hypothesize ways in which virtually any audit procedure may be thwarted. Nevertheless, the committee believes that customary audit procedures properly applied would have provided a reasonable degree of assurance that the existence of fraud at Equity Funding would be detected.
> The nature, extent and timing of audit procedures are normally based on a study and evaluation of the system of internal control in existence in the area under examination. While such procedures would not necessarily reveal a fraud, it appears that internal accounting and administrative controls at Equity Funding were so weak as to raise concern about the reliability of the accounting records. The committee believes that in such circumstances customary procedures would be extended because of the internal control weakness, thereby enhancing the likelihood of detecting fraud.[20]

The committee also concluded that there is never absolute assurance that fraud will be detected even when as *massive* as in Equity Funding.[21]

Implications. The Equity Funding fraud was so completely overt and easily detectible by an audit utilizing proper application of audit procedures, that the entire episode seems to represent the paradigm for the *imperfect* performance of an audit. Even in the kindest light, one could infer from the prosecution's case that the convicted auditors closed their eyes to fraud which cried out to be detected. In the worst light possible, it would have to be said that they suspected the fraud and cooperated in its concealment.

The following points are only a few of the more obvious factors which existed and would contribute to the weight of evidence against any auditor in a similar situation of criminal liability:

1. In many areas, management failed to maintain any semblance of orderly books and records. As a result, the internal control was weak and inadequate to such a degree that the performance of any legitimate audit would have been virtually impossible.

2. Circumstances made the auditors' independence suspect, both as to mental attitude and appearance. First, Equity Funding accounted for a substantial percentage of the billings of Wolfson Weiner, the firm doing the EFCA audits. Second, Equity Funding was an important selling point for Wolfson Weiner in its merger discussions with other firms. Wolfson Weiner eventually merged with Ratoff & Lapin in 1968, which was later combined with Seidman & Seidman. Third, Marvin Lichtig, the audit manager with Wolfson Weiner, became a vice president with Equity Funding. Fourth, Solomon Block, the new audit manager, maintained an office at Equity Funding, was listed in the Equity Funding phone directory, and generally gave the appearance of being an employee of Equity Funding.[22] Fifth, after the merger with Seidman & Seidman, Block still remained in charge of the EFCA audit despite the fact that he was not a certified public accountant.

3. Fictitious general ledger accounts and entries should have been detected by the auditors because of the fact that supporting source documentation was nonexistent in many situations and little attempt had been made to forge such documentation. In addition, inconsistencies in the records between EFCA and its subsidiaries, which were not covered up, also went undetected.[23]

The impact of the Equity Funding fraud will not be as enormous on the accounting profession in the way of changes in standards, procedures, and rules as was initially predicted.[24]   However, Equity Funding is almost certain to lead to new developments in the area of accountant criminal liability.

National Student Marketing--The Natelli Case

In the controversial case of *United States v. Natelli*,[25] two independent auditors were convicted in a New York Federal District Court for false and misleading statements of material facts willfully and knowingly made in a proxy statement filed with the SEC for National Student Marketing Corporation (NSMC) in violation of Section 32(a) of the Securities Exchange Act of 1934.

Anthony Natelli, a partner of Peat, Marwick, Mitchell & Co. (PMM) and in charge of the NSMC engagement, received a one-year sentence and $10,000 fine with all but sixty days of imprisonment suspended. Joseph Scansaroli, an employee of PMM and audit supervisor of the NSMC engagement, also received a one-year sentence and a $2,500 fine with all but ten days of imprisonment suspended. On appeal to the United States Court of Appeals for the Second Circuit, the conviction of Natelli was affirmed while the conviction of Scansaroli was reversed and remanded for a new trial.

NSMC was in the business of providing its clients with fixed-fee advertising, promotional, and marketing programs designed to reach the youth market. This fixed fee was the amount that the client agreed to be charged to participate in the programs. NSMC had been using an accounting method whereby the fixed-fee contracts were recognized as income at the time the clients committed themselves. When PMM took on the engagement in August 1968, Natelli decided to recognize income on a percentage-of-completion basis. However, not only were the commitments not booked by NSMC during the fiscal year, but neither were they in writing. Since a refusal to book these oral commitments would have resulted in a loss for the fiscal year of approximately $232,000, Natelli ordered Scansaroli to verify these commitments.   Rather than obtain written verifications, Scansaroli communicated by telephone with representatives of companies which had indicated interest in using NSMC's services. In addition, he accepted a schedule showing approximately $1.7 million in purported commitments which had been prepared by NSMC's comptroller. He also received estimates from account executives of (1) gross amounts of client commitments, (2) printing and distribution costs for the program, and (3) the percentage completed of the program.

Based on this evidence, Natelli allowed the books to be adjusted for unbilled accounts receivable in the amount of $1.7 million after the close of the fiscal year. As a result, NSMC was able to turn a loss for the year into a profit of $388,031. However, once the audited annual report for the fiscal year ended August 31, 1968, had been certified, Natelli informed the NSMC officers that in the future only written commitments "supported by contemporaneous logs" would be accepted.

By May 1969, over $1 million of the $1.7 million in sales had been written off by NSMC. Of this amount, $350,000 had already been written off by subtracting it from the 1969 current year sales figures. The auditors were asked to write off the additional $678,000 against 1968 prior year sales. In so doing, 1968 earnings were not reduced commensurately. Instead, the write-off (an unrelated ordinary item) was netted with a newly discovered 1968 tax credit (extraordinary item) of approximately the same amount of profit required to be written off. Thus, the material decrease in earnings for fiscal 1968 was never shown. In addition, the sales were not written off against fiscal 1968 sales figures of NSMC, but were written off, at the direction of Natelli, against 1968 sales figures of seven companies acquired subsequent to the 1968 report through a pooling of interests.

The events leading up to the conviction of the auditors revolved around a proxy statement prepared by the auditors, dated September 27, 1969, and filed with the SEC on September 30, 1969. The proxy statement contained the audited statement for the fiscal year ended August 31, 1968, and an unaudited statement for the nine months ended May 31, 1969.

The Audited Statement. In preparing the proxy statement, the auditors drafted a footnote to the audited statement reconciling the prior fiscal 1968 NSMC net sales and earnings with the retroactively restated earnings of the pooled companies.

However, the footnote failed to disclose either the write off of over $1 million of NSMC's adjusted performance in fiscal 1968 minus the sales and earnings of the pooled companies. Natelli had stricken all narrative disclosures in the footnote. This resulted in a violation of APB Opinion No. 9 which requires disclosure of the effect of prior period adjustments on net income of the prior periods.

The Unaudited Statement. The nine months' unaudited statement required in the proxy statement was prepared by NSMC with the assistance of PMM using the same percentage-of-completion method. On the day that the proxy statement was to be printed, Natelli informed the president of NSMC, Cortes Randell, that a commitment for more than $1 million from the Pontiac Division of General Motors would not be accepted as valid during this nine months' fiscal period because the letter from Pontiac did not constitute a legally binding obligation. That very same day, however, another commitment of $280,000 from Eastern Airlines was miraculously produced through a purported letter from Eastern dated the previous day confirming a commitment entered into on May 14, only seventeen days prior to the close of the nine-month period. In the final proxy statement, the Pontiac sale had been replaced with the Eastern commitment.

In addition to the Eastern commitment, Oberlander, a PMM accountant assigned by Natelli to review NSMC's accounts, found $177,547 worth of bad 1968 contracts and recommended to the NSMC comptroller that these and other contracts totaling over $320,000 be written off in addition to the previous $1 million in bad contracts. The comptroller informed Scansaroli, who in turn consulted with Natelli, which resulted in a decision not to make the write-off.

Conviction of Natelli. The Court of Appeals found that there was sufficient evidence for the jury to find Natelli guilty of willfully and knowingly filing a materially false proxy statement with the SEC. First, the court found the requisite criminal intent present. The court's reasoning was that "[c]ircumstantial evidence, particularly with proof of motive, where available, is often sufficient to convince a reasonable man of criminal intent beyond a reasonable doubt." Thus, the jury could infer that Natelli was motivated by a desire to conceal the uncollectibility and non-existence of receivables which had been booked as unbilled sales after the fiscal period closed, because "the revelation stood to cause Natelli severe criticism and possible liability." These sales had been sufficient to convert a loss into a profit. The jury could also infer that the netting of the extraordinary item (the tax credit) against the ordinary item (the $678,000 write-off of 1968 sales) was motivated by the same factor.

Next, the court examined the question of the footnote in the audited statement. In finding that the footnote to the fiscal 1968 audited statement should have disclosed the loss for the year resulting from the write-offs, the court found that the absence of a formal reaudit for 1968 did not in any way lessen the accountant's duty to correct the statement once he had knowledge that it was false or misleading.

Finally, the court took up the question of the Eastern commitment and the nine months' unaudited statement. Natelli contended that he had no duty to verify the Eastern commitment which had been substituted for the Pontiac commitment because the statement was unaudited. In rejecting this, the court noted that the auditors were "associated" with the statement, cited *SAS No. 1*, § 516, and concluded:

We do not think this means, in terms of professional standards, that the accountant may shut his eyes in reckless disregard to his knowledge that highly suspicious figures, known to him to be suspicious, were being included in the unaudited earnings figures with which he was "associated" in the proxy statement.[26]

The court noted that the Eastern commitment "was a matter of deep suspicion" because of a combination of circumstances: its spectacular appearance after the end of the fiscal year; its similarity in amount to the Pontiac commitment; no record of expenditures on it; no record of billing for services to Eastern; no other documents from Eastern other than the letter; and the "history of post-period bookings and the dismal consequences later discovered" all of which were known to Natelli. Thus, Natelli had a duty to pursue the Eastern commitment further.

Conviction of Scansaroli. Scansaroli's conviction as to the footnote in the audited statement was also affirmed based on similar reasoning used to affirm Natelli's conviction. The court determined that "the jury could properly find. . . that both the netting of the tax credit against earnings and the subsequent subtracting of the write-offs from the pooled earnings in the footnote without further explanation were done in order to conceal the true retroactive decrease in the Marketing earnings for fiscal 1968."

However, the Eastern commitment was another matter and the court found that the evidence was insufficient to support Scansaroli's conviction beyond a reasonable doubt. Under orders by his superior Natelli, he merely adjusted the figures to reflect the Eastern commitment. There was insufficient evidence to establish that Scansaroli exercised any discretion, engaged in related conversations, or participated in any attempt at verification. As a result, the court remanded Scansaroli's case back for a new trial because of the possibility that the jury might have convicted him based solely upon the insufficient evidence presented of the nine months' unaudited statement.

AICPA's Brief. The AICPA filed a brief as *amicus curiae* before the U.S. Court of Appeals for the Second Circuit on the issue of the trial court's failure to instruct the jury as to the "distinct difference between the responsibility of an independent accountant with respect to financial statements he has audited and reported on and his very limited responsibility with respect to financial statements which he has not audited and on which he has not reported."[27] The instructions given to the jury were as follows:

While I have stated that negligence or mistake do not constitute guilty knowledge or intent, nevertheless, ladies and gentlemen, you are entitled to consider in determining whether a defendant acted with such intent if he deliberately closed his eyes to the obvious or to the facts that certainly would be observed or ascertained in the course of his accounting work or whether he recklessly stated as facts matters of which he knew he was ignorant.

If you find such reckless deliberate indifference to or disregard for truth or falsity on the part of a given defendant, the law entitles you to infer therefrom that the defendant willfully and knowingly filed or caused to be filed false financial information of a material nature with the SEC.

But such an inference, of course, must depend on the weight and credibility extended to the evidence of reckless and indifferent conduct, if any.

I repeat: Ordinary or simple negligence or mistake alone would be insufficient to support a finding of guilty knowledge or willfulness or intent.[28]

However, the trial court refused to supplement the instructions with the following request of the defendants as to the unaudited earnings statement:

The defendants' *only* responsibility as to this statement [unaudited statement of earnings for the nine months ended May 31, 1969] was to be satisfied that, *as far as they knew,* the statement contained no misstatement of material facts.[29] [Emphasis in original.]

In their brief, the AICPA argued that an independent accountant who becomes associated with unaudited statements does not have the same responsibility as when he expresses an opinion on audited statements. The court did not challenge this point. What the court did say, however, was that "[t]he issue on this appeal is not what an auditor is *generally* under a duty to do with respect to an unaudited statement, but what these defendants had a duty to do in these unusual and highly suspicious circumstances."[30] [Emphasis in original.] And given these sets of facts, the court concluded that the duty with respect to the unaudited statement was not so different from that of a full audit as to require jury instructions different from those given by the trial court.

As for the AICPA's fear of exposing "independent accountants to criminal liability with respect to unaudited financial statements with which they are 'associated' unless a full audit is undertaken," the court reiterated the following:

We expound no rule, to be sure, that an accountant in reviewing an unaudited company statement is bound, without more, to seek verification and to apply auditing procedures. We lay no extra burden on the normal activities of accountants, nor do we assume the role of an Accounting Principles Board. We deal only with such deviations as fairly come within the common understanding of dishonest conduct which jurors bring into the box as applied to the particular conduct prohibited by the particular conduct prohibited by the particular statute.

It was not for Judge Tyler in his instructions to deal with the abstract question of an accountant's responsibility for unaudited statements, for that was not the issue. So long as we find that the Judge explicated the proper test applicable to the facts of this case, the duty inherent in the circumstances, and we do, we must also find that he gave the appellants [defendants] a fair charge.[31]

MAIL, WIRE AND OTHER FRAUD STATUTES

The federal mail fraud statute, section 1341, imposes criminal sanctions for using the mail to defraud and provides:

> Whoever, having devised or intending to devise any scheme or artifice to defraud, or for obtaining money or property by means of false or fraudulent pretenses, representations, or promises, or to sell, dispose of, loan, exchange, alter, give away, distribute, supply, or furnish or procure for unlawful use any counterfeit or spurious coin, obligation, security, or other article, or anything represented to be or intimated or held out to be such counterfeit or spurious article, for the purpose of executing such scheme or artifice or attempting to do so, places in any post office or authorized depository for mail matter, any matter or thing whatever to be sent or delivered by the Postal Service, or takes or receives therefrom, any such matter or thing, or knowingly causes to be delivered by mail according to the direction thereon, or at the place at which it is directed to be delivered by the person to whom it is addressed, any such matter or thing, shall be fined not more than $1,000 or imprisoned not more than five years, or both.[32]

Similarly, the federal wire fraud statute prohibits the use of the airwaves for fraudulent purposes. The federal mail and wire fraud statutes contain provisions that can be used against accountants. In the case of *United States v. Simon*, the Department of Justice secured mail convictions of three accountants for fraudulently drawing up and certifying false financial statements, and then mailing them in via the U.S. mails.[33] In that case, the falsehood for which the accountants were convicted was the inclusion of an officer's account receivable as an asset of the company, when the solvency of the company (and the collectibility of the account) was in question.

Enforcement of Other Laws with Fraud Convictions

The Federal Bureau of Investigation has used tax laws to gain convictions of organized criminals over the years. Similarly, U.S. prosecutors have used non-tax statutes, such as mail and wire fraud laws, to augment their cases against federal, state and local tax evaders.[34]

The *Flaxman* Case. The case of *U.S. v. Flaxman*[35] provides an example of the use of non-tax criminal provisions in a tax case. The case involved a certified public accountant who prepared Illinois occupational tax returns and federal income tax returns for his client.

The Illinois retail occupational tax is measured by the gross receipts from sales of tangible personal property at retail. It is designed to cover retail sales only.[36] The returns prepared in the *Flaxman* case called for 'Total Receipts from sales of Tangible Personal Property and Services,' followed by 'Total Deductions Authorized by Law,' the first category of which was 'Receipts From-- Sales Made for Purposes of Resale,' i.e., wholesale sales. In the process of preparing the returns, one of the office workers would give the accountant the total sales figures for each of the client's thirteen retail stores.

According to the testimony given by the accountant at trial, when he first prepared a retailers' occupation tax return and showed it to the president of the company, the president told him that he had not taken into account the wholesale sales. From a notebook, the president gave the accountant the amounts of wholesale sales which the president said should have been deducted. The accountant then prepared the return showing the gross receipts and the net figures after deducting the supposed wholesale sales amounts. After he showed this to the president, the president insisted that he wanted only the net taxable figure stated on the return. The accountant accordingly prepared the return and all subsequent returns in this fashion.

In accepting the wholesale figures from the president of the company, the accountant relied upon the client's assertion that the client could prove the wholesale figures. At trial, the accountant testified that it was not his responsibility to look behind the figures furnished by the taxpayer, and that he had been told that the net figure could be used for the total sales amount when he had been an employee of the Illinois Department of Revenue. At trial it was learned that the wholesale sales amounts furnished by the president were fictitious and generally amounted to 90 percent of the total sales.

Despite the accountant's efforts to prepare the returns for the signature of the president in a manner that accommodated the client, the court concluded that the accountant was participating in a representation to the state taxing authority that the amounts reported were the total or gross sales including wholesale sales, whereas in fact the figure reported would have been a net figure after deducting the purported wholesale sales.

The accountant was convicted of conspiracy to commit mail fraud in a U.S. District Court, and sentenced to two years imprisonment.

Adding Criminal Sanctions to Civil Laws. The *Flaxman* case demonstrates how U.S. mail fraud statutes have provided an avenue for a federal prosecution of a state law violation. In *Flaxman*, the underlying statute requiring payment of the occupational tax had its own criminal penalties, but these were ignored by the U.S. court.

Other cases have gone even further, by adding criminal penalties (via the U.S. mail fraud statute) to non-criminal violations. This happened in the case of *U.S. v. Porcelli*,[37] a situation similar to that in the *Flaxman* scenario. In *Porcelli*, the defendant filed over a hundred fraudulent New York State sales tax returns with respect to sales at twelve of his retail gasoline stations. But in New York, unlike Illinois, intentional violation of the state sales tax laws is considered a civil, rather than criminal, infraction.[38] In upholding the conviction of the defendant, the U.S. Circuit Court concluded that since the specific intent required under the mail fraud statute is the intent to defraud, and not necessarily the intent to violate a civil or criminal statute.[39] For that reason, it was not improper to apply the mail fraud statute when a defendant purposely acts to defraud a state or local government agency from funds due to them.

Bank Fraud

The federal bank fraud statute makes it illegal to defraud a financial institution, to obtain any of the funds or assets of a financial institution by means of false or fraudulent pretenses, representations, or promises.

Banks, like telephone wires, radio waves, and the U.S. mail, are used in everyday business and personal financial transactions. The U.S. bank fraud statute can be used, like the other statutes described above, as a "hook" to allow the U.S. to prosecute what is essentially a local infraction.

The *Morgenstern* Case. An accountant was convicted under the bank fraud statute in the case of *U.S. v. Morgenstern*.[40] The accountant had been employed on a part-time basis to handle the tax affairs of three separate business entities engaged in the manufacturing and marketing of sweaters (the sweater companies). He prepared the federal, state and local tax returns, as well as the accompanying checks made payable to the tax depository bank, for the sweater companies.

The accountant initiated a scheme to divert money designated to cover the sweater companies' payroll tax liability to an account under his own personal control at the company's tax depository bank. He did this by misrepresenting the amount of payroll taxes the sweater companies owed. He presented the officers of the sweater companies with checks made out to the depository bank, which the accountant indicated were necessary for payment of payroll taxes although the total sum of such checks vastly exceeded the companies' actual payroll tax obligations. Relying on the accountant's assurance that payroll taxes were due in the amounts on the checks, the officers signed the checks and gave them to the accountant, assuming that he would deposit them in the tax depository bank.

Rather than doing that, however, the accountant deposited a large number of sweater company checks in a corporate account he controlled at the bank. He eventually withdrew nearly all the funds from that account, spending them on a wide array of personal expenses.

After several years, responsibility for drafting and depositing the sweater companies' payroll tax checks was shifted from the accountant and given to a firm hired to print employee paychecks. This change compelled the accountant to modify his scheme. He began to alter checks made out to various tax authorities, e.g., New York State or the Internal Revenue Service, which the officers had signed and given to him for mailing. Using a pen eraser, he erased the name of the original payee on the checks and then rewrote the payee as the depository bank. He also altered the dollar amounts on the face of many of these checks, generally increasing the amounts to between $1500 and $6000. He then presented these checks--now made out to the depository bank and signed by his employer--to his neighborhood branch for deposit in the Amerco account. In sum, the accountant deposited into his own corporate account a number of sweater company checks on which he had altered the payee.

Counting the payroll tax checks the accountant had previously diverted, a total of approximately 225 checks made out to "Chemical Bank" were deposited in the accountant's own account. These checks totaled roughly $728,000.

In upholding the accountant's conviction and 27 month prison sentence, the U.S. Circuit Court determined that even if the bank was not harmed, the bank fraud conviction was proper.

The bank fraud statute, which makes it unlawful to "defraud a financial institution," was interpreted broadly. The Court held that the bank was deceived by the accountant's pretense that the accountant had authority to deposit the checks in his own account, and that the deception was part of a large fraudulent scheme. In addition, the accountant's removal of the funds for his own personal use constituted the fraudulent taking of money "under the custody and control" of the bank, even if the money did not belong to the bank.[41] Hence, the deception of the bank was fraudulent, and covered by the statute.[42]

Other Bank and Savings & Loan Statutes. In response to the problems associated with the U.S. savings and loan crisis, Congress has enacted legislation imposing criminal sanctions on individuals committing banking crimes. Two statutes in particular, The Financial Institutions Reform, Recovery and Enforcement Act of 1989 (FIRREA),[43] and the Comprehensive Thrift and Bank Fraud Prosecution and Taxpayer Recovery Act of 1990 (Comprehensive Act),[44] include language targeted at such professionals as accountants and lawyers.

The Comprehensive Act adds to U.S. law, among other new federal crimes, a new felony for concealment of assets from the Federal Deposit Insurance Corporation (FDIC),[45] and a new felony for obstructing a financial institution examination.[46]

FIRREA serves to increase the criminal penalties to as many as 30 years imprisonment for violations of certain banking-related crimes, such as false entries,[47] false statements,[48] concealment of assets,[49] and bank fraud.[50] The statute also expands the class of liable persons to include accountants,[51] and specifically prescribes minimum sentencing requirements in situations involving violations that "substantially jeopardize" federally-insured financial institutions.[52] FIRREA also extends the statute of limitations for fraud and other criminal offenses affecting banking institutions from five to ten years.[53]

Conspiracy

In addition to the anti-fraud statutes, the U.S. statutes include a general anti-conspiracy provision that allows the enforcement of the fraud statutes (and others) to be expanded to include other defendants in addition to the primary perpetrators.[54] No formal agreement is necessary to constitute a conspiracy to commit an offense under the anti-conspiracy statute.[55] The Government may rely upon circumstantial evidence of the concert of action among the defendants. And a conspirator need not participate in all the activities of a conspiracy in order to be held liable for the unlawful scheme.[56]

FEDERAL AND STATE TAX LAWS

Federal Tax Laws. Civil penalties under the Internal Revenue Code[57] for negligence, fraud, failure to file a tax return, failure to file the return on time, and failure to pay the tax are always imposed upon the taxpayer, not the tax practitioner. The taxpayer then may sue the practitioner to recover any damages incurred.

The tax practitioner is, however, subject to the criminal tax provisions of the Internal Revenue Code.[58] **Table I**, below, lists those provisions of the Code which may subject the tax practitioner to criminal liability.

Table I.   **Tax Crimes Under the Internal Revenue Code (IRC)**

IRC §	Title
7201	Attempt to Evade or Defeat Tax
7203	Willful Failure to File Return, Supply Information, or Pay Tax
7206	Fraud and False Statements
7207	Fraudulent Returns, Statements, or Other Documents
7210	Failure to Obey Summons
7212	Attempts to Interfere with Administration of Internal Revenue Laws
7216	Disclosure or Use of Information by Preparers of Returns

Sentencing of violators of criminal tax provisions is accomplished pursuant to the Guidelines Manual of the U.S. Sentencing Commission.[59] Generally, an "offense level" is assigned to such cases, based on the amount of the "tax loss" associated with the criminal activity. Tax losses are calculated by multiplying the taxpayer's highest marginal tax rate times the understated taxable income (or, if higher, gross income), plus 100 percent of any false credits claimed against the tax. Offense codes are then assigned, ranging from an offense level of 6 (assigned to tax losses of less than $2,000) to a level of 24 (assigned to tax losses of greater than $80 million). Multi-year criminal tax cases have a minimum offense level of 9, irrespective of the amount of tax loss.

Fines and/or imprisonment are, in turn, imposed based on the offense level and, in the case of imprisonment, prior criminal history, **Table II.**

Table II.   Tax Crimes Fines and Prison Terms

Offense Level	Minimum Tax Loss	Maximum Fine	Maximum Term in Months (No Prior History)	Maximum Term in Months (Prior History)
6-7	$1	$5,000	7	18
8-9	$5,000	$10,000	10	27
10-11	$20,000	$20,000	14	33
12-13	$70,000	$30,000	18	41
14-15	$200,000	$40,000	24	51
16-17	$500,000	$50,000	30	63
18-19	$1.5 Mill.	$60,000	37	78
20-21	$5 Mill.	$75,000	46	96
22-23	$20 Mill.	$100,000	57	105
24	$80 Mill.	$100,000	63	115

Accountants can also be imprisoned for refusing to turn over tax returns or other records to a judge, magistrate or grand jury pursuant to court order or subpoena duces tecum.[60]

State Tax Laws. State revenue laws are also supported by criminal sanctions in many states. These sanctions serve to punish tax practitioners when fraudulent returns (or no required returns) are submitted. They also serve to strengthen the enforcement of the collection of franchise taxes, payroll taxes, and other obligations of accounting firms and their clients.[61]

OTHER CRIMINAL PROVISIONS

Civil Statutes with Criminal Sanctions. Under the federal securities laws, accountants have exposure to criminal prosecution in the context of issuing financial statements on behalf of any publicly held corporation. In particular, a term of imprisonment, a fine, or a combination of both, are imposed upon (i) any person who willfully and knowingly makes or causes to be made any false or misleading statement in any application, report or document required to be filed under Securities Exchange Act; (ii) any undertaking contained in a registration statement; or (iii) any self-regulating organization in connection with an application for membership or participation or association with a member.[62] In this regard, the Insider Trader Sanctions Act of 1984 increased the maximum fine from $10,000 to $100,000.[63] And the Trading and Securities Fraud Enforcement Act of 1988 increased tenfold the maximum fine from $100,000 to $2.5 million, and increased the maximum prison term from five to ten years.[64]

The Foreign Corrupt Practices Act (FCPA), the Racketeering Influenced and Corrupt Organizations Act (RICO), and other federal statutes also have criminal provisions. Under the FCPA, for example, the anti-bribery and the accounting provisions of the FCPA are enforced via civil liabilities, but the anti-bribery provisions also contain criminal sanctions.[65] The SEC has jurisdiction to investigate issuers who may have violated the anti-bribery and accounting provisions, and may bring a civil injunction action against an issuer as well as refer a bribery case to the Department of Justice for prosecution.[66] The Department of Justice has authority to investigate American companies other than issuers, and handles all criminal prosecutions.[67] RICO, similarly, allows the Department of Justice to utilize its provisions to pursue criminal convictions.

Transportation of Stolen Property. The National Stolen Property Act prohibits the interstate transportation of stolen property to the extent that the person transporting the property knows that the property is "stolen, converted, or taken by fraud."[68] In the case of *United States v. Gullett*,[69] two partners in an accounting firm engaged in a scheme in which clients of the firm wrote checks to the firm for services that were never performed. In turn, the clients took a tax deduction and ultimately shared in the proceeds of the checks.

The defendants, the accounting firm partners, were convicted under the National Stolen Property Act, rather than under the tax fraud statutes. The U.S. prosecutors apparently determined that it would be easier to prove that the accountants transported funds obtained by fraud over state lines, than to prove all of the elements of tax fraud.

Foreign Laws. U.S. law is not the only source of criminal prosecution in today's world of multinational corporations engaging in international transactions. The United Kingdom, for example, has an entire array of securities fraud statutes containing criminal provisions. The Financial Securities Act 1986, in particular, imposes criminal penalties, including imprisonment, for any behavior which is proven to have created a false or misleading impression as to the investment and securities markets.[70]

Disclosure of a client's confidential information can subject an accountant to a civil action in the U.S. But in some countries, most notably Switzerland[71] and France,[72] disclosure of confidential information by an accountant can lead to criminal prosecutions.

State statutes covering a variety of subjects often contain criminal provisions that can ensnare accountants. The California Corporate Criminal Liability Act of 1989, for example, requires that accountants, consultants, and other third parties, as well as corporate officers and employees, file reports with the State of California whenever a "serious concealed [environmental] danger" is discovered.[73] Fines of up to $25,000, and imprisonment of up to three years, can be applied to individuals who do not file such reports. And information regarding an environmental infringement that would convince a "reasonable person in the circumstances," rather than actual knowledge, triggers the reporting responsibility, making a prosecution under the Act much easier than ordinary criminal prosecutions.

CONCLUSION

Jail terms and fines are not the only penalties associated with the conviction of an accountant. Loss of state certification, as a certified public accountant, is also likely, even if the crime is a relatively minor one, or is unrelated to the accountant's professional activities.

In the case of *Stubenhause v. State Education Department*, for example, a certified public accountant gave minimal assistance to an estate for whom his brother served as attorney.[74] When the attorney was convicted for converting the estate's assets for his personal benefit, however, the accountant's conviction for criminal facilitation was held to be sufficient to result in the loss of the accountant's license.

In another case, *Ashe v. Department of Prof. Regulation*, convictions for wire fraud and for transportation of forged securities were essentially based on gambling activities, not fraud in the accountant's professional efforts.[75] But in that case as well, loss of certification as a C.P.A. was upheld.

In addition to loss of certification, suspension from practice before the Internal Revenue Service can occur.[76] Finally, the loss of reputation is a cost that cannot be measured.

NOTES

1. 15 U.S.C.S. § 77x (1992).
2. 328 F. 2d 854 (2d Cir. 1964).
3. 328 F. 2d at 861.
4. *Ibid.*
5. 328 F. 2d at 862.
6. 328 F. 2d at 863.
7. *Ibid.*
8. 15 U.S.C.S. § 78ff(a) (1992).
9. 18 U.S.C.S. § 1001 (1992).
10. 425 F. 2d 796 (2d Cir. 1969), *cert. denied*, 397 U.S. 1006 (1970).
11. 425 F. 2d at 800.
12. 425 F. 2d at 801.
13. 425 F. 2d at 806.
14. 425 F. 2d at 806.
15. 425 F. 2d at 805.
16. 425 F.2d at 805.
17. *See* U.S. v. Weiner, 578 F.2d 757 (9th Cir. 1978), *cert. denied by* Lichtig v. U.S., 439 U.S. 981 (1978), *reh den* 439 U.S. 1135 (1979).
18. *See*, LEE J. SEIDLER, FREDERICK ANDREWS, & MARC J. EPSTEIN, THE EQUITY FUNDING PAPERS (John Wiley: 1977).
19. *Ibid*, "Report of the Trustee of Equity Funding Corporation of America," p. 139.
20. *Ibid*, "Report of the Special Committee on Equity Funding (AICPA)."
21. *See*, Seidler, Andrews, & Epstein, *supra* note 18.
22. F. Andrews, "Why Didn't Auditors Find Something Wrong With Equity Funding?" in *Wall Street Journal*, May 4, 1973 at p.1, Col. 6.
23. *See*, Seidler, Andrews, & Epstein, *supra* note 18.
24. *Ibid.*
25. 527 F. 2d 311 (1975).
26. 527 F. 2d at 320.
27. "AICPA Brief in Natelli-Scansaroli," *Journal of Accountancy* CXXXIX (May 1975), 71.
28. 527 F. 2d at 322, fn. 9.
29. 527 F. 2d at 324.
30. 527 F. 2d at 323.
31. 527 F. 2d at 324.
32. Federal Mail Fraud Statute, 18 U.S.C.S. § 1341 (1992).
33. 425 F. 2d 796 (2d Cir. 1969), *cert. denied*, 397 U.S. 1006 (1970).
34. *See* United States v. Melvin, 544 F.2d 767 (5th Cir.), *cert. denied*, 430 U.S. 910 (1977); United States v. Brewer, 528 F.2d 492 (4th Cir.1975); United States v. Mirabile, 503 F.2d 1065 (8th Cir.1974), *cert. denied*, 420 U.S. 973 (1975).

35. 495 F.2d 344 (7th Cir. 1974); *cert. denied*, 419 U.S. 1031 (1974).
36. Theo. B. Robertso Products Co. v. Nudelman 389 Ill. 281, 59 N.E.2d 655 (1945).
37. 865 F.2d 1352 (2nd Cir. 1989).
38. *See* People v. Valenza, 60 N.Y.2d 363, 370; 457 N.E.2d 748, 750; 469 N.Y.S.2d 642, 645 (1983).
39. 865 F.2d at 1358, *citing* United States v. Rodolitz, 786 F.2d 77, 80-81 (2d Cir.), *cert. denied*, 479 U.S. 826 (1986).
40. 933 F.2d 1108 (2nd Cir. 1991).
41. *See* 18 U.S.C.S. § 1344(a)(2) (1992).
42. 933 F.2d at 1113.
43. Pub.L. No. 101-73, 103 Stat. 183.
44. Pub.L. No. 101-647, 104 Stat. 4859.
45. Pub.L. No. 101-647, § 2501, 104 Stat. 4859; codified at 18 U.S.C.S. § 1032 (1992).
46. Pub.L. No. 101-647, § 2503, 104 Stat. 4861; codified at 18 U.S.C.S. § 1517 (1992).
47. 18 U.S.C.S. § 1006 (1992).
48. 18 U.S.C.S. § 1014 (1992).
49. 18 U.S.C.S. § 1032 (1992).
50. 18 U.S.C.S. 1344 (1992).
51. Pub. L. No. 101-73, § 204(u), 103 Stat. 193, codified at 12 U.S.C.S. § 1813 (1992); Pub.L. No. 101-73, § 901(a), 103 Stat. 446, codified at 12 U.S.C.S. § 1786 (1992).
52. 101 Pub.L. No. 101-73, § 961, 103 Stat. 501; 28 U.S.C.S. § 994 (1992).
53. *See* 18 U.S.C.S. § 3293 (1992).
54. 18 U.S.C.S. § 371 (1992).
55. United States v. Robinson, 470 F.2d 121, 123 (7th Cir. 1972).
56. United States v. Cardi, 478 F.2d 1362, 1368-1369 (7th Cir. 1973); United States v. Fellabaum, 408 F.2d 220, 224 (7th Cir. 1969), *cert. denied*, 396 U.S. 858.
57. I.R.C. (26 U.S.C.S.) §§ 6651-6689 (1992).
58. I.R.C. (26 U.S.C.S.) §§ 7201-7216 (1992).
59. UNITED STATES SENTENCING COMMISSION, FEDERAL SENTENCING GUIDELINES MANUAL § 11.2 (1991). The Comprehensive Crime Court Act of 1984 created the Commission to achieve uniformity in tax and other criminal prosecutions.
60. Donnelly v. U.S., 201 F.2d 826 (9th Cir. 1953).
61. Even a well-intentioned international accounting firm can find itself as the subject of a criminal investigation when state payroll taxes of its employees are not remitted. *See* Scott R. Schmedel & Lee Berton, "Arthur Andersen Copes With Effects of Tax Scandal," *Wall Street Journal*, August 6, 1992, p.B1.
62. 15 U.S.C.S. § 78ff(a) (1992).
63. Insider Trader Sanctions Act of 1984, Pub. L. No. 98-376, 98 Stat. 1264, 1265 (Aug. 10, 1984), codified at 15 U.S.C.S. §§ 78a, 78c, 78o, 78t, 78u, 78ff (1992).
64. 15 U.S.C.S. § 78ff(a) (1992); *See* § 4 of the Insider Trading and Securities Fraud Enforcement Act of 1988, Pub. L. No. 100-704, 102 Stat. 4680 (Nov. 19, 1988) (codified at 15 U.S.C.S. § 78a (1992)).
65. 15 U.S.C.S. §§ 78m(b)(6), 78dd-1(a), 78dd-2(a)-(c), 78ff (1992).
66. 15 U.S.C.S. § 78u(d) (1992).
67. 15 U.S.C.S. § 78dd-2(c) (1992).
68. 18 U.S.C.S. § 2314 (1992).
69. 713 F2d 1203 (6th Cir.1983), *cert. denied*, 464 U.S. 1069 (1984).
70. § 47(2) of the Financial Services Act 1986. *See*, Caird Forbes-Cockell, "Financial Services Regulation in the United Kingdom," PLI Order No. B4-6916, *Practicing Law Institute Corporate Law and Practice Course Handbook Series*, 683 PLI/Corp 711, March 15, 1990.
71. StGB, Cp, art. 162 (Swiss Penal Code prohibition against disclosure of bank secrets).
72. C. pen., art. 378.

73. Added by Stats. 1990, c. 1616 (A.B.2249).
74. 453 N.Y.S.2d 69 (1982).
75. 467 So.2d 814 (1985).
76. 31 F.F.R. § 10.51, Circular 230 (U.S. Treasury Department).

Chapter Six

Detection of Fraud and Systemic Weaknesses

What does an auditor actually do? Does he or she issue the equivalent of a "clean bill of health" for the audited client? Or are his or her services limited merely to the performance of certain auditing procedures? The answer to these questions frame the discussion of an accountant's liability for negligence in performing audits and audit-related services.

TASKS AND LIMITATIONS

One approach to an understanding of the work of an auditor is to view the tasks performed, and the limitations under which those tasks are performed.

The work of an auditor generally includes the following five steps:

a. First, the auditor plans the audit by gathering information about the entity's operation, organization, and accounting systems.

b. Second, the auditor evaluates the client's internal control structure.

c. Third, the auditor determines whether the execution and recording of financial transactions is subject to a proper control and approval process.

d. Fourth, the auditor performs tests to confirm validity of the accounting information. The extent and depth of these tests are determined, in part, by the auditor's analysis of the internal and accounting controls in place.

e. Finally, the auditor renders an audit opinion in a report stating that the audit was conducted in accordance with generally accepted auditing standards (GAAS), and that the corporation's financial statements present its financial position fairly, in accordance with generally accepted accounting principles (GAAP).[1]

All of the above steps are, in turn, conducted within certain restraints, including:

1. **Costs.**   Even though an auditor serves as a "public accountant," and owes a duty of care to investors, creditors, and to some extent the general public, the auditor is paid by the client it audits.   And that client has limited resources, requiring the auditor to compete for the engagement by keeping its fees to a minimum in comparison to the auditor's own competitors.

2. **Time.** The bylaws of a corporate client establish the time and place of the corporation's annual shareholder meeting. The time period between the end of a fiscal year and the shareholder meeting generally constitutes the maximum time during which an audit must be completed. That time frame is further shortened by creditor demands for current financial information, management needs, and other tensions. Due to these time constraints, the auditor must limit the number of transactions tested, the extent of sampling, and other time-dependant tasks.

3. **Sampling.** The time and cost restraints necessitate the testing of transactions and accounting information. This is

usually done on a statistical basis, but serves nevertheless to constitute a restraint on the breadth of the audit.

4. **Sources of Information.** Most of the figures, data, documents, computer reports, and related information examined by the auditor are provided by management. Even managers who are not involved in fraud have a vested interest in a positive outcome of the audit. Hence, auditor is, for the most part, examining information that is possibly "tainted" due to its source.

5. **Promulgations.** The art of accounting, and the science of auditing, are dynamic disciplines that must adapt to changes in technology, industry, and culture. In the practice of their profession, however, auditors are expected to implement volumes of Financial Standards Accounting Board (FASB) pronouncements pertaining to GAAP, and SAS's and other audit-related directives issued by the AICPA pertaining to the audit process. In so doing, auditors must master such a massive profusion of technical promulgations that their ability to develop new and innovative applications of sound theoretical principles in specific, sometimes unusual audit situations is often stymied. And so the very promulgations that are intended to provide guidance can become an additional restraint upon the audit process.

6. **Internationalization of Business.** Nearly every country in the world has its own version of generally accepted accounting principles. In addition, a growing body of international accounting principles is being developed. But business organizations based in the U.S., including those with operations, affiliates, and sales outside of the U.S., must convert non-U.S. financial information into a format that complies with U.S. generally accepted accounting principles. In the process, many decisions regarding interpretation of sales contracts, currency valuations, foreign exchange, and accounting principles, must be made. The final U.S. version of a multinational corporation's financial statements must necessarily be limited by the fact that much of the data is not only aggregated, it is converted or otherwise interpolated from a variety of disparate sources.

DIFFERING VIEWS OF WHAT ACCOUNTANTS DO

The Profession's View

Perhaps a better approach to the understanding of the auditing process is to examine the scope and limitations of the audit function. In so doing, however, the answer to the question, "What do auditor's do?" will depend, under this approach, on who is asked the question.

For many years, accountants held to a view that the audit function is a limited process involving the verification of specific information contained in financial statements prepared by an entity. This verification is accomplished by an examination of the entity's books and records, and by the performance of certain audit procedures in accordance with generally accepted auditing standards (GAAS). If the auditor concludes that the financial statements are a fair representation of the entity's financial position, results of operations, and cash flows, the auditor issues an unqualified opinion.

Significance of Unqualified Opinions. An unqualified opinion is not, according to the accounting profession, a "clean bill of health." Instead, an unqualified opinion provides only the following assurances:

1. The accounting principles used by the entity are generally accepted.
2. The accounting principles are appropriate for the entity's operation.
3. The accompanying disclosures are sufficient for a reader's understanding of the financial statements.
4. Classifications and summarizations of data are reasonable.
5. The significant economic events and transactions of the entity are reflected.[2]

The Views of Financial Statements Users and the Public

Financial statement users, and the general public, have attributed more to the work product of the accountant than has the accountant. When an unqualified opinion is issued, for example, it is not uncommon for that opinion to be referred to as a "clean bill of health."[3] And nonaccountants often presume that a financial audit includes an effort to detect fraud within the organization.[4]

In 1988, an effort to close the "expectation gap" between the accountant's perception of the scope of an audit, and that of the general public, the AICPA issued nine new statements on auditing standards.[5]

Although these new promulgations clarify the profession's position with regard to its duty to detect fraud and discover other errors, they do not completely bridge the expectation gap.[6]

Statement of Auditing Standards No. 53 (SAS No. 53), for example, entitled *The Auditor's Responsibility to Detect and Report Errors and Responsibilities*, clarifies certain limitations accountants place on the scope of their audit services. Unless expanded services are explicitly agreed to pursuant to an engagement agreement, financial auditors limit their responsibility for the detection of fraud to the detection of material misstatements that result from errors and regularities. "Material" misstatements are defined as only those misstatements which have the effect of causing the financial statements to be something other than a fair representation of the entity's operation as a whole.

In controlling for the possibility of material errors and omissions, and in planning the audit itself, auditors examine the internal financial control structure of the entity. This includes the performance of certain control tests and substantive tests in order to attain an assessment of the control environment, an appraisal of the integrity of the accounting system, and a review of the internal control procedures. As the AICPA points out in SAS no. 53, however, the analysis of internal controls is not designed to provide a "guarantee" or similar level of assurance,[7] since some irregularities are the result of sophisticated subterfuge, such as forgeries, collusion, and complex computer fraud.

The Views of the Legal System

Despite the profession's efforts to define the audit function in terms of the performance of specific tasks, rather than in terms of the issuance of a "clean bill of health," clients and other financial statement users have been quick to turn to the legal system when problems arise after the issuance of unqualified opinions. And, to the chagrin of the accounting profession, the judiciary has generally become more and more sympathetic of such plaintiffs.

Typical of such lawsuits are those accusing the auditors of negligently failing to detect employee fraud. If SAS no. 53's "no guarantee" language were to be taken at face value by the courts, such lawsuits would be dismissed out of hand. But they have not been dismissed. Instead, courts have been willing to grant judgments against auditors, even in cases where employees have crafted careful artifices specifically designed to dupe auditors and to survive standard audit procedures.[8]

CONTRIBUTORY NEGLIGENCE DEFENSE

In the past, accountants have not been left without their defenses in court. The defense of contributory negligence has, in years past, provided some aid to the beleaguered auditor. Under a "strict" legal theory of contributory negligence, a plaintiff with any hint of fault of negligence on his or her part was completely barred from recovering against a defendant.[9] But as courts began to limit the availability of the strict rule of contributory negligence in more and more cases, defendants were not as easily protected.[10]

The *Craig* Case. The 1925 case of *Craig v. Anyon*[11] was the first case to discuss the principle of contributory negligence as a defense, in an action of accountant, in any depth. In *Craig*, the plaintiffs were stockbrokers and commodities brokers who hired the defendant accounting firm to audit their books. After approximately five years of services, during which the accounting firm regularly reported that the company was profitable and the books were proper, the person in charge of plaintiff's commodities department confessed to embezzling over $1,250,000. The plaintiffs sued their accountants alleging breach of contract and negligence. The jury found the accountants liable, and determined the damages to be $1,177,805.26.

The appellate court in the *Craig* case reversed, stating that while it was clear that the accountants were negligent, the plaintiffs were not blameless for their losses. The plaintiffs, in effect, had contended that the defendants were chargeable with negligence because of failure to detect the wrongdoing of the commodities department, wholly overlooking the fact that the plaintiffs were themselves negligent in failing properly to supervise the department or to learn the true condition of their own business and to detect the wrongdoing.[12] And the accountants were able to successfully argue that the plaintiffs had contributed to the problem by, among other things, failing to put in place internal financial controls to protect the company from embezzlement.

THE COMPARATIVE NEGLIGENCE APPROACH

Although the *Craig* case represented the majority view at one time, only a handful of states still retain strict contributory negligence.[13] Most judicial jurisdictions have turned to a "comparative negligence" approach in lieu of the old contributory negligence doctrine.[14] Under this newer approach, plaintiffs are not barred from recovery simply because they might have also been negligent. Instead, the courts compare the relative negligence of plaintiff and defendant, and allocate liability in proportion to that comparison.

Courts faced with lawsuits against accountants now look to the dissenting opinion in the *Craig* case for guidance. In that dissent, Justice Clark reasoned as follows:

> [t]he contract of audit was not one merely to discover if inadvertent clerical errors had been made in the bookkeeping, but was one of protection of the plaintiffs' firm from their own failure to find any error in their books of account. * * * [T]he defendants' work in pursuance of the contract, owing to the manner in which it was performed, failed to save plaintiffs from the consequences of such failure and neglect, which was the very subject of the contract.[15]

The *National Surety* Case. The 1939 case of *National Surety*[16] followed Justice Clark's dissent. In *National Surety*, during an audit, the accountants failed to discover that a cashier was embezzling funds from a stockbroker. The court rejected the accountant's defense that the client had been contributorily negligent in running its business such that it was impossible to determine that the cashier was embezzling funds. In opting for comparative negligence as a preferred approach to the resolution of the case, the court stated:

> We are. . . not prepared to admit that accountants are immune from the consequences of their negligence because those who employ them have conducted their own business negligently. . . . Accountants, as we know, are commonly employed for the very purpose of detecting defalcations which the employer's negligence has made possible. Accordingly, we see no reason to hold that the accountant is not liable to his employer in such cases. Negligence of the employer is a defense only when it has contributed to the accountant's failure to perform his contract and report the truth.[17]

The *National Surety* line of reasoning is now followed in most jurisdictions.[18] The most prominent application in recent years has been in the 1984 case of *Lincoln Grain, Inc. v. Coopers & Lybrand*.[19] In reaching its decision to disregard the old contributory negligence rule, Nebraska Supreme Court stated in the *Lincoln Grain* case:

> [A]ccountants are not to be rendered immune from the consequences of their own negligence merely because those who employ them may have conducted their own business negligently. Allowing such a [contributory negligence] defense would render illusory the notion that an accountant is liable for the negligent performance of his duties.[20]

Burden of Proof of Plaintiff Complicity. *National Surety* not only ushered in the doctrine of comparative negligence in accountants' liability cases, but it also raised the burden of proof that an accountant must meet in order to successfully require the sharing of fault by the client. Under *National Surety*, an accountant can reduce liability if the accountant can provide convincing evidence that the client "has contributed to the accountant's failure to perform his contract and to report the truth."[21] In other words, the accountant would have discovered a material problem **but for** the wrongoing or negligence of the client. This standard is generally considered a difficult one to establish.

The earlier *Craig* burden of proof, on the other hand, invited judicial consideration of any negligence, or any fraud, on the part of the client that **may have** colored the accountant's work product.

The *Devco Premium* Case. The Florida case of *Devco Premium Fiance Co. v. North River Ins. Co.*[22] illustrates the application of the *Craig* burden of proof as compared to that of *National Surety*. In that case, Devco Premium Finance Company (Devco) served clients who desired to purchase insurance policies but who could not afford to pay the initial lump-sum premiums on those policies. Each client paid to the agent of the insurer a stated percentage of the lump-sum premium, generally 30 percent, and Devco then paid the insurer the remainder of the premium. In return for Devco's payment to the insurance company on behalf of the client, the client: (1) agreed to make monthly payments to Devco, amortizing the balance due on the premium plus interest; (2) assigned the unearned premium held by the insurance company to Devco as a security interest; and (3) provided Devco with a power of attorney. When a client failed to make a monthly payment, Devco used its power of attorney to cancel the client's insurance policy. Upon cancellation, the insurance company refunded to Devco the portion of the client's premium which was as yet unearned. Devco thereby protected itself from loss because the premium returned by the insurance company should always be greater than the amount owed by the client to Devco.

Timely notification to the client that he was in arrears on his payment and prompt cancellation of the insured's policy upon the insured's failure to become current in his payments were critical to the success of Devco. Because Devco did not subject its clients to credit checks and did not require the pledge of collateral, its only security lay in the interest which it held in the client's unearned premium. If it failed to promptly cancel the insurance policy of a client who defaulted on his payments, more of the premium would be earned by the insurance company, and Devco stood not only to lose its profit but also its initial investment.

Initially, Devco subscribed to a monthly computer service which provided it with reports of the aging of its accounts receivable. The reports showed the accounts receivable on which payments were 0 to 30 days overdue, 31 to 60 days overdue, and more than 60 days overdue. Devco received these monthly computer aging reports from 1976 through May 1980. On 1 June 1980, Devco began converting to an in-house computer system. Although the problem had existed before the conversion, the company soon began to experience severe problems with failure to properly cancel delinquent accounts. Although Dan Crisp, the President of Devco and a member of its Board of Directors, had available the monthly printouts with their aging schedules from 1976 through May 1980, he never reviewed them during that time.

During the 1979 and 1980 audits of the company, the auditors devised a statistical confirmation test to determine the number and size of doubtful accounts receivable. The auditors omitted numerous pre-1980 contracts from the sample used for this test even though those contracts were still outstanding and were included as accounts receivable on the company's financial statements. The auditors relied upon the opinion of a manager of Devco, as to the collectibility of the pre-1980 accounts which were omitted from the confirmation sample used. The auditors selected 240 Devco accounts receivable to test by confirmation procedures in both the 1979 and 1980 audits.

It appears, however, that in each year the auditors in fact tested only 100 of the 240 accounts and neglected to test the remainder because they concluded, after completing the 100 accounts, that no problems existed. In fact, many of the accounts selected for testing were deficient. Of the 100 accounts actually tested in one of the years, 80 were debit accounts on which payments from the client were owed. Of these 80 accounts, 27 were accounts on which the security--the unearned insurance premium--had been lost. The auditors ignored the results of the statistical sample testing and instead established a doubtful accounts receivable allowance of .5% of the outstanding premium contracts receivable.

In reviewing the actions of the auditors, the *Devco* court observed that the existence of an accountant's duty to perform an audit with due care does not relieve management of its responsibility for the establishment and maintenance of a system of internal accounting controls, nor does it convert the auditor into something of management's agent who must police the system created by management. The court concluded that the evidence in the case, did not establish that any material weakness in Devco's internal accounting control ever came to the attention of the auditors.

The court also concluded that had the auditors adequately and properly tested Devco's accounts receivable, the material weaknesses in the internal accounting controls established and maintained by management would have been discovered earlier; and the awareness of the existence of those weaknesses would have provided management an opportunity to take remedial action.

But the court found blame on both sides. The court pointed out that Devco did not make use of (or provide to auditors) aged accounts receivable reports and other similar information that would have helped to pinpoint the problem. Devco also attempted to convert to a computerized accounting system without adding the personnel necessary to assure an orderly conversion, and in the process its recordkeeping fell dangerously behind.

Since Florida is a comparative fault jurisdiction, the trial court in the *Devco* case allocated 80 percent of the damages to the client, and 20 percent to the accounting firm. This effectively reduced the judgment against the accounting firm to 20 percent of the damages suffered by third party plaintiffs who relied upon the resulting financial statements, in the manner of *National Surety*.[23]

But the case did not use the *National Surety* standard for the accountants' burden of proof. That is, the *Devco* court did not insist, before reducing judgment against the accountants, that the accountants prove that their negligence was entirely dependent upon the actions of the client. Instead, the *Devco* court took into consideration all negligence on the part of the client (such as the installation of a computer without sufficient personnel) that **might** have affected the accounting firm's ability to perform its audit without negligence.

The *Devco* court's willingness to consider any and all relevant negligence or wrongdoing on the part of the client leaves accountant-defendants with a burden of proof closer to that of the *Craig* case, than to the *National Surety* case.

Figure 7 depicts this relationship between *Craig* and *National Surety*. To ascertain the effect of these two cases and their progeny, it must first be determined whether a lawsuit is governed by the laws of a contributory negligence state, or by those of a comparative negligence jurisdiction. If the case is subject to the comparative negligence doctrine, it is then necessary to determine if the accountant's burden of proof is established under the restrictive *National Surety* approach, or under the more accommodating *Craig* approach (as in the *Devco* case). Once these questions are answered, the liability of the accountant can be ascertained.

Figure 7. Application of *Craig* and *National Surety* Cases.

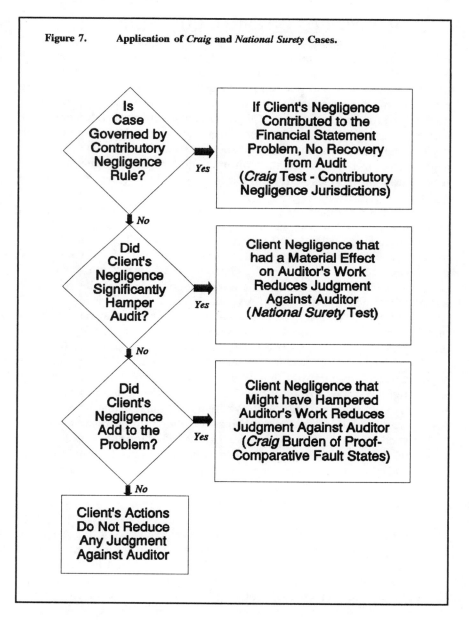

ANALYSIS OF INTERNAL CONTROL

Even though the expectation gap is still alive and well, accountants still contend that their work is not designed, and should not be expected, to uncover employee fraud and similar schemes unless such defalcations are material and are reasonably discoverable given the tests and procedures normally conducted by auditors. Clients and other financial statement users, with the backing of the legal system, insist that even when an audit client does not have sufficient internal controls, and even when the client has been negligent or overtly fraudulent, auditors should, at least in some cases, be held at least partially liable for not discovering such irregularities during an audit.

The second standard of field work, as defined by SAS no. 55, requires that before an auditor plan an audit, he or she must first obtain a sufficient understanding of a client's internal control structure. This understanding, in turn, will determine the nature, timing, and extent of tests to be performed. SAS no. 55 defines the elements of an entity's internal control structure, and provides guidance on assessing control risk in the context of a financial audit. Although SAS no. 55 also upgrades an auditor's responsibility for assuring that internal controls are sufficient so that a material misstatement would be detected, the Statement contains language assuring that the audit report does not constitute a "clean bill of health."

Irregularities that do not appear to be "material" or particularly significant, and irregularities that do not cause financial statements to be an unfair representation of an entity's condition and operation, are treated under SAS no. 55 as unimportant. Whether the courts would be so cavalier toward such "small" internal control breaches when faced with an accounting malpractice action is unclear. But the SAS no. 55 emphasis on only certain types of internal control issues prevents the promulgation (and its implementation) from completely closing the expectation gap.

Foreign Corrupt Practices Act

Despite the accounting profession's circumscribed view of the extent to which internal controls are examined and evaluated during an audit, other voices have been less reserved. The U.S. Congress elevated the importance of internal controls to the level of statutory law when it enacted the Foreign Corrupt Practice Act of 1977 (FCPA).[24] The FCPA is an anti-bribery statute prohibiting U.S. corporations from granting bribes or kickbacks to foreign officials in exchange for favored treatment overseas.

The FCPA contains specific provisions requiring U.S. corporations with foreign operations to maintain books, records, and accounts that accurately and fairly reflect the transactions and dispositions of their corporate assets.

In addition, U.S. companies are required to maintain a system of internal accounting controls sufficient to accomplish the objectives of the FCPA. By enacting the FCPA, Congress expressed a public policy that acknowledges that adequate internal controls can serve as an antidote to illegal uses of corporate funds.[25]

Securities and Exchange Commission

In its 1979 "Statement of Management on Internal Accounting Controls,"[26] the Securities and Exchange Commission attempted to impose mandatory internal control reporting requirements on all publicly held U.S. corporations. This proposal, like the FCPA, was founded on the principle that the effectiveness of an entity's internal control system is critical to the reliability and credibility of financial statements and other management disclosures. Although the Statement regulation, and similar proposals raised in 1988 and 1989, were never finalized, their initial publication reflect the SEC's concern that management provide investors and analysts with reliable assurances as to the internal control systems in place.

Federal Deposit Insurance Corporation Improvement Act

The Federal Deposit Insurance Corporation Improvement Act of 1991 (FDICIA)[27] was enacted to reduce the risk of depletion of FDIC assets.[28] Section 112 of the FDICIA requires banks and thrift organizations to publish management reports providing assessments of their compliance with certain banking laws and regulations, and evaluations of the effectiveness of their internal controls and financial procedures.[29] Section 112(b) provides, in part, as follows:

(b) *Management responsibility for financial statements and internal controls.* Each insured depository institution shall prepare--

(1) annual financial statements in accordance with generally accepted accounting principles and such other disclosure requirements as the Corporation and the appropriate Federal banking agency may prescribe; and
(2) a report signed by the chief executive officer and the chief accounting or financial officer of the institution which contains--

(A) a statement of the management's responsibilities for-- (i) preparing financial statements; (ii) establishing and maintaining an adequate internal control structure and procedures for financial reporting; and (iii) complying with the laws and regulations relating to safety and soundness which are designated by the Corporation or the appropriate Federal banking agency; and

(B) an assessment, as of the end of the institution's most recent fiscal year, of-- (i) the effectiveness of such internal control structure and procedures; and (ii) the institution's compliance with the laws and regulations relating to safety and soundness which are designated by the Corporation and the appropriate Federal banking agency.[30]

Treadway Commission

In 1985, the AICPA, American Accounting Association (AAA), Financial Executives Institute (FEI), Internal Auditors Association (IIA), and the National Association of Accountants (NAA) [now the Institute of Management Accountants (IMA)] formed a joint National Commission on Fraudulent Financial Reporting (Treadway Commission). Among the Commission's objective were the identification of those factors causing fraudulent internal reporting, and the development of recommendations to reduce such fraudulent reporting.

The 1987 report issued by the Treadway Commission included general recommendations for corporate managers, boards of directors, the public accounting profession, the SEC and other regulatory and law enforcement bodies, and academics. A four volume follow-up report, "Internal Control -- Integrated Framework," was issued in 1992. The 1992 report defines internal control as follows:

> Internal control is broadly defined as a process, effected by an entity's board of directors, management and other personnel, designed to provide reasonable assurance regarding the achievement of objectives in the following categories:
>
> • Effectiveness and efficiency of operations.
> • Reliability of financial reporting.
> • Compliance with applicable laws and regulations.[31]

Although the Treadway Commission's 1992 report gives recognizance to the fact that internal controls can only provide reasonable assurance that an entity's control objective will be achieved, the report provides specific guidance for the organizational development of each of the nine listed components.

In addition, the draft 1992 report renews the call for management reporting as to the internal controls in place.[32] The 1992 report has been received favorably by some factions of industries plagued by internal control difficulties, including the Federal Deposit Insurance Corporation.[33] It has been criticized by the U.S. General Accounting Office, however, because it:

1. Does not require public reporting on internal controls, and explicit disclosures of internal control deficiencies;
2. Does not emphasize the role that an independent auditor can play in the evaluation of internal controls;
3. Is not as comprehensive and specific as the set of guidelines provided in the FDICIA.[34]

CONCLUSION

In view of a general consensus within the business and professional communities that the upgrading of internal controls is a critical element in the production of more reliable financial statements, the public accounting profession must be prepared to play a significant role in the development of internal control standards.

Individual accountants and auditors must determine, on a case by case basis, the extent to which they should go beyond the requirements *SAS No. 53*, and the related AICPA publications and promulgations, in their analysis of a client's internal controls. For even if they follow promulgated GAAS, but suffer exposure to malpractice lawsuits because a client's internal controls were too weak, the auditors' compliance with GAAS will not necessarily shield them from liability (especially in comparative negligence jurisdictions).

NOTES

1. *See* J. Sullivan, R. Gnospelius, P. Defliese & H. Jaenicke, Montgomery's Auditing 203-07 (10th ed.1984).
2. American Institute of Certified Public Accountants, *Statements on Auditing Standards No. 58: Reports on Audited Financial Statements* (New York: AICPA, 1988).
3. *See* Travis Morgan Dodd, Accounting Malpractice and Contributory Negligence: Justifying Disparate Treatment Based upon the Auditor's Unique Role, 80 Geo. L.J. 909, at n.33, *citing* Cenco Inc. v. Seidman & Seidman, 686 F.2d 449, 452 (7th Cir.) (auditors continued to give client "a clean bill of health"), *cert. denied,* 459 U.S. 880 (1982). *See also* Allison Leigh Cowan, "Accountants Fear S&L Backlash," *New York Times,* July 31, 1990, at D1, D5 ("Many of these [failed institutions] got clean bills of health from their auditors just before being identified by regulators as insolvent . . . ."); Allison Leigh Cowan, "S.E.C. Inquiry is Reported On Loans to Accountants," *New York Times,* Feb. 7, 1991, at D1, D9

        ("All through its tenure as its auditor, Arthur Young gave Republicbank a clean bill of health."); John R. Wilke, "Ernst & Young Gave Clean Opinion Of Failed Rhode Island Deposit Insurer," *Wall Street Journal*, Feb. 1, 1991, at A4 ("Ernst & Young gave a clean bill of health last year to the private deposit insurer whose collapse precipitated Rhode Island's banking crisis.").

4.   *See* Dan M. Guy & Jerry Sullivan, "The Expectation Gap Auditing Standards," *Journal of Accountancy*, Apr. 1988, p.37.

5.   *Ibid.* The nine new statements, all issued by the AICPA, are: SAS no. 53, *The Auditor's Responsibility to Detect and Report Errors and Irregularities*; SAS no. 54, *Illegal Acts by Clients*; SAS no. 55, *Consideration of the Internal Control Structure in a Financial Statement Audit*; SAS no. 56, *Analytical Procedures*; SAS no. 57, *Auditing Accounting Estimates*; SAS no. 58, *Reports on Audited Financial Statements*; SAS no. 59, *The Auditor's Consideration of an Entity's Ability to Continue as a Going Concern*; SAS no. 60, *Communication of Internal Control Structure Related Matters Noted in an Audit*; and SAS no. 61, *Communication with Audit Committees*.

6.   *See* Goldstein & Dixon, New Teeth for the Public's Watchdog: The Expanded Role of the Independent Accountant in Detecting, Preventing, and Reporting Financial Fraud, 44 Bus.Law. 439, 442 (1989) (discussing expectation gap and various proposals to close it).

7.   Au. § 316.08.

8.   *See, e.g.,* Maryland Casualty Co. v. Cook, 35 F.Supp. 160, 165-67 (D.Mich.1940) (liability established because audit procedures allowed defalcators to go undetected); Dantzler Lumber & Export Co. v. Columbia Casualty Co., 115 Fla. 541, 543, 156 So. 116, 116-17 (1934) (defalcations would have been detected had auditors followed certain procedures); Bonhiver v. Graff, 311 Minn. 111, 115-16, 248 N.W.2d 291, 295-96 (1976) (action against auditors for failure to discover defalcating company officers); Smith v. London Assurance Corp., 109 A.D. 882, 883-84, 96 N.Y.S. 820, 821 (1905) (client sued auditors for failure to detect employee defalcations). *See also* Annotation, Accountants' Malpractice Liability to Client, 93 A.L.R. 3d 396, 411 (1979).

9.   *See* WILLIAM KEETON, DAN B. DOBBS, ROBERT E. KEETON AND DAVID G. OWEN, PROSSER & KEETON ON THE LAW OF TORTS, §65, at 451-452 (1984).

10.   *Id* at §66-67, 462-70. *See generally* James, Last Clear Chance: A Transitional Doctrine, 47 Yale L.J. 704 (1938).

11.   212 A.D. 55, 208 N.Y.S. 259, (1925), *aff'd mem.,* 242 N.Y. 569, 152 N.E. 431 (1926).

12.   *Id.* at 67, 212 N.Y.S. at 269.

13.   The only remaining strict liability states, as of the writing of this book, are Alabama, Maryland, North Carolina, South Carolina, and Virginia.

14.   *See* Sobelsohn, Comparing Fault, 60 Ind. L.J. 413, 414 & N.14 (1985).

15.   *Supra* note 11, 212 A.D. at 67-68, 212 N.Y.S. at 269-70.

16.   256 A.D. 226, 9 N.Y.S.2d 554 (1939).

17.   *Id* at 235-36, 9 N.Y.S.2d at 563.

18.   *See* Halla Nursery, Inc. v. Baumann-Furrie & Co., 454 N.W.2d 905 (Minn. 1990); Shapiro v. Glekel, 380 F.Supp. 1053, 1058 (S.D.N.Y.1974); Cereal Byproducts Co. v. Hall, 8 Ill.App.2d 331, 336, 132 N.E.2d 27, 29-30 (1956), *aff'd,* 15 Ill.2d 313, 155 N.E.2d 14 (1958); Hall & Co. Inc., v. Steiner & Mondore, 147 A.D.2d 225, 228, 543 N.Y.S.2d 190, 191-92 (1989); Jewelcor Jewelers & Distrib., Inc. v. Corr, 373 Pa.Super. 536, 551-52, 542 A.2d 72, 80 (1988); Greenstein, Logan & Co. v. Burgess Marketing, Inc., 744 S.W.2d 170, 190 (Tex.Ct.App.1987). *See generally* Menzel, The Defense of Contributory Negligence in Accountant's Malpractice Actions, 13 Seton Hall L.Rev. 292, 310 (1983).

19.   216 Neb. 433, 345 N.W.2d 300 (1984).

20.   *Ibid,* 345 N.W.2d at 306.

21.   256 A.D. at 236; 9 N.Y.S.2d at 563.

22.   450 So.2d 1216 (Fla.App.1984).

23. 450 So.2d at 1220. *See also* Capital Mortgage Corp. v. Coopers & Lybrand, 142 Mich. App. 531, 369 N.W.2d 922 (1985).
24. 15 U.S.C.S. §§ 78dd-1, 78dd-2 (As Amended in 1988) (1992).
25. *See* Alan Reinstein & Albert Spalding, "Complying with the Foreign Corrupt Practices Act Amendments of 1988," *International Journal of Accounting Education and Research*, Vol. 26, pp 18-26 (1991).
26. Release Nos. 33-6789; 34-25925; IC-16485; 17 CFR Parts 229, 240, 249, 270 and 274, 1988 SEC LEXIS 1491 (July 19, 1988).
27. Pub. L. 102-242, 105 Stat. 2236-2494 (1991).
28. *See*, Martha L. Ellett & Josiah O. Hatch III, "New Banking Legislation Charts a Dangerous Course for Officers And Directors," *Insights*, August, 1992; Vol. 6, No. 8; p. 5.
29. 12 U.S.C.S. § 1831m (1992).
30. *Ibid.*
31. Committee on Sponsoring Organizations,"Internal Control -- Integrated Framework," (1992) (Executive Summary, p.1).
32. *Ibid.*
33. "COSO Internal Control Guidance Weakens Oversight and Reporting, GAO Charges," *Thomson's International Bank Accountant*, November 16, 1992, Vol. 2; No. 43; p. 3.
34. *See*, 12 U.S.C.S. § 1831m (1992).

Chapter Seven

Auditor's Reporting Responsibility

When the auditor has completed his or her examination of the client's financial statements, which present the financial condition, results of operations and the cash flow of the client's operation, the auditor must then render a report. It is the language of this report which communicates the auditor's representations to the client and third parties as to the auditor's opinion on the reliability of the financial statements. It is upon these representations that potential legal liability is attached.

THE REPORTING FUNCTION

The auditor's report is governed by the generally accepted auditing standards (GAAS) of the accounting profession. Pursuant to the professional standards of the AICPA the auditor's report includes the following:

1. A conclusion as to whether or not the financial statements comply with generally accepted accounting principles (GAAP);
2. A conclusion as to whether or not the GAAP reflected in the current period is consistent with the accounting principles applied in the prior period;
3. The implication (unless otherwise stated in the auditor's report) that the disclosures contained in the financial statements, including the footnotes, are adequate; and
4. A conclusion as to whether or not the financial statements, taken as a whole, present a fair representation of the financial circumstances of the audited client.[1]

GAAS includes the various *Statements on Auditing Standards (SAS)*, and related technical promulgations, issued by the AICPA. Rule 203 of the AICPA's Code of Professional Conduct, in fact, requires that AICPA members either follow its *SAS* system, or be prepared to justify departures from the system.

GENERALLY ACCEPTED ACCOUNTING PRINCIPLES

GAAP has been promulgated by a succession of authoritative bodies. For several years from the time of the inception of the AICPA, the AICPA's Committee on Accounting Procedures, and its Committee on Terminology, issued a series of pronouncements called Accounting Research Bulletins (ARB). In 1953, the ARB's to date were revised, restated and combined, and issued as ARB No. 43 and Accounting Technology Bulletin (ATB) No. 1. From 1953 to 1959, three additional ATB's and eight new ARB's were issued. ARB Nos. 43 through 51 and ATB Nos. 1 through 4 remain in force except to the extent modified by subsequent pronouncements.

From 1959 to 1973 the Accounting Principles Board (APB) replaced the two AICPA committees, and issued 31 opinions (APBO's), most of which are still fully or partially in effect. The APB also issued several "statements," only one (No. 3) of which is still in effect.

In 1973, the APB was replaced by the Financial Accounting Standards Board (FASB). The FASB has issued over a hundred Statements, almost half as many Technical Bulletins, and several dozen Interpretations, explaining or interpreting those Statements. The FASB usually maintains between six and twelve Exposure Drafts designed to solicit professional comment with regard to proposed new pronouncements.

The above pronouncements are subject to Rule 203 of the AICPA's Code of Professional Conduct, which requires compliance with those pronouncements unless there is good reason justifying noncompliance. All of the above pronouncements, as well as those of the Government Accounting Standards Board (GASB), are properly referred to as "promulgated GAAP."

Promulgated GAAP are only a subset of all GAAP. That is because there are accounting principles and practices that are not encompassed by promulgated GAAP, including those that have not been reduced to writing. *SAS No. 52*, itself an example of "promulgated GAAS," describes a hierarchy of GAAP wherein promulgated GAAP are identified as having priority, but other non-promulgated GAAP are also taken into consideration.

Non-promulgated GAAP are applied in the exercise of professional judgment by accountants. Accounting is itself an art, rather than a science, and certain underlying concepts, such as reliability, substance over form, and materiality, take precedence over the specific accounting rules that may have evolved in the context of promulgated GAAP.

Disclosures in the Financial Statements and Footnotes

One of the more significant reporting issues involving professional judgement is the matter of disclosure. Promulgated GAAP provide detailed rules for the disclosure of hundreds of categories of information, ranging from contingent liabilities, to lease information, to pension assets and liabilities, to stock issued to employees.

The absence of a "rule" issued by an authoritative body does not, however, preclude the necessity of disclosure. The courts have consistently required accountants to disclose adverse information that comes to their attention (or should have come to their attention) during an engagement.

The case of *Herzfeld v Laventhol, Krekstein, Horwath & Horwath* provides an example of this judicially imposed super-disclosure requirement.[2] That case involved an accountant who was retained by a real estate syndicate for purposes of preparing an audit for the 11 month period ending November

30, 1969. His report, intended to generate capital investment, reflected current earnings purportedly derived from the sale of certain nursing home properties. The sale in reality was no more than an option exercisable at the discretion of the buyer. The court reviewed the procedures which the accountants had followed in certifying this transaction as a sale and concluded that, although there was no outright fraud, defendants had knowledge of material facts which they failed to disclose. Specifically, the court found inter alia that the accountants, upon a review of the contract of sale, had knowledge of and a duty to report the ambiguity of the supporting documentation, the nature and worth of the buyer, the magnitude of the transaction and the impact on the company should the transaction abort. The court further found that the disclaimer issued by the accountant was itself misleading, particularly in its use of the word "acquired." Thus, despite the precautionary efforts of the accountants in obtaining the opinions of other accountants and lawyers regarding the contract of sale, the court found the audit seriously deficient and imposed liability.

The accountant in the *Herzfeld* case had, in fact, followed GAAP in disclosing the client's purchase and subsequent sale of some nursing homes. The client accepted a purchase money mortgage as part of the purchase and sale transaction, the likelihood of collection of the mortgage note was considered questionable by the court. The court ruled that an individual who invested in the accounting firm's client, in reliance upon the financial statements audited by the accounting firm, could recover from the accounting firm due to a lack of "full and fair disclosure" as required under the securities laws. The court pointed out that accountants have a duty to go beyond GAAP-required disclosures, stating:

> Compliance with generally accepted accounting principles is not necessarily sufficient for an accountant to discharge his public obligation. Fair presentation is the touchstone for determining the adequacy of disclosure in financial statements. While adherence to generally accepted accounting principles is a tool to help achieve that end, it is not necessarily a guarantee of fairness.

Nondisclosure of a material item, even if disclosure is not required by GAAP, can cause other problems. If a plaintiff can convince the court that the nondisclosure is tantamount to an "omission" of a material fact under the U.S. securities laws, for example, the defendant-accountant will lose an important defense in his or her trial strategy. Under § 10(b) of the securities law, it is necessary to prove that a plaintiff-investor relied upon financial statements (and the accompanying auditor's opinion) before the court will allow a recovery against the auditor. But reliance is presumed in cases involving an omission (as opposed to a misstatement) of material fact.

As the U.S. Supreme Court pointed out in the case of *Affiliated Ute Citizens v. United States*,[3] a disclosure, even if improperly or inelegantly made, of a problem at least warns the financial statement user of a problem. But nondisclosure necessarily leaves the user in the dark.

The judicial standard for materiality, for purposes of disclosure, is not necessarily the same as that of GAAP, either. While *SAS No. 47, Audit Risk and Materiality in Conducting an Audit*, recognizes that materiality is often a matter of professional judgment, taking into consideration both qualitative and quantitative factors, the U.S. Supreme Court has expressed a preference for making a disclosure in any doubtful circumstance. In the decision of *TSC Industries, Inc. v. Northway, Inc.*, the Court laid down the following standard:

> An omitted fact is material if there is a substantial likelihood that a reasonable shareholder would consider it important in deciding how to vote . . . . What the standard does contemplate is a showing of a substantial likelihood that, under all the circumstances, the omitted fact would have assumed actual significance in the deliberations of the reasonable shareholder. Put another way, there must be a substantial likelihood that the disclosure of the omitted fact would have been viewed by the reasonable investor as having significantly altered the "total mix" of information made available.[4]

This judicial standard of disclosure is required whenever an accounting firm is "associated" with financial statements. And in addressing the disclosure requirements, the courts will not be bound by GAAP promulgations (such as *SAS No. 26*, discussed below) in determining whether an accountant is associated with financial statements. If an accounting firm is named in a memorandum describing a new offering of stock, for example, the courts will deem the accounting firm as having been associated with any enclosed financial statements or projections. As the court in the case of *Roberts v. Peat, Marwick, Mitchell & Co.*:

> [I]nvestors have alleged that Peat, Marwick knew of the alleged violation but allowed the use of its name in offering memoranda despite that knowledge. These facts may be sufficient to create a duty to disclose in Peat, Marwick. Investors can reasonably be expected to assume that an accounting firm would not consent to the use of its name on reports and offering memoranda it knew were fraudulent. Thus, it may be reasonable to expect an accountant to disclose fraud in this type of situation, where the accountant's information is superior and the cost to the accountant of disclosure is minimal.[5]

Even if an accounting firm's name is used without its permission, the accounting firm can be held liable if material information is not disclosed. The courts require that accounting firms take positive action to "disassociate" themselves from financial information, even seeking out potential recipients of that information, if the accounting firm learns that its name is being used. As the court in *Rudolph v. Arthur Andersen & Co.* noted:

> Standing idly by while knowing one's good name is being used to perpetuate a fraud is inherently misleading. An investor might reasonably assume that an accounting firm would not permit inclusion of an audit report it prepared in a placement memo for an offering the firm knew to be fraudulent, and that such a firm would let it be known if it discovered to be fraudulent an offering with which it was associated.[6]

The extent to which an accounting firm must seek out potential investors or financial statement users, whenever its name is mentioned (without permission) in an offering circular or other promotional item, is not clear. Once court concluded that accounting firms are not required to take out advertisements in the *Wall Street Journal*, but this "limitation" on the accountant's obligation is not necessarily very helpful.[7] Suffice it to say that the accountant placed in the unenviable situation of learning that his or her name is being used to tout a stock offering or other promotional effort, without permission, should seek out an attorney who can help him or her determine the duty, under both state and federal law, to remedy the problem.

Expression of an Opinion

Each of the four elements of an auditor's report constitutes an "opinion." That is, the auditor exercises judgement and professional skill in determining whether the financial statements conform to GAAP, are consistent with the prior year, are sufficiently detailed and revealing, and constitute a fair representation of the economic condition of the firm.

It is the last "opinion," pertaining to fair representation, however, that implies that the financial statements are free from any material misstatement. To arrive at this conclusion, the auditor strives to "reasonably assure" himself or herself that the information provided by management is reliable. He or she does this by examining evidence supporting the financial information, conducts certain tests, and reviews any significant estimates made by management.

If financial statements contain a material error or misstatement, they do not represent fairly the financial circumstances of the audited entity. This results in a cause of action for the injured plaintiff. As one court put it:

> When an accountant certifies that a firm's financial statements 'present fairly' its financial position . . . it is certifying the absence of materially misleading omissions, a source of primary liability.[8]

ASSOCIATION WITH FINANCIAL STATEMENTS

Whenever an auditor's name is associated with audited financial statements,[9] the auditor should indicate the degree of responsibility being assumed for the reliability of the statements. The auditor is deemed to be associated with financial statements if the auditor actually prepares those financial statements (or assists in their preparation).[10]

Implicit in the fourth standard of reporting are four degrees of responsibility which the auditor may choose to assume: (1) an unqualified opinion, (2) a qualified opinion, (3) an adverse opinion, or (4) a disclaimer of opinion. It is the objective of the fourth standard of reporting to "prevent misinterpretation of the degree of responsibility the auditor is assuming."[11]

The court made reference to this standard as established by the AICPA in *Stanley L. Bloch, Inc. v. Klein.*[12] In this case, the plaintiff sought to recover damages sustained as the result of the defendant accountants issuing a balance sheet containing errors in the inventory and surplus account, which had not been verified by an independent check or sampling process. In observing the defendants' failure to place any qualification notice on the balance sheet, the court held:

> . . . Defendants' failure to place any qualification notice on the subject balance sheet, therefore, clearly constituted a violation of the emphasized portion of the cited rule [fourth standard of reporting] which, without any doubt, fixes the existing and accepted standards of the profession.
> The balance sheet on the defendants' professional letterhead was unqualified and in effect, an audited financial statement upon which plaintiff had the right to rely in order to determine and evaluate its financial condition as of April 30, 1957. It is clear that in order to relieve themselves of liability for errors contained in this April 30, 1957, balance sheet, defendants could have and should have indicated on its face all items that were not independently verified.[13]

The accountants prepared the financial statements on their letterhead but did not indicate the degree of responsibility assumed, so the court treated the statements as though the accountants had issued an unqualified opinion.

THE AUDITOR'S REPORT

If an auditor assumes responsibility for an unqualified opinion, the following scope and opinion paragraphs are usually issued when the standard report is utilized:

Introductory paragraph

We have audited the accompanying balance sheet of X Company as of [at] December 31, 19xx, and the related statements of income, retained earnings and cash flows for the year then ended. These financial statements are the responsibility of the Company's management. Our responsibility is to express an opinion on these financial statements based on our audit.

Scope paragraph

We conducted our audit in accordance with generally accepted auditing standards. Those standards require that we plan and perform the audit to obtain reasonable assurance about whether the financial statements are free of material misstatement. An audit includes examining, on a test basis, evidence supporting the amounts and disclosures in the financial statements. An audit also includes assessing the accounting principles used and significant estimates made by managements, as well as evaluating the overall financial statement presentation. We believe that our audit provides a reasonable basis for our opinion.

Opinion paragraph

In our opinion, the financial statements referred to above represent fairly, in all material respects, the financial position of X company as of [at] December 31, 19xx, and the results of its operations and its cash flows for the year then ended, in conformity with generally accepted accounting principles.[14]

In essence, the auditor represents in the scope of the paragraph that his audit was made in accordance with generally accepted auditing standards and that based on this audit, the opinion paragraph represents that in his opinion the financial statements present fairly the client's financial position, results of operations, and changes in financial position in conformity with generally accepted accounting principles applied on a basis consistent with that of the preceding year.

During an audit, the auditor might conclude that an unqualified report is not merited. Based on the deficiencies encountered, the auditor may issue one of the following report forms:

1. **Qualified Opinion.** When a qualified opinion is intended by the independent auditor, the reasons for the qualified opinion are set forth in a separate paragraph, and that explanatory paragraph is inserted ahead of the opinion paragraph. The explanatory paragraph refers specifically to the subject of the qualification and should give a clear explanation of the reasons for the qualification and of the effect on financial position and results of operations, if reasonably determinable. The opinion paragraph, in turn, makes reference to the explanatory paragraph. The opinion expressed is limited by the deficiency described in the explanatory paragraph, and makes clear the nature of the qualification. However, when a qualification is so material as to negate an expression of opinion as to the fairness of the financial statements as a whole, either a disclaimer of opinion or an adverse opinion is required.

2. **Adverse Opinion.** An adverse opinion is an opinion that the financial statements *do not* present fairly the financial position or results of operations in conformity with generally accepted accounting principles. An adverse opinion is required in any report where the exceptions as to fairness of presentation are so material that in the independent auditor's judgment a qualified opinion is not justified.

3. **Disclaimer of Opinion.** When the auditor has not obtained sufficient competent evidential matter to form an opinion on the fairness of presentation of the financial statements as a whole, the independent auditor's report should state that the auditor is unable to express an opinion on such statements. The necessity of disclaiming an opinion may arise either from a serious limitation on the scope of examination or from the existence of unusual uncertainties

concerning the amount of an item or the outcome of a matter materially affecting financial position or results of operations, causing the independent auditor not to be able to form an opinion on the financial statements as a whole.[15]

Departure from the unqualified standard report is necessitated by the following circumstances:

1. The scope of the auditor's examination is affected by conditions that preclude the application of one or more auditing procedures he considers necessary in the circumstances.
2. The auditor's opinion is based in part on the report of another auditor.
3. The financial statements are affected by a departure from a generally accepted accounting principle.
4. The financial statements are affected by a departure from an accounting principle promulgated by the body designated by the AICPA Council to establish such principles.
5. Accounting principles have not been applied consistently.
6. The financial statements are affected by uncertainties concerning future events, the outcome of which is not susceptible of reasonable estimation at the end of the auditor's report.
7. The auditor wishes to emphasize a matter regarding the financial statements.
8. Disclosure is insufficient.[16]

Some of these circumstances have represented greater legal complications for the accountant than others, and those will be examined closer later in the chapter.

SIGNIFICANCE OF THE AUDITOR'S REPORT LANGUAGE

It should be emphasized that the language being communicated in an audit report is all that the reader has available as to the meaning of a qualification. What the accountant intended to communicate and how the report was interpreted by the reader may ultimately be decided through litigation unless extreme care is taken.

For example, in the case of *C.I.T. Financial Corporation v. Glover*,[17] plaintiff C.I.T. sued the defendant accountants for losses incurred as a result of loans made to Manufacturers Trading Corporation. The loans were not called in reliance upon representations made as to the financial condition of M.T.C. in an audit conducted by the defendants. The plaintiffs claimed the audit failed to disclose that receivables in the form of loans were overvalued and that the allowance for uncollectible accounts was inadequate due to the stagnancy and concentrated types of certain collateral securing the loans. The defendants contended that they had never asserted any special competence as to appraising such collateral and stated so as a qualification in their report:

> While it was not within our province to pass upon or assume responsibility for the legal or equitable title to the commercial receivables purchased by the companies or the valuation of any security thereto accepted and held by them, it was apparent from their books and records and by opinion of counsel, that there contractual and assignment forms are adequate for their legal protection in connection with the collection and liquidation of commercial receivables purchased.[18]

The crux of the case was whether the qualified language was limited merely to the valuation of the collateral as argued by plaintiff, or was equally applicable to the valuation of the receivables as contended by defendants. The meaning of the language in the qualification was left to the jury which was instructed as follows:

> Defendants contend that by this disclaimer or qualification anyone who read their reports would take notice that the defendants assumed no responsibility for the valuation of the collateral held by Manufacturers Trading Corporation. This much plaintiff apparently concedes, but plaintiff contends that this disclaimer [qualification] did not permit the defendants to close their eyes to facts and to give up the alertness which an accountant should apply during his audit. Plaintiff contends that if the defendants had reasonable ground to suspect that the collateral was not worth the amounts which the management thought it was worth, the disclaimer [qualification] did not cover the situation. There was testimony of expert accounting witnesses bearing on the issue. The question of the accounting principles involved is a question of fact which you, as jurors, are to decide and the true meaning and application of the disclaimer or qualification, in light of that testimony and the other facts of the case, is for you to decide.[19]

The jury found for the defendants and on appeal the decision was affirmed. Though the accountants were spared any liability, the language in the qualification was still unclear enough to go to the jury as a question of fact, and it should be the accountant's objective to avoid such a situation.

RESTRICTIONS ON SCOPE OF EXAMINATION

Situations develop in which restrictions are imposed upon the scope of the auditor's examination "by the client or by circumstances such as the timing of his work, the inability to obtain sufficient competent evidential matter, or an inadequacy in the accounting records. . . ."[20] The most common of the scope limitations are those involving confirmation of accounts receivable and observation of physical inventories.

In *Stephens Industries, Inc. v. Haskins and Sells,*[21] the defendant accountants were engaged by the owner of rent-a-car companies to conduct an audit for the benefit of the plaintiff who was a potential buyer of the companies. In examining accounts receivable, the defendants found poorly kept records and a discrepancy between the subsidiary ledger and general ledger. Because of the added expense, the client requested that the defendants not reconcile the records or adjust for uncollectibility. Thus, receivables were not confirmed and the audit opinion was qualified. The scope paragraph contained the following language:

> Our examination was made in accordance with generally accepted auditing standards, and accordingly included such tests of the accounting records and such other auditing procedures as we considered necessary in the circumstances, excepting that in accordance with your instructions we did not request any of the customers to confirm their balance nor did we review the collectibility of any trade accounts receivable.[22]

The defendants also attached a note to the balance sheet disclosing that the accounts receivable balance was taken from the detail accounts receivable records and was not adjusted to reflect uncollectible accounts.

> In finding for the defendant accountants, the Court of Appeals held:
> . . . the care and competence of appellees [defendants] is reflected in the notes attached to the balance sheet and in the separate accountant's opinion. In both places the accounts receivable had not been adjusted to reflect collectibility.
> From this evidence we are satisfied that appellees exercised the care and competence required of their profession. They followed the

scope of audit as outlined by their clients, and carefully limited their work product results to coincide exactly with the undertaking.[23]

It is certainly questionable whether merely qualifying the scope paragraph and opinion was sufficient. One could argue that the client-imposed restriction on the confirmation of receivables significantly limited the scope of the audit requiring the auditor to disclaim an overall opinion. Dependant upon the materiality of receivables, the AICPA has provided that:

> Restrictions imposed by the client on the scope of the examination most commonly concern the omission of the observation of inventory-taking or the confirmation of receivables by direct communication. In such cases when inventories or receivables are material, the independent auditor should indicate clearly in the scope paragraph (or in a middle paragraph) the limitations on his work and, generally, disclaim an opinion on the financial statements taken as a whole.[24]

Irrespective of the fact that the court found the qualification appropriate, the case could still have been decided in favor of the accountants because of the lack of privity between the defendants and the third-party plaintiffs.

The fact that an auditor disclaims making any opinion on the financial statements taken as a whole may still not completely shield the accountant from liability which was the situation in *Rhode Island Hospital Trust National Bank v. Swartz, Bresenoff, Yavner & Jacobs*[25] (discussed in Chapter Three). Bank loans made by the plaintiff to the client *specifically* for leasehold improvements were applied instead to operating expenses. However, fictitious leasehold improvement expenses were capitalized and thus constituted two-thirds of net assets. The balance sheet showed a substantially overinflated net worth and the income statement failed to show a loss. The audited financial statements required to be furnished to the plaintiff bank contained a disclaimer of opinion by the defendant accountants as to the valuation of the improvements. The disclaimer issued by the accountants concluded with:

> Because of the limitations upon our examination expressed in the preceding paragraphs and the material nature of the items not confirmed directly by us, we are unable to express an opinion as to the fairness of the accompanying statements.

In the description of work performed, the accountants expressed the reason for the disclaimer stating that "fully complete detailed cost records were not kept of these capital improvements and no exact determination could be made as to the actual cost of said improvements." On the face of it, this would appear to be an adequate disclaimer and explanation in accordance with the authority of Chapter Ten of the *Statement on Auditing Procedure No. 33* which the court chose to cite, and which provides in pertinent part that "[t]he report shall either contain an expression of opinion regarding the financial statements, taken as a whole, or an assertion to the effect that an opinion cannot be expressed. When an overall opinion cannot be expressed, the reasons therefor should be stated. . . ."

However, there was undisputed testimony that if the bank had known that the leasehold improvements were fictitious, "it would have refused further loans and immediately begun efforts to effect collection of the amount outstanding." The reason given for the disclaimer by the accountants stated their reservations about the precise value of the improvement, which was insignificant for the bank's purposes when compared to reservations as to its very existence. The court addressed itself specifically to this point by commenting that "[t]his disclaimer. . . followed other reference to the purported leasehold improvements which expressed no reservation about their existence but only their precise value." The court then went on to observe that "[w]hen Accountants said only that 'fully complete detailed cost records were not kept of these capital improvements, and no exact determination could be made as to the actual cost of said improvements,' we do not think that the reasons assigned were sufficiently stated."[26]

Thus, it seems that the accountant should be as careful in formulating the content of a qualification or disclaimer as he is in indicating, in form, the degree of responsibility assumed. If the basis for the reader's reliance is not included in the explanation given for the disclaimer, then the disclaimer does not shield the accountant from liability to that reader.

UNAUDITED FINANCIAL STATEMENTS

The accountant is often engaged to perform accounting services which result in the preparation of unaudited financial statements. For many accountants, providing this form of accounting service may be the most significant aspect of their practice and, therefore, taking precautions to avoid uncertain legal liability is extremely important.

The accountant should first determine whether the services he has been engaged to perform involve unaudited financial statements.

By definition, "[f]inancial statements are unaudited if the certified public accountant (a) has not applied any auditing procedures to them, or (b) has not applied auditing procedures which are sufficient to permit him to express an opinion concerning them. . . ."[27] In essence, then, it is a judgment decision that the accountant must resolve based on various factors, the most important of which is the purpose of the engagement. The purpose, of course, is whatever the client and accountant mutually understand it to be. This understanding is most efficiently reached by exploring the client's objectives and intended use of the statements.

The Engagement Letter

The use of an engagement letter is the surest and safest way of defining the nature and scope of the services to be performed. The following information has been recommended to comprise the engagement letter:

1.   Address the letter to the party who retained the accountant.
2.   Describe the accounting services to be performed, and indicate that no audit is to be made.
3.   Specify that a disclaimer of opinion will be issued on the financial statements including reservations as to known departures from generally accepted accounting principles.
4.   Only those procedures the client specifies to be performed should be referred to in the letter.
5.   Indicate the limited responsibility for detecting defalcations and fraud.
6.   Completely describe all relevant information pertaining to the fee arrangement.[28]

Unaudited financial statements "are representations of management, and the fairness of their representation is management's responsibility."[29] But when the accountant becomes associated with such statements, he must be careful to take certain protective measures to avoid liability. The accountant is associated when he consents "to the use of his name in a report, document, or written communication setting forth or containing the statements" or when he "submits to his client or others, with or without a covering letter, unaudited financial statements which he has prepared or assisted in preparing" regardless of the fact that his name is not appended to the statements.[30]

Compliance with SSARS No. 1

SSARS No. 1, discussed in Chapter Two generally divides unaudited statements into two categories: "compilation" and "review." A compilation is the presentation of financial information that is the representation of management without an undertaking by the accountant to express any assurance on the statements; a review, on the other hand, involves the performance of inquiry and analytical procedures that provide the accountant with a reasonable basis of expressing limited assurance that there are no material modifications that should be made to the statements in order for them to be in conformity with generally accepted accounting principles.[31]

SSARS No. 1 states that in a compilation engagement, the CPA "is not required to make inquiries or perform other procedures to verify, corroborate, or review information supplied by the entity."[32] Even if the CPA happens to learn of problems or negative information during a prior engagement, the problem or negative information need not be divulged if the CPA simply includes a paragraph in the report letter which states that substantially all disclosures have been omitted. As indicated above, however, courts generally are unforgiving in situations where the accountant actually knew (or should have known) about a problem and did not disclose it.

In a review engagement, similarly, the aim of a CPA's investigation has less to do with verification, corroboration, or review of data supplied by management for the purpose of substantiating its accuracy, than it has to do with assuring that the financial statements are themselves in conformity with generally accepted accounting principles (GAAP) or are otherwise consistent with the non-GAAP method of accounting selected. There is a *SSARS No. 1* directive that, in review engagements, the CPA obtain "specialized knowledge" regarding the client's industry and specific business, but it is the integrity of the accounting system itself, and the internal consistency of the resultant financial statements, that receive the greatest emphasis. And, again, even if the CPA does become aware of financial information that is incorrect, incomplete, or otherwise unsatisfactory, it is the relationship of that information to the financial statements themselves that becomes the issue; unless, of course, the accountant is authorized to omit substantially all disclosures, in which case the materiality of the omitted information does not matter.[33] Again, *SSARS No. 1* does not reflect the view of courts, which generally require accountants to disclose material information. Nevertheless, *SSARS No. 1* does require that even errors, irregularities or illegal acts which are not disclosed in the financial statements be reported to management.[34]

SUBSEQUENTLY DISCOVERED FACTS

GAAP Requirements

Promulgated GAAP does not impose upon the auditor a duty to monitor an audited client once the auditor's report has been issued. However, if the auditor later becomes aware of facts that may have existed prior to the date of the report letter and which might have affected his report had he been aware of such facts, the auditor, in cooperation with the client, is obligated to make such further investigations as deemed necessary to determine the reliability of these facts and whether they existed at the date of the report. Once the auditor is convinced as to the existence and reliability of this information, further action as prescribed should be taken if "(a) his report would have been affected if the information had been known to him at the date of his report and had not been reflected in the financial statements, and (b) he believes there are persons currently relying or likely to rely on the financial statements who would attach importance to the information."[35]

When the auditor has concluded, after considering that his report would have been affected if the undisclosed information had been known to him and that there are "persons currently relying or likely to rely on the financial statements,"[36] that action should be taken to prevent future reliance on his report, he should advise his client to make appropriate disclosure of the newly discovered facts and their impact on the financial statements to persons who are known to be currently relying or who are likely to rely on the financial statements and the related auditor's report. When the client undertakes to make appropriate disclosure, the method used and the disclosure made will depend on the circumstances.

When it appears that revision of the statements will cause delay appropriate disclosure would consist of notification by the client to persons who are known to be relying or who are likely to rely on the financial statements and the related report that they should not be relied upon, and that revised financial statements and auditor's report will be issued upon completion of an investigation.[37]

Significantly, promulgated GAAP also directs the auditor with a cooperating client to "satisfy himself that the client has made the disclosures specified."[38] However, when the client is not cooperative, the auditor should notify each member of the board of directors of such refusal and of the fact that, in the absence of disclosure by the client, the auditor will take steps as outlined below to prevent future reliance upon his report. The steps that can appropriately be taken will depend on the degree of certainty of the auditor's knowledge that there are persons who are currently relying or who will rely on the financial statements and the auditor's report, and who would attach importance to the information, and the auditor's ability as a practical matter to communicate with them. Unless the auditor's attorney recommends a different course of action, the auditor should notify each person known to the auditor to be relying on the financial statements that his report should no longer be relied upon.[39] If the client is publicly held, SEC notification may also be required.

Judicial Requirements

The duty to disclose facts discovered after the issuance of an audit report was confirmed by the court in the case of *Fischer v. Kletz*.[40] In that case, the defendant firm of public accountants was engaged to audit the financial statements of Yale Express System, Inc., which were to be included in the annual report issued to shareholders for the year ending December 31, 1963. After certification of the figures and completion of the audit, the defendant was again engaged by Yale, this time to study past and current income and expenses. Sometime toward the end of 1964, the defendant discovered that the annual report had contained substantially false and misleading figures. However, the defendant did not disclose this to the exchanges, the SEC, or to the public at large until May 5, 1965, when the results of the special studies were released. Plaintiffs filed a class action suit against the defendant claiming damages based, in part, on common law deceit.

The court was faced with the question of whether liability for deceit extended beyond the customary requisite of *affirmative* misrepresentation to that of mere silence and nondisclosure of known facts. Acknowledging the general rule against such liability, the court made reference to an exception cited by Dean Prosser that "one who has made a statement and subsequently acquires new information which makes it untrue or misleading, must disclose such information to any one whom he knows to be still acting on the basis of the original statement. . . ."[41]

Reference was also made to the *First Restatement of Torts*. Section 551 provides that "one who fails to disclose to another a thing which he knows may justifiably induce the other to act or refrain from acting in a business transaction is subject to the same liability to the other as though he had represented the nonexistence of the matter which he has failed to disclose, if, but only if, he is under a duty to the other to exercise reasonable care to disclose the matter in question."[42] The *Restatement* position was then cited as to the circumstances giving rise to a duty to disclose. "One party to a business transaction is under a duty to exercise reasonable care to disclose to the other before the transaction is consummated. . . (n) any subsequently acquired information which he recognizes as making untrue or misleading a previous representation which when made was true or believed to be so."[43]

The defendant contended that the *Restatement* applied only to "a business transaction" and that the defendant was in no way a party and had no pecuniary interest. To this the court responded with the following:

> Generally speaking, I can see no reason why this duty to disclose should not be imposed upon an accounting firm which makes a representation it knows will be relied upon by investors. To be sure, certification of a financial statement does not create a formal business relationship between the accountant who certifies and the individual who relies upon the certificate for investment purposes. The act of certification, however, is similar in its effect to a representation made in a business transaction: both supply information which is naturally and justifiably relied upon by individuals for decisional purposes. Viewed in this context of the impact of nondisclosure on the injured party, it is difficult to conceive that a distinction between accountants and parties to a business transaction is warranted. The elements of "good faith and common honesty" which govern the businessman presumably should also apply to the statutory "independent public accountant."[44]

The fact that an auditor was discharged by a client does not change the auditor's duties with regard to events subsequent to the date of the auditor's report.[45] Even though an auditor is expected to maintain a certain degree of confidentiality with regard to client information not actually required by promulgated GAAP to be disclosed, pursuant to *SAS No. 32, Adequacy of Disclosure in Financial Statements*, the duty to disclose material information subsequent to the issuance of a report letter overrides this concern. As the Wisconsin Court of Appeals, affirming a Wisconsin Board of Accountancy regulation, pointed out in *Chevron Chemical Company v. Touche Ross*:

> The prohibition against disclosure of confidential information obtained in the course of a professional engagement does not apply to disclosure of such information when required to properly discharge the certified public accountant's or public accountant's responsibility according to the profession's standards. The prohibition would not apply, for example, to disclosure, as required by section 561 of *Statement on Auditing Standards No. 1*, of subsequent discovery of facts existing at the date of the auditor's report that would have affected the auditor's report had he been aware of such facts.[46]

INQUIRY OF CLIENT'S LAWYER

One area which has grown in significance over the years, partially in response to potential liability for failure to provide more complete disclosures, has been the auditor's demand for disclosure of any pending and threatened litigation, claims and contingent liabilities by means of letters of inquiry to the client's lawyer. The purpose of such disclosure was to protect the accountant, but resulted in undesirable consequences for the attorney, especially as to unasserted claims. The lawyer had to ensure that the attorney-client relationship was protected as to both client confidences and evidentiary privileged communications, which could be waived as to an entire subject matter by merely disclosing one related communication. Also, requests by auditors for predictions of outcomes of threatened or pending litigation against the client jeopardized potential settlements, weakened the client's position, and even encouraged new or nuisance litigation which might have never occurred.

The lawyer, of course, could refuse to respond to such inquiries made by the auditor. However, the auditor would have to qualify his opinion probably making the financial statements unacceptable to the SEC. This undoubtedly would not be pleasing to the client.

The controversy between the two professions was finally resolved by reaching a workable accord between the American Bar Association and the AICPA, the provisions of which are contained in *Statement on Auditing Standards No. 12*, "Inquiry of a Client's Lawyer Concerning Litigation, Claims, and Assessments."[47]

The object of the letter of audit inquiry to the client's lawyer is to corroborate the information obtained from management regarding litigation, claims, and assessments. A list of asserted and unasserted claims and assessments prepared by management is included in the letter requesting the lawyer, with respect to asserted claims, to describe "the nature of the matter, the progress of the case to date, and the action the company intends to take"; to evaluate "the likelihood of an unfavorable outcome and an estimate, if one can be made, of the amount or range of potential loss"; and identify "the omission of any pending or threatened litigation, claims, and assessments or a statement that the list of such matters is complete."[48] With respect to management's list of unasserted claims, the lawyer need only comment if he differs with such description and evaluation.[49]

Refusal by the lawyer to furnish the requested information is treated as a limitation on the scope of the auditor's examination, and a lawyer's inability to furnish such information because of uncertainties is treated as "an uncertainty concerning the outcome of a future event which is not susceptible of reasonable estimation."[50] In either situation, the auditor would probably have to issue a qualified opinion or disclaimer.

NOTES

1. 1 Prof. Stand. [AICPA] *Auditing, Management Advisory Services, Tax Practice, Accounting and Review Services* (Chicago: Commerce Clearing House, Inc.) [hereafter AU], *Statement on Auditing Standards No. 1, Codification of Auditing Standards and Procedures,* AU §§ 410.01, 420.01, and 430.01). *See also, Statement on Auditing Standards No. 26, Association with Financial Statements* (AU § 504.01) (1992).
2. 378 F. Supp 112, 122 (S.D.N.Y. 1974), *aff'd in part and rev'd in part on other grounds,* 540 F.2d 27 (2nd Cir. 1976), *quoting* Sonde, 68 N.W.U.L.Rev. 4 (1968).
3. 406 U.S. 152 (1972).
4. 426 U.S. 438, 449 (1976).
5. 857 F.2d 646, 655 (9th Cir. 1988), *cert. denied,* 493 U.S. 1002 (1989).
6. 800 F.2d 1040, 1044 (11th Cir. 1986), *cert. denied,* 480 U.S. 946 (1987).
7. Latigo Ventures v. Laventhol & Horwath, 876 F.2d 1322, 1327 (7th Cir. 1989).
8. DiLeo v. Ernst & Young, 901 F.2d 624, 628 (7th Cir. 1990), *cert. denied,* 111 S. Ct. 347, 112 L.Ed.2d 312 (1990).
9. AICPA, *Statement on Auditing Standards No. 26: Association with Financial Statements* (New York: AICPA).
10. 1 Prof. Stand. [AICPA] (CCH) *SAS No. 26, Association with Financial Statements,* AU § 504.03 (1992).
11. 1 Prof. Stand. [AICPA] (CCH) AU § 509.05 (1992).
12. Stanley L. Bloch, Inc. v. Klein, 258 N.Y.S. 2d 501 (1965).
13. 258 N.Y.S. 2d at 506-7.
14. AICPA, *Statement on Auditing Standards No. 58: Reports on Audited Financial Statements* (New York: AICPA).
15. AICPA, *Statement on Auditing Procedure No. 33: Auditing Standards and Procedures,* 1963.
16. 1 Prof. Stand. [AICPA] (CCH) AU § 509.09 (1992).
17. C.I.T. Financial Corporation v. Glover, 224 F. 2d 44 (2d Cir. 1955).
18. 224 F. 2d at 46.
19. Instructions given by Judge Ryan, U.S. District Court for the Southern District of New York.
20. 1 Prof. Stand. [AICPA] (CCH) AU § 509.10 (1992).
21. Stephens Industries, Inc. v. Haskins and Sells, 438 F. 2d 357 (10th Cir. 1971).
22. 438 F. 2d at 360-61 fn 1.
23. 438 F. 2d at 360-61.
24. AICPA, *Statement on Auditing Standards No. 1*, pp. 97-98 (New York: AICPA).
25. Rhode Island Hospital Trust National Bank v. Swartz, Bresenoff, Yavner & Jacobs, 455 F. 2d 847 (4th Cir. 1972).
26. 455 F. 2d at 852.
27. 1 Prof. Stand. [AICPA] (CCH) AU § 516.02 (1992).
28. AICPA, *Guide for Engagements of CPAs to Prepare Unaudited Financial Statements,* 1975, pp. 12-13.
29. 1 Prof. Stand. [AICPA] (CCH) AU § 516.01 (1992).
30. 1 Prof. Stand. [AICPA] (CCH) AU § 516.03 (1992).
31. AICPA *SSARS No. 1*, 1978, § 4.
32. AICPA *SSARS No. 1*, 1978, § 12.
33. AICPA *SSARS No. 1*, 1978, § 29.
34. AICPA *SSARS No. 1*, 1978, § 29.
35. 1 Prof. Stand. [AICPA] (CCH) AU § 561.05 (1992).
36. 1 Prof. Stand. [AICPA] (CCH) AU § 561.05(a) & (b) (1992).
37. 1 Prof. Stand. [AICPA] (CCH) AU § 561.06 (1992).

38. 1 Prof. Stand. [AICPA] (CCH) AU § 561.07 (1992).
39. 1 Prof. Stand. [AICPA] (CCH) AU § 561.08 (1992).
40. Fischer v. Kletz, 266 F. Supp. 180 (1967).
41. 266 F. Supp. at 185.
42. Restatement of Torts § 551(1) (1938).
43. *Ibid.*, § 551(2).
44. 266 F. Supp. at 186.
45. *Auditing Interpretation* (February 1989).
46. 483 N.W.2d 314, 319 (Ct. App., Wisc., 1991), quoting Wis. Adm. Code § Accy 1.301(4)(a) (effective January 1, 1975).
47. AICPA, *Statement of Auditing Standards No. 12* (1976).
48. AICPA, *SAS No. 12*, p. 5.
49. *Ibid.*
50. *SAS No. 12*, pp. 6-7.

Chapter Eight

Liability of the Tax Practitioner

R eference has previously been made to legal liability based on the contractual relationship between two parties. When a client engages the services of a tax practitioner, potential liability to the client exists for either breach of contract if the tax practitioner fails to perform in accordance with the provisions of the contract, or for negligence. It will be recalled that liability for negligence requires the breach of a duty to exercise due care which results in damages. Thus, the tax practitioner may perform that which he has contracted to perform, but in so doing has breached his duty owed to the client to exercise professional due care.

BASIS OF CIVIL LIABILITY

The Engagement Contract

The scope of the obligation which the tax practitioner undertakes should be carefully defined by an agreement in the form of a contract or engagement letter.   Such written agreement clarifying the tax practitioner's responsibilities should be prepared prior to commencement of the engagement and any unnecessary delay can only lead to uncertainty and risk. The courts have tended to show little sympathy toward tax practitioners who have not taken steps to protect both sides such as merely outlining the services to be performed.

In constructing the written agreement, the following areas should be taken into consideration.

   a.   Avoid undertaking to achieve a specific *result.*
   b.   Make reference to any conversations and oral agreements.
   c.   Indicate the specific nature of services to be performed.
   d.   Indicate whether data or information is to be supplied by the taxpayer.
   e.   Indicate whether audit or other verification is to be performed upon submitted data.
   f.   Discuss the fee arrangement and whether there are any subsequent services covered or not covered by the fee such as the appeal of a decision of a taxing authority.
   g.   Request that a copy of the agreement be signed and returned.

Working Papers

Working papers used in the preparation of tax returns or for analytical purposes in rendering tax advice are similar in significance to those used in performing an independent audit.   The working papers, in whatever form most convenient, serve an evidentiary function of indicating exactly what the tax practitioner has accomplished and exactly how it was accomplished.

In preparing a tax return, working papers make it possible to trace back to the source the figures appearing in the return. The working papers should contain reasons, dates, and agreements by taxpayer as to any corrections or adjustments made to data furnished by the taxpayer. Tax return items involving uncertain or gray areas of the law in substantial amounts should be discussed with the taxpayer by presenting alternatives, pros and cons, and potential risk, thereby leaving the ultimate decision to the taxpayer. The working papers should explain the options adopted and the basis for arriving at them.

In addition to added organizational efficiency, working papers may represent one of the few reliable sources indicating the work performed and the reasonable care and effort taken in performing such work in the event of litigation.

PRACTICE BEFORE THE IRS

To effectively serve a client's tax needs, the tax practitioner must maintain his or her privilege to appear before the IRS, and in Tax Court, on behalf of the client. The Treasury Department's regulations governing such representation are found in *Circular 230, Rules for Practice Before the Internal Revenue Service*.[1] Those regulations require that the practitioner exercise "due diligence" in representing the taxpayer, taking care to make an independent determination as to the correctness of oral or written representations made by him or her to the IRS (or to the client in conveying tax advice).[2] To the extent that the due diligence standard is consistent with professional standards, discussed below, it does not present a problem. To the extent that a CPA, in exercise of his or her professional duties, must choose between the possible suspension of practice before the IRS, and the exercise of professional due care on behalf of his or her client, however, the regulations serve as a wedge between the CPA and his or her client.

Any certified public accountant or attorney may practice before the Internal Revenue Service by filing a written declaration with the Service that he is currently qualified as a CPA or attorney and is authorized to represent the party on whose behalf he acts provided he is not currently suspended or disbarred from practice before the Service.[3] And any other individual who demonstrates special competence in tax matters in a written examination administered by the Service may be enrolled to practice.[4]

Practice before the Internal Revenue Service consists of all matters presented to the Service relating to the client's rights, privileges, or liabilities under the laws or regulations administered by the IRS. The following are considered to include such presentations:

a. Preparation and filing of necessary documents;
b. Correspondence with and communications to the IRS;
c. The representation of a client at conferences, hearings, and meetings.[5]

The following are not considered to constitute practice before the Service:

a. Preparation of a tax return;
b. Appearance as a witness for the taxpayer;
c. Furnishing information at the request of the IRS or any of its officers or employees.[6]

An individual may engage in limited practice without enrolment both on his own behalf and in representing the following:

a. His regular full-time employer;
b. A partnership in which he is a member or regular full-time employee;
c. A member of his immediate family without compensation;
d. Corporations, trust, estates, associations, or organized groups in which he is a bona fide officer or regular full-time employee;
e. A governmental unit, agency, or authority in which he is an officer or regular employee in the course of his official duties;
f. Outside the United States before IRS personnel;
g. A taxpayer for whom he signed a return as having prepared it or prepared a return not requiring it to be signed by the person who prepared it;
h. Anyone, if authorized by the Commissioner, for the purpose of a particular matter.[7]

Fees and Solicitation

Circular 230 prohibits the tax practitioner from charging an unconscionable fee for representation of a client in any IRS matter.[8]

The tax practitioner is also prohibited from directly or indirectly soliciting employment in IRS-related matters.[9] Examples of solicitation include the following:

a. Advertising of professional attainments or services;
b. Employment of, or the forming of an association or partnership with, any person, partnership, corporation or other organization which solicits in a manner prohibited to attorneys, certified public accountants, and enrolled agents;
c. Use of signs, printing, or other written matter indicating some past or present connection with, or relationship to, the IRS.[10]

Disbarment or Suspension to Practice Before the IRS

The tax practitioner may be suspended or disbarred from practice before the IRS for incompetence, disreputable conduct, refusal to comply with the rules and regulations of Circular 230, or for willfully and knowingly deceiving, misleading, or misleading, or threatening any claimant by word, circular, letter, or advertisement with intent to defraud.[11]

The disreputable conduct referred to is defined to include, though not limited to, the following:

a. Conviction of any criminal offense under U.S. revenue laws, or any offense involving dishonesty or breach of trust;
b. Giving or participating in the giving of false or misleading information to the IRS;
c. Solicitation of employment in matters related to the IRS;
d. Procurement of employment by the use of intentionally false or misleading representations;
e. Intimating that special consideration or action can be improperly obtained from the IRS by the tax practitioner;
f. Federal tax evasion or counseling a plan to evade federal taxes;
g. Willful failure to make a federal tax return;
h. Failure to properly and promptly remit funds to IRS received from client for payment of taxes or misappropriation of such funds;
i. The use of threats, false accusations, duress, or coercion against or bribery of any IRS officer or employee;
j. Suspension or disbarment from practice by a state;
k. Aiding and abetting or maintaining a partnership with another person to practice before the IRS knowing that person to be under suspension, disbarment, or ineligibility to so practice;
l. Contemptuous conduct before the IRS.[12]

Privileged Communications

For the sake of public policy and an orderly society, there are certain classes of communications between persons standing in a confidential or fiduciary relationship to each other in which the law recognizes a privilege to prevent disclosure of such confidential communications. At common law, there was no privilege recognized between the accountant and his client. However, many states have adopted statutes recognizing an accountant-client privilege.

Although there is no federal accountant-client privilege, the state privilege statutes are often applied in federal *civil* cases, especially when the issues do not involve federal questions. However, federal *criminal* cases are another matter and state accountant-client privilege statutes are not recognized in these cases.

Public policy considerations are different for an accountant as tax practitioner, and therefore state accountant-client privilege statutes will probably never be recognized by federal courts in IRS administrative proceedings or IRS investigations requiring enforcement of a summons. However, other measures have recently been used, but they still fall short of an accountant-client privilege such as the one rejected by the United States Supreme Court.

In *Couch v. United States*,[13] the United States Supreme Court examined the confidential nature of the accountant-client relationship. The taxpayer was the sole proprietress of a restaurant. Her accountant was not a personal employee, but had numerous other clients. Beginning in 1955, the accountant was yearly given possession by the taxpayer of bank statements, payroll records, and sales and expenditure records for the purpose of preparing the taxpayer's income tax returns.

In 1969, an investigation was commenced by the IRS of the taxpayer's tax returns. With the accountant's permission, the taxpayer's books and records were examined in the accountant's office. When indications of a substantial understatement of gross income were found, the Intelligence Division of the IRS was brought into the case. The taxpayer was given her *Miranda* warnings and the accountant was issued a summons pursuant to 26 U.S.C. § 7602 which provides:

Examination of Books and Witnesses
For the purpose of ascertaining the correctness of any return, making a return where none has been made, determining the liability of any person for any internal revenue tax or the liability at law or in equity of any transference or fiduciary of any person in respect of any internal revenue tax, or collecting any such liability, the Secretary or his delegate is authorized --

(1) To examine any books, papers, records, or other data which may be relevant or material to such inquiry;

(2) To summon the person liable for tax or required to perform the act, or any officer or employee of such person, or any person having possession, custody, or care of books of account containing entries relating to the business of the person liable for tax or required to perform the act, or any other person the Secretary or his delegate may deem proper, to appear before the Secretary or his delegate at a time and place named in the summons and to produce such books, papers, records, or other data, and to give such testimony, under oath, as may be relevant or material to such inquiry; and

(3) To take such testimony of the person concerned, under oath, as may be relevant or material to such inquiry.[14]

At the taxpayer's request, the accountant delivered all of the records and documents to the taxpayer's attorney before the return day of the summons arrived. The U.S. District Court was thereupon petitioned for enforcement of the summons pursuant to 26 U.S.C. § 7402(b) and 7604(a) which provide:

Section 7402. *Jurisdiction of District Courts.*
(b) *To enforce summons.* If any person is summoned under the internal revenue laws to appear, to testify, or to produce books, papers, or other data, the district court of the United States for the district in which such person resides or may be found shall have jurisdiction by appropriate process to compel such attendance, testimony, or production of books, papers, or other data.[15]

Section 7604. *Enforcement of Summons*
(a) *Jurisdiction of district court.* If any person is summoned under the internal revenue laws to appear, to testify, or to produce books, papers, records, or other data, the United States district court for the district in which such person resides or is found shall have jurisdiction by appropriate process to compel such attendance, testimony, or production of books, papers, records, or other data.[16]

However, the taxpayer intervened asserting her Fifth Amendment privilege against self-incrimination. The District Court and the Court of Appeals rejected the taxpayer's claim and the United States Supreme Court affirmed their decisions.

The Court also rejected the taxpayer's claim of a confidential accountant-client privilege by stating:

> Petitioner [taxpayer] further argues that the confidential nature of the accountant-client relationship and her resulting expectation of privacy in delivering the records protect her, under the Fourth and Fifth Amendments, from their production. Although not in itself controlling, we note that no confidential accountant-client privilege exists under federal law, and no state-created privilege has been recognized in federal cases, Falsone v. United States, 205 F. 2d 734 (5th Cir. 1953), *cert. denied*, 346 U.S. 864; Gariepy v. United States, 189 F. 2d 459, 463-464 (6th Cir. 1951); Himmelfarb v. United States, 175 F. 2d 924, 939 (9th Cir. 1949), *cert. denied,* 338 U.S. 860; Olender v. United States, 210 F. 2d 795, 806 (9th Cir. 1954). Nor is there justification for such a privilege where records relevant to income tax returns are involved in a criminal investigation or prosecution. In *Boyd*, a pre-income tax case, the Court spoke of protection of privacy, 116 U.S., at 630, but there can be little expectation of privacy where records are handed to an accountant, knowing that mandatory disclosure of much of the information therein is required in an income tax return. What information is not disclosed is largely in the accountant's discretion, not petitioner's [taxpayer's]. Indeed, the accountant himself risks criminal prosecution if he willfully assists in the preparation of a false return. 26 U.S.C. Section 7206(2). His own need for self-protection would often require the right to disclose the information given him. Petitioner [taxpayer] seeks extensions of constitutional protection against self-incrimination in the very situation where obligations of disclosure exist and under a system largely dependent upon honest self-reporting even to survive. Accordingly, petitioner [taxpayer] here cannot reasonably claim, either for Fourth of Fifth Amendment purposes, an expectation of protected privacy or confidentiality.[17]

The AICPA has recognized the existence of a confidential relationship between the accountant and his client under Rule 301 which provides:

> A member shall not disclose any confidential information obtained in the course of a professional engagement except with the consent of the client.[18]

The only exceptions permitted to this rule are (a) when necessary to meet one's obligation to comply with auditing standards and accounting principles, (b) when necessary to comply with a valid subpoena or summons enforceable by court order, (c) when participating in a voluntary quality review of one's professional practices under AICPA authorization, and (d) when responding to inquiries made by the AICPA ethics division or Trial Board, state CPA society investigative or disciplinary body, or under state statutes.

STATEMENTS ON RESPONSIBILITIES

The federal tax division of the AICPA has published a numbered series of *Statements on Responsibilities in Tax Practice* (SRTP) which to date consists of eight statements.[19] They are intended to represent a body of advisory opinion as to what constitutes good standards of tax practice.

The *Statement on Responsibilities in Tax Practice*, however, lack the force of authority of those rules contained in the IRS regulations and requirements (discussed below), and therefore depend on general acceptability for their authority where they tend to be more restrictive. The principal objectives of the SRTP have been stated as follows:

a. To recommend appropriate standards of responsibilities in tax practice and to promote their uniform application by CPAs.
b. To encourage the development of increased understanding of the responsibilities of the CPA by the Treasury Department and Internal Revenue Service and to urge their officials to promote the application of commensurate standards of responsibilities by their personnel.
c. To foster increased public understanding of, compliance with, and confidence in our tax system through awareness of the recommended standards of responsibilities of CPAs in tax practice.[20]

Thus, the Statements are educational in nature and help delineate the extent of the tax practitioner's responsibility to his or her client, the public, the government, and his or her profession. In so doing, however, they establish a minimum standard of care to be exercised in the context of tax engagements.

The SRTP do not, on the other hand, constitute the only standards an accountant follows while performing tax-related services.[21] The AICPA's Code of Professional Conduct, for example, requires attitudes and habits of truthfulness and integrity in all of a CPA's practice, including tax practice. Rule 102 of the Code of Professional Conduct states:

> In the performance of any professional service, a member shall maintain objectivity and integrity, shall be free of conflicts of interest, and shall not knowingly misrepresent facts or subordinate his or her judgment to others.[22]

Tax Return Positions

A critical area of application of Rule 102 is the accountant's involvement with the preparation of clients' tax returns. *Statement on Responsibilities in Tax Practice (1988 Rev.) No. 1* provides that, with respect to the tax return positions, a certified public accountant should comply with the following standards:

a. A CPA should not recommend to a client that a position be taken with respect to the tax treatment of any item on a return unless the CPA has a good faith belief that the position has a realistic possibility of being sustained administratively or judicially on its merits if challenged.

b. A CPA should not prepare or sign a return as an income tax return preparer if the CPA knows that the return takes a position that the CPA could not recommend under the standard expressed in paragraph a, above.

c. Notwithstanding the above paragraphs, a CPA may recommend a position that the CPA concludes is not frivolous so long as the position is adequately disclosed on the return or claim for refund.

d. In recommending certain tax return positions and in signing a return on which a tax return position is taken, a CPA should, where relevant, advise the client as to the potential penalty consequences of the recommended tax return position and the opportunity, if any, to avoid such penalties through disclosure.

e. The CPA should not recommend a tax return position that:

   i.   Exploits the Internal Revenue Service audit selection process; or

     ii.   Serves as a mere "arguing" position advanced solely to obtain leverage in the bargaining process of settlement negotiation with the Internal Revenue Service.

    f.   A CPA has both the right and responsibility to be an advocate for the client with respect to any positions satisfying the aforementioned standards.

Realistic possibility. *SRTP No. 1* requires that there be "realistic possibility" of success in upholding a particular position, either on appeal at the IRS or in court, before a CPA recommend that position to his or her client. This standard has also been adopted by the legal profession.[23] The AICPA, in addition, has issued SRTP Interpretation 1-1, which provides fifteen examples interpreting the standard in light of various nuances of differing tax law authority available in support of tax issues.[24]

The Internal Revenue Service uses a similar standard for two purposes: first, in determining whether to suspend an accountant from practicing before in the IRS in the representation of clients; and second, in determining whether to impose preparer penalties. But the interpretation of the "realistic possibility" standard by the IRS is the same for both purposes.

According to Treasury Regulations issued with regard to the preparer penalty provisions of the Internal Revenue Code, a position is considered to have a realistic possibility of being sustained on its merits if a reasonable and well-informed analysis by a person knowledgeable in the tax law would lead such a person to conclude that the position has approximately a one in three, or greater, likelihood of being sustained on its merits. In making this determination, the possibility that the position will not be challenged by the Internal Revenue Service (e.g., because the taxpayer's return may not be audited or because the issue may not be raised on audit) is not to be taken into account.[25]

The Treasury Regulations also provide that in order to sustain the position that there was a realistic possibility of succeeding with regard to a tax issue, the practitioner must be able to show that substantial authority for that position existed. According to the Regulations, there is substantial authority for the tax treatment of an item only if the weight of the authorities supporting the treatment is substantial in relation to the weight of authorities supporting contrary treatment. All authorities relevant to the tax treatment of an item, including the authorities contrary to the treatment, are taken into account in determining whether substantial authority exists. The weight of authorities is determined in light those authorities, as well as in light of the pertinent facts and circumstances.

There may be substantial authority for more than one position with respect to the same item. Because the substantial authority standard is an objective standard, the taxpayer's belief that there is substantial authority for the tax treatment of an item is not relevant to the Internal Revenue Service in making a determination as to whether there is substantial authority for that treatment.[26] The Regulations provide a hierarchy of tax authorities for the purpose of ascertaining the relative weight of sources of tax law,[27] and provides eight examples of the interpretation of the these standards.[28]

Due Diligence as to Accuracy. Regulations § 10.22, meanwhile, state the federal government's position with regard to the areas in which due diligence should be exercised, for purposes of practice before the IRS:

a.   In preparing or assisting in the preparation of, approving, and filing returns, documents, affidavits, and other papers relating to Internal Revenue Service matters;

b.   In determining the correctness of oral or written representations made by him to the Internal Revenue Service; and

c.   In determining the correctness of oral or written representations made by him to clients with reference to any matter administered by the Internal Revenue Service.[29]

Representations made by the tax practitioner to the Treasury Department are made in the form of tax returns filed with the Internal Revenue Service. Thus, the due diligence requirement seems to indicate the exercise of reasonable care in the preparation of a return based on the standard of the tax profession. It would seem to be reasonable that in addition to accepting data furnished by the client, the tax practitioner should also make simple inquiries into such areas as omissions and client classifications of items into possible wrong categories, and then to follow up on any irregularities seemingly uncovered.

Adequate Disclosure. In stating that a CPA may recommend a position that the CPA concludes is not frivolous so long as the position is adequately disclosed on the return or claim for refund, *SRTP No. 1* creates a conflict between the CPA and his or her client. Although it allows the CPA to advise his or her client that a position as a "realistic possibility" of success, it also requires that the CPA's client co-operate by including sufficient information in the return so as to put the IRS on notice as to the questionable position.

If a client is unwilling to make such a disclosure, the CPA must determine if he or she must disassociate himself or herself from the return.

Professionalism versus Compliance. None of the regulations referred to above have been "tested" by the fires of litigation. Whether the IRS will be able to enforce its own "realistic possibility" standard in view of the right of self-assessing taxpayers to interpret tax authorities for themselves, at the risk of losing in court, remains to be seen.

The tax practitioner, meanwhile, is left with two separate standards applying the concept of "realistic possibility." The AICPA approach, as illustrated with its fifteen examples, and the Treasury Department approach, including its own eight illustrations, provide overlapping, but noncontiguous, parameters. It is left to the professional accountant to sift through such promulgations, and to make an independent determination as to the proper handling of a specific tax issue.

Answers to Questions on Returns

Statement on Responsibilities in Tax Practice No. 2 provides that a CPA should make a reasonable effort to obtain from the client, and provide, appropriate answers to all questions on a tax return before signing as preparer.[30] This provision is tempered by Rule 301 of the AICPA's Code of Professional Conduct, which prohibits disclosure of confidential client information unless required by law, requested by the client, or required by a court subpoena.

In making an effort to answer all questions on a return, reasonable grounds may exist for omitting an answer such as the following:

a. The information is not readily available and the answer is not significant in terms of taxable income or loss, or the tax liability shown on the return.

b. The answer might prove to be significant as to the particular return, but, either:

   i. genuine uncertainty exists regarding the meaning of the question in relation to the particular return, or

   ii. the information which is obtainable is not sufficiently reliable to warrant reporting on the return.

c. The answer to the question is voluminous; however, assurance should be given on the return that the data will be supplied to the revenue agent in the course of his examination.

Section 7701(a)(36) of the Internal Revenue Code defines a tax return "preparer," and the Code and Treasury Regulations impose several duties, with penalty sanctions attached, on such preparers. The Code imposes, for example, a negligence penalty under § 6694(a), and a wilfulness penalty under § 6694(b), when tax return information is clearly insufficient or incorrect. By signing the declaration that the information contained therein is true, correct and complete on the best of his knowledge and belief "based on all information of which he has knowledge," the CPA not only fulfills his or her professional responsibilities under *SRTP No. 2*--but the CPA also places himself or herself at risk with regard to such penalties.

Furnishing Requested Information to the IRS. Circular 230 prohibits the neglect and refusal to *promptly* submit records or information in any matter before the IRS upon a *proper and lawful request*, or the interference with any proper and lawful effort by the IRS to obtain such record or information unless there is a *good faith belief* based on *reasonable grounds* that the record or information is privileged or that the request or effort is of *doubtful legality*.[31]

The questions of what is proper and lawful, or what constitutes a good faith belief based on reasonable grounds, or how the legality is doubtful are often beyond the expertise of the average tax practitioner. It may become necessary to turn to legal counsel in order to comply with Circular 230 and at the same time not breach his ethical duty to the client.

A summons served by the IRS upon the tax practitioner is made pursuant to 26 U.S.C. § 7602. The tax practitioner is allowed ten days in which to respond to the summons and therefore will have sufficient time to secure adequate legal advice. It should be noted that an IRS summons is usually only the tip of the iceberg of unknown legal consequences for the client. When the tax practitioner becomes aware that his client is under investigation, he should inform the client of the subpoena power of the IRS, that the client's records he possesses are not protected by an accountant-client confidential privilege, and advise the client to obtain legal counsel without further disclosures to the tax practitioners.

Certain Procedural Aspects of Preparing Returns

Statement on Responsibilities in Tax Practice No. 3 provides that preparing or signing a return, the CPA may in good faith rely without verification upon information furnished by the client or by third parties. However, the CPA should not ignore the implications of information furnished and should make reasonable inquiries if the information furnished appears to be incorrect, incomplete, or inconsistent either on its face or on the basis of other facts known to the CPA.[32] In this connection, the CPA should refer to the client's returns for prior years whenever feasible.

Where the Internal Revenue Code or income tax regulations impose a condition with respect to deductibility or other tax treatment of an item (such as taxpayer maintenance of books and records or substantiating documentation to support the reported deduction or tax treatment), *SRTP No. 3* requires the CPA to make appropriate inquiries to determine to his or her satisfaction whether such condition has been met. The individual CPA who is required to sign the return should consider information actually known to that CPA from the tax return of another client when preparing a tax return if the information is relevant to that tax return, its consideration is necessary to properly prepare that tax return, and use of such information does not violate any law or rule relating to confidentiality. If a CPA prepares a federal return, he should sign it without modifying the preparer's declaration.[33]

In the preparation of tax returns, the tax practitioner must often use data and information supplied by the taxpayer. The practitioner should always anticipate that such information may be incorrect or incomplete. Blind reliance is unacceptable, although the Statement permits the tax practitioner to rely on information furnished by his client unless it appears incorrect or incomplete.

The reasonableness of furnished data can be tested by comparing previous tax returns and making reference to trade statistics. This does not require an involved investigation, but merely an inquisitive approach.

Use of Estimates

Statement on Responsibilities in Tax Practice No. 4 provides that a CPA may prepare tax returns involving the use of the taxpayer's estimates if it is impracticable to obtain exact data, and the estimated amounts are reasonable under the facts and circumstances known to the CPA. When the taxpayer's estimates are used, they should be presented in such a manner as to avoid the implication of greater accuracy than exists.

The application of accounting judgments by use of approximations such as salvage value, obsolescence, and useful life in computing depreciation are not considered estimates.

Estimates arise in cases where expenditures are too small to achieve accuracy in recording them or whether either records are missing or precise information is not available at the time of filing. However, care should be taken to avoid implying greater accuracy than exists or presenting a deceptive or misleading impression of the facts.

Recognition of Administrative Proceeding of a Prior Year

Statement on Responsibilities in Tax Practice No. 5 provides that the recommendation of a position to be taken concerning the tax treatment of an item in the preparation or signing of a tax return should be based on the facts and the law as they are evaluated at the time the return is prepared or signed by the CPA. Unless the taxpayer is bound to a specified treatment in the later year, such as by a formal closing agreement, the treatment of an item as part of concluding an administrative proceeding or as part of a court decision does not restrict the CPA from recommending a different tax treatment in a later year's return. Therefore, if the CPA follows the standards in *SRTP No. 1*, the CPA may recommend a tax return position, prepare, or sign a tax return that departs from the treatment of an item as concluded in an administrative proceeding or a court decision with respect to a prior return of the taxpayer.

There is very sound reasoning behind this statement. In determining whether to recommend a departure from the treatment, on a current year tax return, of an item differs from that consented to by the taxpayer for a similar item as a result of an administrative proceeding concerning a prior year's return, the tax practitioner should consider several factors. First, the Internal Revenue Service is obliged to examine each return as a new matter. Second, the taxpayer may presently have adequate supporting data which was lacking at the administrative proceedings. Third, the taxpayer may have had adequate supporting data at the administrative proceeding but instead chose to settle. Fourth, since the administrative proceeding, subsequent court decisions and revenue rulings may have placed the taxpayer in a more favorable position. What these factors should indicate to the tax practitioner is that each return should be prepared based on the facts and circumstances that now exist.

Knowledge of Error: Return Preparation

Statement on Responsibilities in Tax Practice No. 6 provides that a CPA should inform the client promptly upon becoming aware of an error in a previously filed return or upon becoming aware of a client's failure to file a required return.

The CPA should recommend the measures to be taken. Such recommendation may be given orally. The CPA is not obligated to inform the Internal Revenue Service, and the CPA may not do so without the client's permission, except where required by law.

If the CPA is requested to prepare the current year's return and the client has not taken appropriate action to correct an error in a prior year's return, *SRTP No. 6* indicates that the CPA should consider whether to withdraw from preparing the return and whether to continue a professional relationship with the client. If the CPA does prepare such current year's return, the CPA should take reasonable steps to ensure that the error is not repeated.

Subsequent discovery of errors in client's tax returns or client's failure to file tax returns places certain responsibilities upon the tax practitioner. Immediately upon discovery, the taxpayer should be notified as to the extent of the error and the recommended corrective measures to be taken. Such advice should always eventually be put into writing.

Once the taxpayer has been adequately informed, it is his decision alone as to what course of action will be taken. The tax practitioner has no further obligation other than refraining from disclosing such information to taxing authorities, and possibly terminating the professional relationship in the event the taxpayer fails to take corrective measures.

Knowledge of Error: Administrative Proceedings

Statement on Responsibilities in Tax Practice No. 7 provides that when the CPA is representing a client in an administrative proceeding with respect to a return which contains an error of which the CPA is aware, the CPA should inform the client promptly upon becoming aware of the error. The CPA should recommend the measures to be taken. Such recommendation may be given orally. The CPA is neither obligated to inform the Internal Revenue Service nor is he or she permitted to do so without the client's permission, except where required by law.

SRTP No. 7 also points out that the CPA should request the client's agreement to disclose the error to the Internal Revenue Service. Lacking such agreement, the CPA should consider whether to withdraw from representing the client in the administrative proceeding and whether to continue a professional relationship with the client.

There can be no question that when the Internal Revenue Service raises a question in the course of an administrative proceeding concerning an error that has resulted or may result in a material understatement of tax liability, the tax practitioner, in representing his client, must avoid being false or devious.

However, when the tax practitioner has knowledge of an error that has not been raised by the Internal Revenue Service, the client should be requested to agree to a disclosure of the error. In the event that the client refuses to so disclose, the tax practitioner, rather than violate the confidential relationship with his client, should determine whether he should withdraw from the engagement.

If an error exists which had it been known at the time the return was prepared would have resulted in the tax practitioner refusing to sign the preparer's declaration, then this constitutes a patent error requiring disclosure. But such is not the case in what is merely a debatable issue. As long as there is reasonable support, the tax practitioner has a right and responsibility to advocate his client's position and not disclose any weaknesses inherent in that position.

IRS Requirements. Circular 230 requires a tax practitioner, retained by a client with respect to a matter administered by the IRS, to promptly advise the client of known noncompliance with revenue laws or an error in or omission from any return, document, affidavit, or other paper required by law to be executed by the client in connection with such matter.[34]

This language is very similar to that contained in *SRTP Nos. 6* and *7* in that the tax practitioner is not required to notify the IRS of such noncompliance, error, or omission. Only the client need be informed. However, unlike the *Statements*, the regulation does not indicate what course of action the tax practitioner should consider in the event that the client refuses or fails to make a disclosure to the IRS.

There seems to be a distinction as to the materiality of the error. Whereas *SRTP No. 6* specifies concern only "with errors that have resulted or may result in a material understatement of the tax liability," the regulation does not state whether the error must be material, which may indicate that any error regardless of materiality is covered by this section.

Advice to Clients

Statement on Responsibilities in Tax Practice No. 8 governs the tax practitioner's role as tax advisor. It provides as follows:

a. In providing tax advice to a client, the CPA should use judgment to ensure that the advice given reflects professional competence and appropriately serves the client's needs. The CPA is not required to follow a standard format or guidelines in communicating written or oral advice to a client.

b.   In advising or consulting with a client on tax matters, the CPA should assume that the advice will affect the manner in which the matters or transactions considered ultimately will be reported on the client's tax returns. Thus, for all tax advice the CPA gives to a client, the CPA should follow the standards in *SRTP No. 1* relating to tax return positions.

c.   The CPA may choose to communicate with a client when subsequent developments affect advice previously provided with respect to significant matters. However, the CPA cannot be expected to have assumed responsibility for initiating such communication except while assisting a client in implementing procedures or plans associated with the advice provided or when the CPA undertakes this obligation by specific agreement with the client.

Providing tax advice should consistently involve two objectives: (1) reflecting professional competence, and (2) serving the client's needs. In reaching these objectives, it is stated in *SRTP No. 8*:

In deciding on the form of advice provided to a client, the CPA should exercise professional judgment and should consider such factors as the following:

i.   The importance of the transaction and amounts involved.

ii.   The specific or general nature of the client's inquiry.

iii. The time available for development and submission of the advice.

iv.   The technical complications presented.

v.   The existence of authorities and precedents.

vi.   The tax sophistication of the client and the client's staff.

vii. The need to seek legal advice.

When communicating advice orally to a client, it is recommended that written confirmation should follow. This confirmation has the effect of limiting misunderstandings and also establishing a written record for future reference.

Other aspects to consider in providing advice:

a.   Explain the assumptions made at arriving at a conclusion.
b.   Indicate that the validity of the conclusion possessed the
     same degree of dependability as the validity of the
     assumptions.
c.   Tax consequence should be fully developed.
d.   Indicate the point in time to which the advice applies.

In the event that the taxpayer relies on negligently provided erroneous
tax advice, the tax practitioner may be liable for damages thereby sustained.
In *Rassieur v. Charles*,[35] the court awarded damages to the client to the
extent of restoring her to her former position. In that case, the client was
advised to sell certain securities at a loss that would offset the gain on the
previous sale of other securities thereby reducing the client's taxes. Instead
of the gain erroneously calculated by defendants in using incorrect cost
figures, there had been a loss. Thus, the tax advice resulted in offsetting a
loss against a loss rather than a gain and, therefore, no tax saving. The
client was permitted to recover the difference between the sale price and the
cost of replacing the securities after the thirty-day statutory repurchase
period.

Continuing Duty to Provide Advice. It is a common occurrence for tax
laws to change and new interpretations to develop all of which tend to affect
in some manner past tax advice. The question then arises as to what extent
the tax practitioner must follow up the advice previously given.

SRTP No. 8 indicates that the duty continues only so long as the tax
practitioner is actively participating in implementing the procedures or plans
associated with the advice, but beyond that point, such a duty should be
specifically provided for in the contract agreement. *Statement No. 8* provides
the following explanation:

Sometimes the CPA is requested to provide tax advice but does not
assist in implementing the plans adopted. While developments such
as legislative or administrative changes or further judicial
interpretations may affect the advice previously provided, the CPA
cannot be expected to communicate later developments that affect
such advice unless the CPA undertakes this obligation by specific
agreement with the client. Thus, the communication of significant
developments affecting previous advice should be considered an
additional service rather than an implied obligation in the normal
CPA-client relationship. The client should be informed that advice
reflects professional judgment based on an existing situation and
that subsequent developments could affect previous professional
advice. CPAs should use precautionary language to the effect that

their advice is based on facts as stated and authorities that are subject to change.

This ongoing duty is consistent with the legal expectation of a continuing duty to inform the client of erroneous tax advice. In the case of *Bancroft v. Indemnity Insurance Co. of North America*,[36] for example, the taxpayer was erroneously advised that the sale of stock in one corporation to a related corporation by the common shareholding taxpayer would result in capital gains, whereas in fact, it resulted in ordinary income. The taxpayer not only transacted the present sale, but also completed a similar transaction a couple of years later. The court held that the taxpayer was justified in relying upon the advice, and that the tax practitioner's professional insurer was liable for the excess income taxes.

UNAUTHORIZED PRACTICE OF LAW

There is another area of potential liability for the tax practitioner. Unless the practitioner is an attorney, engaging in tax work might subject him to prosecution for the unauthorized practice of law.

It should be quite apparent that taxation is a very broad and overly complex field requiring the expertise of both the accounting profession and the legal profession. Yet, regardless of how broad the field may be, it is a difficult proposition to ascertain where one profession ends and the other begins. This difficulty has been evidenced over the years by the various litigation which has occurred. And, not so surprising, the state level decisions have resulted in very little uniformity.

The first significant decision was the New York case *In re Bercu*.[37] A certified public accountant was engaged by the president of a company to advise as to the proper year to deduct city taxes. The CPA rendered an opinion based on his research of cases and rulings. No other services were performed and a fee of $500 was charged. In a contempt action brought against the CPA, the court found that he had engaged in the unauthorized practice of law. In so holding, the court stated:

We must either admit frankly that taxation is a hybrid of law and accounting and, as a matter of practical administration, permit accountants to practice tax law, or, also as a matter of practical administration, while allowing the accountant jurisdiction of incidental questions of law which may arise in connection with auditing books or preparing tax returns, deny him the right as a consultant to give legal advice. We are of the opinion that the latter alternative accords to the accountant all necessary and desirable latitude and that nothing less would accord to the public the protection that is necessary when it seeks legal advice.

Respondent [CPA] is most persuasive when he challenges the consistency of recognizing an accountant's right to prepare income tax returns while denying him the right to give income tax advice. As respondent says, precisely the same question may at one time arise during the preparation of an income tax return and at another time serve as the subject of a request for advice by a client. The difference is that in the one case the accountant is dealing with a question of law which is only incidental to preparing a tax return and in the other case he is addressing himself to a question of law alone.

The preparation of an income tax return is not primarily a matter of law and generally and mainly is not a matter of law. It may usually be prepared by one having no legal knowledge, from instructions prepared for lay consumption, or by one having only incidental legal knowledge. A taxpayer should not be required, and is not required to go to a lawyer to have a tax return prepared. It is a practical, reasonable and proper accommodation to businessmen and the accounting profession not only to permit accountants to prepare tax returns but to permit them, despite the risks involved, to assume jurisdiction of the incidental legal questions that may arise in connection with preparing tax return. It is quite another thing to say that apart from preparing a tax return and from doing the accounting work in connection with the return, an accountant should be permitted as an independent consultant to pass upon specific questions which are question of law, especially when the occasion for such consultation is apt to be, as it was in this case, a particularly knotty question of law. The distinction is altogether valid and desirable. The law here, as elsewhere, is a rational and practical adjustment of conflicting interests, objectively calculated to be of the greatest public benefit.[38]

The court's comments seem to indicate, by way of dictum, that the test to be applied in resolving questions of unauthorized practice of law on tax work is whether the tax advice is given as an *incident* to the preparation of tax returns. This court determined that the CPA's tax advice was the only service rendered and therefore constituted the unauthorized practice of law.

In 1949, a Minnesota court took a stricter approach in the case of *Gardner v. Conway*.[39] The defendant was a public accountant who held himself out as an "income tax expert" and "tax consultant."

The tax work at issue performed by the accountant was both the preparation of a return and the rendering of tax advice. However, the court specifically rejected the New York court's "incidental test" and prohibited accountants and laymen from resolving "difficult or doubtful questions of the interpretation or application of statutes, administrative regulations and rulings, court decisions, or general law" regardless of whether incidental to preparation of a tax return. The court noted that the *recognition* of a difficult question was proper as long as no attempt was made to answer it.

In 1951, a Joint Statement of Principles was issued by the National Conference of Lawyers and Certified Public Accountants supporting the preparation of tax returns and determination of transactional tax effects by both professions.

Subsequent to this event, litigation became centered around suits by tax practitioners to collect fees from their clients who set up the defense that the engagement contract required the unauthorized practice of law and therefore was unenforceable. The first such litigation occurred in California in the case of *Agran v. Shapiro*[40] in which the court relied upon the Minnesota decision rejecting the incidental approach. The accountant, who was enrolled to practice before the IRS, prepared an income tax return and engaged in research used by him in representing the client before the IRS. However, the accountant was unsuccessful in collecting his entire fee. Another CPA was more successful in collecting his fee in the California case of *Zelkin v. Caruso Discount Corp.*[41] by demonstrating that he cited no cases, that research performed did not involve legal principles but only accounting methods, and that the tax matter could have been resolved without any reference to the law.

Treasury Department Circular 230 contains the enrollment procedures permitting the non-lawyer CPA to practice before the Internal Revenue Service. This has raised the question as to whether this federal provision preempts state restrictions on the right of the accountant to practice in the area of taxation. Although not precisely on point, the Supreme Court rendered an opinion in *Sperry v. State of Florida ex. rel. Forida Bar*[42] in which Patent Office regulations permitting non-lawyers to practice before the Patent Office was held to take precedence over state regulation irrespective of the provision that these regulations "shall not be construed as authorizing persons not members of the bar to practice law," which is similar language to that contained in Circular 230 regarding the tax field.

The Court stated that "[a] State may not enforce licensing requirements which, though valid in the absence of federal regulation, give 'the State's licensing board a virtual power of review over the federal determination' that a person or agency is qualified and entitled to perform certain functions, or which impose upon the performance of activity sanctioned by federal license additional conditions. . . ."

This holding by the Supreme Court has been believed to be similarly applicable to tax practitioners enrolled to practice before the IRS.

NOTES

1.   31 CFR Part 10.
2.   *Ibid*, §10.22.
3.   Treasury Department Circular 230, Section 10.3(a) and (b).
4.   *Ibid.*, Section 10.4.
5.   *Ibid.*, Section 10.2.
6.   *Ibid.*
7.   *Ibid.*, Section 10.7.
8.   T.D. Circular 230, Section 10.28.
9.   *Ibid.*, Section 10.30.
10. *Ibid.*
11. *Ibid.*, Section 10.50.
12. *Ibid*, Section 10.51.
13. Couch v. United States, 409 U.S. 322 (1972).
14. I.R.C. (26 U.S.C.S.) § 7602 (1992).
15. I.R.C. (26 U.S.C.S.) § 7402(b) (1992).
16. I.R.C. (26 U.S.C.S.) § 7604 (a) (1992).
17. 409 U.S. at 335-36.
18. AICPA, *Rule 301, Confidential Client Information, Code of Professional Conduct.*
19. AICPA, *Statements on Responsibilities in Tax Practice (SRTP)* (1988 Rev.). Prior to the 1988 revision, ten statements had been published. A cross-reference of the previous *Statements* to those of the 1988 revision is contained at the *Appendix* to the 1988 revised *SRTP.*
20. *Ibid.*, p. 1.
21. *See* U.S. v. Simon, 425 F.2d 796 (2nd Cir. 1969), *cert. denied,* 397 U.S. 1006 (1970).
22. AICPA, *Statements on Responsibilities in Tax Practice (SRTP)* (1988 Rev.), p.2.
23. ABA Comm. on Professional Ethics Formal Opinion 85-32, 39 Tax Law. 631, 633-634 (1986).
24. AICPA, *Statement on Responsibilities in Tax Practice, Interpretation No. 1-1* (Dec. 1990).
25. Treas. Reg. § 1.6694-2(b). *See* Mitchell L. Stump, The Realistic Possibility Standard -- Final Regulations, 9-92 T.Tax.Adv. 593 (Sept. 1992).
26. Treas. Reg. § 1.6662-4(d)(3)(i).
27. Treas. Reg. § 1.6662-4(d)(3)(ii) and (iii).
28. Treas. Reg. § 1.6662-4(d)(3)(iv).
29. *Ibid.*, Section 10.22.
30. AICPA, *SRTP No. 2* (1988 Rev.).
31. *Ibid.*, Section 10.20.
32. *See* Brockhouse, 577 F. Supp. 55 (D.C. Ill., 1986), *aff'd* 749 F.2d 1248 (7th Cir. 1984).
33. *SRTP No. 3* (1988 Rev.).
34. *Ibid.*, Section 10.21.
35. Rassieur v. Charles, 354 Mo. 117, 188 S.W. 2d 817 (1945).
36. Bancroft v. Indemnity Insurance Co. of North America, 203 F. Supp. 39 (W.D. La. 1962), *aff'd. mem.*, 309 F. 2d 959 (5th Cir. 1963).
37. *In re Bercu*, 273 App. Div. 524, 78 N.Y.S. 2d 209 (1948), *aff'd.*, 299 N.Y. 728, 87 N.E. 2d 451 (1949).
38. Gardner v. Conway, 234 Minn. 468, 48 N.W. 2d 788 (1951).

39. *Ibid.*
40. 127 Cal. App. 2d 807, 273 P. 2d 619 (Super. Ct. 1954).
41. 186 Cal. App. 2d 802, 9 Cal. Rptr. 220 (Dist. Ct. App. 1960).
42. 373 U.S. 379 (1963).

Chapter Nine

Forensic Accounting

A ccountants are being indicted under an increasing array of criminal statutes and proceedings. All criminal prosecutions require some form or element of criminal intent. Intent, however, is as hard to disprove as it is to prove. And in situations where the accountant's work product reflects some form of negligence or poor work, it is often difficult to avoid being accused of making an intentional effort to defraud or cause harm.

THE ACCOUNTANT'S ROLE IN LITIGATION

As litigation in a complex society becomes more complicated and technical, it is often necessary for the judicial system to seek specialized assistance from technical experts. Accountants are needed to assist lawyers, judges and juries in such tasks as sifting through financial information, interpreting complex accounting issues, and arriving at factual (and legal) conclusions based on the results of financial analysis.

Expert Witnesses

Accountants are often called upon to serve as "expert" witnesses. That is, they are asked to bring their expertise into the judicial analysis of a matter at trial. This task often involves oral testimony by the accountant, as well as his or her introduction of summaries of voluminous data.[1]

The difference between an accountant's services as an expert witness, and his or her services as a consultant to one side or the other of a lawsuit, is described as follows:

> Whether the CPA is asked to testify as an expert witness at trial or act as a consultant to the attorney may impact the CPA's decision to become involved in litigation. As an expert witness the CPA presents opinions publicly in an objective fashion, but as a consultant the CPA advises and assists the attorney or client in private. In the private role, the CPA provides assistance more like that of an advocate to help the attorney identify case strengths and weaknesses or to develop strategy against the opposition.[2]

An accountant's decision to accept a litigation support engagement, then, includes a decision as to the scope of services to be performed as well as to the role to be played by the accountant.[3]

The admissibility of evidence during a trial, including the testimony of expert witnesses, is governed in part by the applicable rules of evidence in the trial court, and in part by the discretion of the trial judge.

Admissibility. In federal courts, Rule 702 of the Federal Rules of Evidence provides as follows:

> If scientific, technical, or other specialized knowledge will assist the trier of fact to understand the evidence or to determine a fact in issue, a witness qualified as an expert by knowledge, skill, experience, training, or education, may testify thereto in the form of an opinion or otherwise.[4]

Whether to admit expert testimony pursuant to the federal Rules of Evidence is a decision left to the discretion of the trial court. Trial courts have broad discretion in determining the extent to which expert testimony is admissible.[5] A federal trial court's admission of expert testimony is usually reversed on appeal only when the appellate court finds an abuse of that discretion.[6]

It is appropriate for experts to testify about the ordinary practices of a profession or trade "to enable the jury to evaluate the conduct of the parties against the standards of ordinary practice in the industry."[7]

Basis of Opinion. The admissibility of expert testimony is governed by Rule 703, as follows:

> The facts or data in the particular case upon which an expert bases an opinion or inference may be those perceived by or made known to the expert at or before the hearing. If of a type reasonably relied upon by experts in the particular field in forming opinions or inferences upon the subject, the facts or data need not be admissible in evidence.[8]

Closely related to Rule 703 is Rule 705, which provides:

> The expert may testify in terms of an opinion or inference and give reasons therefor without prior disclosure of the underlying facts or data, unless the court requires otherwise. The expert may in any event be required to disclose the underlying facts or data on cross-examination.[9]

Rule 703 allows experts to express their opinions on "facts or data . . . perceived by or made known to [them] at or before the hearing." Rule 703 allows an expert to testify based on facts otherwise inadmissible in evidence, but it is not an open door to all inadmissible evidence disguised as expert opinion. Although experts are sometimes allowed to refer to hearsay evidence as a basis for their testimony, such hearsay must be the type of evidence reasonably relied upon by experts in the particular field in forming opinions or inferences on the subject.[10]

If these criteria are met, an expert may testify as to an opinion, even concerning an "ultimate issue" of fact.[11] Mere qualification as an expert is not a license to invade the jury's function by telling the jury what result to reach,[12] nor is it appropriate for an expert to supplant the judge's function to instruct the jury on the law.[13]

In deriving an opinion in federal court, an expert is entitled to rely on facts or data which have not been admitted into evidence if the expert's reliance on those facts or data is reasonable.[14] As noted in Rule 703, such reasonableness is measured against the facts or data upon which experts in the particular field normally rely. This reasonableness determination is a matter requiring the trial court's careful consideration.[15]

THE ACCOUNTANT'S EXPERTISE

Analysis of Financial Data

One of the most common area of litigation support, including testimony as expert witnesses, by accountants is the ascertainment of the financial consequence of a transaction or an action. For example, accountants sometimes calculate the monetary costs of plaintiffs in liability suits. The courts are assisted with such issues as whether to calculate damages in terms of "lost profits,"[16] or in terms of "cash flow;" the extent to which overhead items are includible in damage calculations; and the method by which damages are to be calculated.

The *Electro Services* Case. The case of *Electro Services, Inc., v. Exide Corporation*[17] provides and example of the expertise that an accountant brings to a trial. That case involved a retailer and distributor of automotive batteries (Electro), who brought suit against a manufacturer of automotive batteries (Exide). The lawsuit was brought in order to recover compensatory and punitive damages as result of defect in batteries and manufacturer's conduct in relation to batteries' manufacture and sale.

At trial, the jury heard the testimony of Lanny Tyler, a certified public accountant and an expert witness for Electro, regarding Electro's loss of future profits. Tyler examined 17 commercial accounts and determined when these commercial purchasers bought batteries from Electro and when they stopped buying batteries from Electro. Tyler then determined the average number of batteries purchased per month and, using Electro's financial statements, determined the gross profit percentage on automotive batteries. Tyler then projected the monthly gross profit figure for 60 months and arrived at a figure of $113,039 for lost gross profits. Tyler then used a net profit margin to calculate lost net profits of $100,000 for the 17 commercial accounts. The jury awarded lost profits to the plaintiff, and on appeal the United States Court of Appeals for the Eleventh Circuit affirmed the award.[18]

The *Midland Hotel* Case. Sometimes the outcome of a case is reduced to a "battle of the accounting experts." In the case of *Midland Hotel Corp. v. Reuben H. Donnelley Corp.*, for example, a Chicago hotel (Midland) sued a "Yellow Pages" telephone directory publisher for breach of contract. Midland lost profits arising from the breach of an oral contract to include its hotel in the first issue of a newly published telephone directory.

Midland's expert witness was an accountant who testified that the hotel's damages, as a result of the exclusion from the directory, could be calculated by measuring the variance between the hotel's occupancy percentage and the average occupancy percentage of other downtown Chicago hotels as derived from a trade publication that published occupancy trends. The accountant's calculation of lost occupancy assumed that Midland's occupancy percentage would have equalled the downtown average for a three-year period. The accountant then added the lost revenue from food and beverage sales as well as lost telephone revenue and deducted from this the hotel's variable expenses to arrive at the total lost net profits.

The publisher's expert witness, also an accountant, testified that the hotel's calculation of damages was invalid since it incorrectly assumed that the occupancy percentage would have otherwise equalled the downtown average. The publisher's accountant noted that for numerous months prior to the time of the publication of the directory in question, Midland's occupancy percentage was trailing the downtown average and that therefore there was no basis for the assumption that the plaintiff would have otherwise equalled the downtown average after the publication of the directory.

The jury awarded damages to the hotel in accordance with the calculation offered by its expert. On appeal, the Illinois Supreme Court concluded that the calculation of lost profits did not sufficiently isolate the actual damages resulting from the exclusion from the directory, and the jury award was set aside for lack of certainty.[19]

Types of Cases

In addition to the determination of damages and lost profits, as seen in the previous two cases, accountants may provide litigation support, including expert testimony, in many types of matters. The AICPA Management Advisory Services' Technical Consulting Practice Aid no. 7, Litigation Services, issued in 1986, included the following types of litigation services for which the skills of accountants can be utilized:

Damages
>Lost profits
>Lost value
>Extra cost
>Lost cash flow
>Lost revenue

Accounting
>Bankruptcy
>Family law
>Tracing
>Contract cost and claims
>Frauds, civil and criminal
>Historical analyses

Analysis
> Tax bases
> Cost allocations
> Tax treatment of specific transactions

Valuation
> Businesses and professional practices
> Pensions
> Intangibles
> Property

General Consulting
> Statistical analyses
> Projections[20]

In addition to the above list, accounting experts are often used the following types of claims:

- Product liability
- Commercial contract claims
- Patent, trademark, and copyright infringement[21]
- Mergers and acquisitions
- Insurance claims
- Reorganization and bankruptcy
- Toxic tort claims

Skills Proffered

Accountants contribute more to a court case than mere sifting through computer records, financial documents, or similar data. Accountants also assist such conceptual areas as the development of the appropriate theory of damages, and the analysis of the effect of management decisions on a business entity's financial statements.[22]

In civil RICO cases, accountants can trace the flow of money, and analyze transactions, in the plaintiff's effort to establish a pattern of activities as required under the RICO statute.[23] Many divorce cases, likewise, have been settled only after an accountant has been able to clarify the income tax effects of alimony payments.[24]

Similarly, in tax fraud cases, accounting expertise is required in order to determine the net worth of a tax fraud defendant, and the extent and sources of incremental growth of that net worth.[25] One commentator has pointed out that "the services of an accountant may be of far greater value to one accused of tax fraud than those of his attorney."[26]

So critical is the role of the accounting expert in making sense out of a confusing mass of facts, figures, and financial records, that some have suggested that a proper defense of an indigent defendant accused of tax fraud and similar crimes should include a Constitutionally-protected right to expert assistance.[27] In the case of *United States v. Brodson*, for example, the tax fraud defendant's attorney was unable to persuade the court to release money from a jeopardy tax assessment to allow his client to hire an accountant as an expert witness.[28]

The skills and insights of the accountant are best utilized when they are employed at the outset of the case. Accuracy and precision can, for example, be brought to the initial pleadings if the accountant is consulted at that early stage. In cases involving fraud or complex claims (such as claims brought under RICO), the pleadings can demonstrate a higher degree of particularity of the accountant is involved with them.

ACCOUNTANTS' LIABILITY CASES

Accountants are sometimes called upon to review the work of other members of their profession. As experts in the field of accounting, accountants are generally able to render opinions as to whether the work of a particular defendant-accountant was performed below the professional standards.

From the standpoint of the accountant whose work is the subject of a lawsuit, the "standards of care" are those standards discussed in the first several chapters of this book. An accountant testifying with regard to the work of another accountant should maintain constant awareness of the following two issues:

a. Expert testimony in the context of accountant malpractice or professional liability cases is, like all testimony in expert witness engagements, subject to professional standards of care (discussed below).

b. Attorneys (and, sometimes, judges and juries) tend to treat promulgated GAAP and GAAS as "law." In explaining professional standards, therefore, the accounting expert must always distinguish between promulgated GAAP and GAAS, and other GAAP and GAAS applicable, in the professional judgment of an accountant, in specific situations. In addition, the accounting expert must be ready to discuss the appropriateness of judicially-imposed standards that do not fall within the confines of GAAS and GAAP. If this is not done, a body of case law could develop that would *de facto* transform the FASB, and even the AICPA, into "law-making" bodies.

PROFESSIONAL STANDARDS

From the standpoint of the expert-witness accountant testifying at the request of the plaintiff (the creditor, investor, or other user of the financial statements associated with the defendant-accountant), the expert witness itself constitutes an "engagement" subject to professional standards. A litigation service engagement constitutes the "practice of public accounting" as defined by the AICPA and many state accountancy boards, and is therefore subject to such AICPA promulgations as the *Statements of Financial Accounting Standards, Statements on Auditing Standards, Statements on Standards for Accounting and Review Services, Statements on Standards for Management Advisory Services, Statements of Governmental Accounting Standards, Statement on Standards for Attestation Engagements*, and *Statement on Standards for Accountants' Services on Prospective Financial Information.*[29]

AICPA Professional Conduct Standards

The AICPA's Code of Professional Conduct serves as an excellent "checklist" of professional standards applicable to an accountant engaged as an expert witness or as a consultant to a party involved in litigation.

Principles. The Principles of the Code of Professional Conduct include references to the public interest, as well as to integrity, objectivity, independence, and due care. With regard to the public interest, for example, the Code provides that members of the AICPA should accept the obligation to "act in a way that will serve the public interest, honor the public trust, and demonstrate commitment to professionalism." This principle would require that an accountant testifying in an accountant's liability matter would take care to place the obligation to the public ahead of any obligation to a particular plaintiff or defendant as a result of the engagement.

Keeping the obligation to the general public would, in turn, lead to the implementation of the Principles of objectivity and independence. The Code of Professional Conduct provides for the maintenance of objectivity and independence, even to the point of being independent in both fact and appearance. Again, this principle should contravene any tendency to "slant" expert testimony in favor of a particular plaintiff or defendant.

Rules. The Rules of Applicability contained in the AICPA's Code of Professional Conduct provide further guidance. Rule 201, General Standards, for example, provides, as follows:

A. *Professional Competence.* Undertake only those professional services that the member or the member's firm can reasonably expect to be completed with professional competence.
B. *Due Professional Care.* Exercise due professional care in the performance of professional services.
C. *Planning and Supervision.* Adequately plan and supervise the performance of professional services.
D. *Sufficient Relevant Data.* Obtain sufficient relevant data to afford a reasonable basis for conclusions or recommendations in relation to any professional services performed.

Rules 201C and 201D are particularly important in litigation service engagements. A litigation service engagement that is properly planned and supervised would be one that is not entirely "controlled" by counsel for a plaintiff or defendant. Instead, the accountant-expert would go beyond the requirements of advocacy (which govern an attorney's services) to those of the accountant's own profession. And by requiring sufficient relevant data as a basis for any conclusions, Rule 201D prohibits casual "expert opinions" based on anything less than sufficient data.

Of course, careful planning and analysis, on the one hand, and advocacy, on the other, are not mutually exclusive. As the *Technical Consulting Practice Aid no. 7, Litigation Services,* published by the Management Advisory Services division of the AICPA, points out:

Not knowing what data is available and precisely what analysis to perform makes developing a work plan difficult and potentially harmful to the client's interest. If the CPA is designated as an expert witness, the opposing party can discover his work plan. Furthermore, the steps in the work plan could prove impossible to complete, or the CPA may choose not to complete them because they do not make sense based on (1) subsequent data production, (2) lack of data production, or (3) facts later identified. A skillful lawyer for the other party might make the CPA expert look foolish, or perhaps even discredit him, by highlighting the uncompleted work steps and by obfuscating the rationale for revised work plans.

Other Rules contained in the Code of Professional Conduct are instructive in litigation service engagements, including:

a. *Rule 301--Confidential Client Information*, prohibiting an accountant from volunteering confidential client information.

b. *Rule 302--Contingent Fees*, prohibiting an accountant from accepting a litigation service engagement under conditions that would result in payment only upon a particular outcome of the matter.

Reporting Standards Generally

Some professional reporting standards apply directly to the services of an accountant engaged in the performance of litigation services. For example, an accountant might be requested by a court (or by a party to a lawsuit) to submit audited financial statements. In such a case, all of reporting standards generally applicable to the issuance of such financial statements would apply.

Even if an accountant is requested to provide unaudited financial statements of an entity, that are the representation of management, the reporting standards outlined in *Standards for Accounting and Review Services no. 1, Compilation and Review of Financial Statements*, would generally apply.[30] And reports prepared at the behest of a court or other trier of fact should be made in deference to such promulgations as *Statement on Auditing Standards No. 62, Special Reports, Statement on Auditing Standards No. 35, Special Reports -- Applying Agreed-Upon Procedures to Specified Elements Accounts or Items of a Financial Statement*, and *Statement on Auditing Standards No. 37, Filings Under Federal Security Statutes*.

"Exemptions" from Reporting Standards

Several AICPA promulgations pertaining to reporting standards specifically exclude conclusions rendered in the context of litigation services (or have otherwise been so interpreted by the AICPA), including:

a. *Statement on Attestation Standards*, which excludes from the concept of "attestation" (expressing a conclusion about the reliability of a written assertion) any expression of an opinion of "stipulated facts" (i.e., factual assumptions) in the context of a expert witness engagement.[31]

b. *Statement on Standards for Accountants' Services on Perspective Financial Information*, which does not attempt to "provide standards or procedures for engagements involving prospective financial statements used solely in connection with litigation support services, although it provides helpful guidance for many aspects of such engagements and may be referred to as useful guidance in such engagements. Litigation support services are engagements involving pending or potential formal legal proceedings before a 'trier of fact' in connection with the resolution of a dispute between two or more parties, for example, in circumstances where an accountant acts as an expert witness. This exception is provided because, among other things, the accountant's work in such proceedings is ordinarily subject to detailed analysis and challenge by each party to the dispute. This exception does not apply, however, if the prospective financial statements are for use by third parties who, under the rules of the proceedings, do not have the opportunity for such analysis and challenge. For example, creditors may not have such opportunities when prospective financial statements are submitted to them to secure their agreement to a plan of reorganization."[32]

c. *Interpretation no. 20 of Statement on Standards for Accounting and Review Services no. 1, Compilation and Review of Financial Statements*, which exempts financial statements submitted in conjunction with litigation services that involve pending or potential formal legal or regulatory proceedings before a "trier of fact" (a court, regulatory body, or government authority; their agent; a grand jury; or an arbitrator or mediator of the dispute) in connection with the resolution of a dispute between two or more parties when the:

   i. Service consists of being an expert witness.
   ii. Service consists of being a "trier of fact" or acting on behalf of one.
   iii. Accountant's work under the rules of the proceedings is subject to detailed analysis and challenge by each party to the dispute.
   iv. Accountant is engaged by an attorney to do work that will be protected by the attorney's work product privilege and such work is not intended to be used for other purposes.[33]

Will accountants avoid being held to the profession's generally accepted reporting standards simply because the promulgated standards exempt themselves? The answer to this question depends on the likelihood of courts to be bound by the self-exempting language of promulgated standards. Courts have historically been reluctant to be so bound.

CONCLUSION

An accountant is, in fact, an expert. But the opportunity to be "officially" labelled an expert in a court of law, with the attendant chance to earn significant fees, should be approached with the same level of caution and care as an audit engagement. Limitations on the nature and scope of an accountant's litigation services, imposed by judicial court rules and rules of evidence, by professional standards of care, and by specific GAAP and GAAS promulgations, should be understood and observed.

NOTES

1.   Fed. R. Evid. 1006 (allowing summaries of data to be introduced, in spite of the best evidence rule). *See*, Jack B. Weinstein, and Robert Kushen, Scientific Evidence in Complex Litigation, *ALI-ABA Course of Study*, C607 ALI-ABA 709, n.56 and context.
2.   Michael J. Wagner, and Peter B. Frank, *Technical Consulting Practice Aid no. 7, Litigation Services* (New York: AICPA Management Advisory Services Division, 1986).
3.   *See* Collier, Jesse Newton, "New Opportunities and Challenges for Today's CPA in the Legal Arena," *Journal of Accountancy*, January 1989, p.66.
4.   F.R. Ev. 702.
5.   Scholz Homes, Inc. v. Wallace, 590 F.2d 860, 861, 863 (10th Cir.1979).
6.   *See, e.g.* Ellis v. Miller Oil Purchasing Co., 738 F.2d 269, 270 (8th Cir.1984); WSM, Inc. v. Hilton, 724 F.2d 1320, 1328 (8th Cir.1984).
7.   *Id.* at 509 (citing VII Wigmore on Evidence § 1949, at 66 (3d ed. 1940)).
8.   F.R.Ev. 703.
9.   F.R.Ev. 705.
10.   United States v. Cox, 696 F.2d 1294 (11th Cir.), cert. denied, 464 U.S. 827, 104 S.Ct. 99, 78 L.Ed.2d 104 (1983).
11.   Fed. R. Evid. 702, 704.
12.   *See* Marx & Co. v. Diners Club, Inc., 550 F.2d 505, 510 (2d Cir.), *cert. denied*, 434 U.S. 861, 98 S.Ct. 188, 54 L.Ed.2d 134 (1977); Zenith Radio Corp. v. Matsushita Electric Industrial Co., Ltd., 505 F.Supp. 1313, 1331-2 (E.D.Pa.1981).
13.   Marx & Co., *supra*, 550 F.2d at 509-510.
14.   *See, e.g.*, Almonte v. National Union Fire Ins. Co., 787 F.2d 763, 770 (1st Cir.1986); American Universal Ins. Co. v. Falzone, 644 F.2d 65, 66-67 (1st Cir.1981).
15.   *Id.*, Almonte, 787 F.2d at 770; Falzone, 644 F.2d at 67.
16.   *See, e.g.*, Penthouse v. Dominion Federal Savings & Loan Association, 855 F.2d 963 (2d. Cir. 1988).
17.   847 F.2d 1524 (11th Cir. 1988).
18.   847 F.2d 1524 (11th Cir. 1988).
19.   118 Ill.2d at 318; 515 N.E.2d at 67.

20.   *Supra*, note 2. *See* Reiss, Freddie M., "Litigation Support," *Practicing Law Institute Corporate Law and Practice Course Handbook Series*, PLI Order No. B4-6842, July 1, 1988.

21.   *See* Dratler, Jr., Distilling the Witches' Brew of Fair Use in Copyright Law, 43 U. Miami L. Rev. 233, n. 506 and context.

22.   *See* Wagner, Michael J., Litigation Support: How Do You Measure Damages? Lost Income or Lost Cash Flow?, *Journal of Accountancy*, February 1990, p.28.

23.   *See*, Jarvis, Robert M., The Use of Civil RICO in International Arbitration: Some Thoughts after Shearon/American Express v. McMahon, 1 Transnat'l Law 1 (Spring 1988).

24.   Winer, Edward L., Cross-Examining the Accountant - The Routine Case, 8 Fam. Advo. 20 (Spring, 1986).

25.   *See, e.g.,* United States v. Scrima, 819 F.2d 996, 998 (11th Cir. 1987).

26.   Alexander, Dennis W., Comment, Assistance in Addition to Counsel for Indigent Defendants: The Need for; The Lack Of; The Right To, 16 Vill. L. Rev. 323, 326-27 (1970).

27.   *See, e.g.,* Madine, David, The Constitutional Right to Expert Assistance for Indigents in Civil Cases, 41 Hastings L.J. 281 (January 1, 1990).

28.   241 F.2d 107 (7th Cir. 1957).

29.   *See* AICPA, "Ethics Interpretation," *Journal of Accountancy*, November 1989, p. 170.

30.   *See* AICPA, "Interpretation No. 20," *Journal of Accountancy*, May 1991, p. 144.

31.   2 Prof. Stand. [AICPA] (CCH) AU § 2100.01-2100.03.(1992). *See*, AICPA, Interpretation of Statements on Standards for Attestation Engagements of AT Section 100, *Journal of Accountancy*, July 1990, p. 143.

32.   *Id.*

33.   *Journal of Accountancy*, May 1991, p. 144.

Chapter Ten

Other Special Engagements and Responsibilities

THE ACCOUNTANT AS ADVISOR

As society and business has become more complex, professional accountancy has changed. In one sense, there is less need for low-level accounting and bookkeeping skills, since computers have replaced manual bookkeeping in many organizations. In another sense, the growing number of business enterprises and other organizations, and the increasing need for specialized knowledge in particular industries, have helped to maintain a growing demand for accountants.

Accountants specializing in such technical areas as litigation support, international tax, environmental regulation, and employee benefits, and in certain industries, such as health care, find that their skills are very much in demand, even during economic downturns.[1] And those accounting firms showing continual growth in their revenues (other than from mergers) can point to expanded management consulting services as a significant factor.

Types of Consulting Services

The AICPA's *Statement on Standards for Consulting Services No. 1 (SSCS No. 1)*, entitled *Definitions and Standards*, establishes a framework of reference for non-attestation (and non-tax) engagements. *SSCS No. 1* acknowledges the fact that accountants find themselves involved in a broad range of activities, including:

A. **Consultations,** in which the practitioner's function is to provide counsel in a short time frame, based mostly, if not entirely, on existing personal knowledge about the client, the circumstances, the technical matters involved, client representations, and the mutual intent of the parties. Examples of consultations are:

   • reviewing and commenting on a client-prepared business plan; and
   • suggesting computer software for further client investigation.

B. **Advisory services,** in which the practitioner's function is to develop findings, conclusions, and recommendations for client consideration and decision making. Examples of advisory services are:

   • an operational review and improvement study;
   • analysis of an accounting system;
   • assisting with strategic planning; and
   • defining requirements for an information system.

C. **Implementation services,** in which the practitioner's function is to put an action plan into effect. Client personnel and resources may be pooled with the practitioner's to accomplish the implementation objectives. The practitioner is responsible to the client for the conduct and management of engagement activities. Examples of implementation services are:

   • providing computer system installation and support;
   • executing steps to improve productivity; and
   • assisting with the merger of organizations.

D. **Transaction services,** in which the practitioner's function is to provide services related to a specific client transaction, generally with a third party. Examples of transaction services are:

- insolvency services;
- valuation services;
- preparation of information for obtaining financing;
- analysis of a potential merger or acquisition; and
- litigation services.

E. **Staff and other support services,** in which the practitioner's function is to provide appropriate staff and possibly other support to perform tasks specified by the client. The staff provided will be directed by the client as circumstances require. Examples of staff and other support services are:

- data processing facilities management;
- computer programming;
- bankruptcy trusteeship; and
- controllership activities.

F. **Product services,** in which the practitioner's function is to provide the client with a product and associated professional services in support of the installation, use, or maintenance of the product. Examples of product services are:

- the sale and delivery of packaged training programs;
- the sale and implementation of computer software; and
- the sale and installation of systems development methodologies.[2]

Many of the above services overlap. For example, an accountant might suggest certain computer software to a client (consulting), help the client test and verify the utility of the software (advising), help the client install the software (product services) and use it for the production of financial projections for purposes of obtaining financing (transaction services), and help select personnel to operate the new program (staff and other). In addition, the accountant might, for a fee, assist the client in locating and recruiting a manager to operate the client's expanded data processing department (executive recruiting).

STANDARD OF CARE FOR ADVISORY SERVICES

Professional Relationship Approach to Liability

SSCS No. 1 does not introduce new performance standards for accountants performing consulting services, but it does serve as a reminder that the general standards of the profession apply to all of the types of services listed above.   In particular, Rule 201, requiring professional competence, due professional care, planning and supervision, and the gathering of sufficient relevant data, are noted in the *SSCS* as being applicable to consulting and related activities.

The courts, likewise, have been quick to comprehend the need to apply general standards of care to the expanding role of accountants.   One approach has been to treat standards espoused by the AICPA promulgations, such as Rule 201, as the appropriate standard of care.   The accountant serving as a consultant is held to the same professional standards as an accountant functioning as an auditor.   Under this approach, all of the GAAS pronouncements, and other promulgations by the AICPA (including *SSCS No. 1*), are "interpreted" in view of the services actually performed.

Negligent Misrepresentation Approach to Liability

Courts often look beyond the presumably self-serving pronouncements of professional organizations and trade associations, however, in determining a legally applicable standard of care against which to measure the work of accountant-defendants.   This is especially true when cases involving non-attestation, and non-tax, engagements come before the courts.

One legal theory used by the courts in approaching the issue of consulting services is the doctrine of negligent misrepresentation. Under this approach, the advisory services of an accountant are characterized as the constituting a process of passing information from the accountant to the client.   If each category of services described in *SSCS No. 1*, were examined from this perspective, the relevance of this legal theory can be readily seen, as shown at **Table III.**

Viewed from this perspective, the legal standard of care is applied primarily to the quality of information conveyed by an accountant in an advisory capacity.   In the case of *Greenstein, Logan & Co. v. Burgess Marketing, Inc.*,[3]for example, one of the complaints of the client-plaintiff was that the accountant-defendant recommended an accountant to the client, to be hired as the client's comptroller.

Table III.   Information Provided by Accounting Consultants

SSCS No. 1 Category of Service	Type of Information Conveyed
Consultations	General business knowledge, e.g., knowledge of computer applications.
Advisory Services	Analysis of client's operation, accounting system, or business.
Implementation Services	Technical information regarding subject matter of engagement.
Transaction Services	Technical information regarding valuations, business financing, etc.
Staff and Other Support Services	Expertise regarding technical skills of others; accounting skills.
Product Services	Information regarding specific products and services.

A member of the defendant accounting firm told the client that the particular individual was "a competent accountant, a competent "CPA, with experience in audit and tax."[4]

Those words cost the accounting firm at least some of the $3.5 million damage award granted to the plaintiff-client in that case. Although *SSCS No.1* had not yet been issued at the time of *Greenstein*, the court found other standards to apply.   In finding the accounting firm liable for negligent personnel recruitment practices, the court turned to § 552 of the *Restatement (Second) of the Law of Torts* (a generalized statement of law written by legal scholars and jurists), which provides:

§ 552 Information Negligently Supplied for the Guidance of Others.
(1) One who, in the course of his business, profession or employment, or in any other transaction in which he has a pecuniary interest, supplies false information for the guidance of others in their business transactions, is subject to liability for pecuniary loss caused to them by their justifiable reliance upon the

information, if he fails to exercise reasonable care or competence in obtaining or communicating the information.[5]

The argument can be made that **any** consulting services, including all of those listed in *SSCS No.1*, constitute the supplying of information by the accountant to others, in the course of the accountant's professional services. Hence, any consulting services that are deemed by a court of law to have been "negligently" performed could, under the *Greenstein* approach, render the accountant liable.

Fiduciary Relationship Approach to Liability

Another legal theory used by courts in assessing the quality of consulting services, performed by accountants, is the fiduciary relationship theory. Under this approach, a court follows these steps:

A. Determine whether a fiduciary relationship existed between the accountant and his or her consulting client.
B. If a fiduciary relationship did exist, decide whether the accountant acted with good faith and with due regard for the interests of the client.

Existence of Fiduciary Relationship. The existence of the fiduciary relationship is to be determined from the actualities of the relationship between the persons involved.

The usual fiduciary relationships are those such as between attorney and client, partners, joint venturers, and close family members such as parent and child.[6] A fiduciary relationship may arise outside these usual situations where the dealings between the parties have continued for such a period of time that one party is justified in relying on the other to act in his best interest.[7]

A fiduciary relationship between client and accountant exists where a client is in fact accustomed to being guided by the judgment or advice of the accountant, or is justified in placing confidence in the belief that the accountant will act in the client's interest.[8] Where a client is accustomed to being guided by the judgment or advice of an accountant in tax and financial accounting matters, and there exists a long association in a business relationship, as well as a personal friendship, courts are easily convinced that the client placed a large degree of confidence in the belief that the accountant will act in his or her best interest. Under these circumstances, a fiduciary relationship has been held to exist.[9]

The fiduciary is one who is bound in equity and good conscience to act in good faith and with due regard for the interests of the beneficiary of the relationship.[10] In the case of *Cafritz v. Corporation Audit Co.*,[11] for example, plaintiff hired an accounting firm, of which a Mr. Robins was general manager and executive officer. The firm failed to deposit certain of plaintiff's checks in the bank, Robins being actively involved in this failure. Plaintiff brought an action for discovery and accounting against the firm and against Robins's wife individually and as administratrix of his estate. The court held, inter alia, that the accounting firm and Robins were fiduciaries as to plaintiff.[12] In so holding, the court stated that the existence of a fiduciary relationship is a question of fact, and that "an accounting party" may be a fiduciary "because of money or property intrusted to him."[13]

Another general test for determining the existence of such a relationship is whether it is clear that the parties did not deal on equal terms.[14] If, for example, a client turned over control of a portion of his or her business to an accountant, the accountant would be considered a fiduciary with respect to those business assets.[15]

Fiduciary Standard of Care. Once a court determines that the accountant is a fiduciary of the client, the accountant is held to a fiduciary standard of care. The standard is higher than a mere business relationship (where the standard of care is prescribed by the contractual arrangement), and it is higher than a professional relationship (where the standard of care is determined by reference to the standards of the profession).

A professional, for example, is expected to place the interests of the client ahead of his or her own interests, but is nevertheless expected to charge a fair fee for services rendered. A fiduciary, however, is expected to uphold the client's interests "at all costs." Where a fiduciary benefits in any way from a transaction with a client, in fact, there is a legal presumption of undue influence.[16] The mere existence of a fiduciary relationship prohibits the dominant party from seeking any selfish benefit whatsoever.[17]

Incident to the relationship, the fiduciary is considered an agent, who must tell his or her principal about anything which might affect the principal's decision whether or how to act.[18] In the case of *Allen Realty Corp. v. Holbert*,[19] a client engaged an accounting firm to assist in the liquidation of the client's real estate. The accountants helped to gather information regarding offers, provided analysis as to the relative value of the offers to the client, and performed related services. The client expected the accountants to disclose and discuss all offers, and when the accountants failed to report an offer the accountants were held liable for breach of fiduciary duty.

A fiduciary must exercise diligence in providing services. In *Dominguez v. Brackey Enterprises, Inc.*[20] an accountant advised some investors to advance $59,000 to a seafood broker. The investors had no knowledge of seafood business. The accountant, however, was a shareholder, officer and director of the broker, and in order to persuade the investors to advance the funds the accountant made assurances to the investors regarding the quality of the investments. The accountant introduced the investors to the president of the brokerage company, and represented that the president of knew the seafood business and could be relied upon. The accountant indicated that the broker was in the seafood brokerage business on a "very, very" large scale, that the president of the brokerage was knowledgeable in the business and could be instructive to the investors. The accountant vouched for the trustworthiness of the president of the brokerage. The investors, were made so confident by the assurances provided by the accountant that the investors entered into the transaction after having relied on the accountant's assurances and financial advice.

In holding the accountant personally liable for the investors' losses, the court in *Dominguez* determined that the accountant had breached a fiduciary duty to the investors. In particular, the accountant had a duty to determine whether his statements were, in fact true.[21]

SPECIAL ENGAGEMENTS

Sometimes accountants are engaged to assist with a specific project. These types of engagements constitute "transaction services" and often one or two other categories of consulting services covered by *SSCS No.1*. But often these engagements are also covered by separate standards of performance. Two examples of such "special engagements" are engagements to express an opinion on an organization's system of internal control, and an engagement by the trustee of a marital trust after one of the spouses has died. Each example is discussed briefly below.

Special Internal Control Engagements

How reliable is financial information produced by someone else? This is the question asked by:

- Trustees of employee benefit plans, who receive reports from the banks and investment companies hired by the trustees to invest and hold plan assets;
- Mortgage note holders, whose mortgages notes are collected and serviced by mortgage bankers; and

- Small business enterprises, whose bookkeeping and routine transaction summaries are produced by an electronic data processing (EDP) firm.

Among those who make this type of inquiry are organizations, like employee benefit plans, who are required to have their financial statements audited.

Accountants are often asked to look into the reliability of reports produced by banks, mortgage bankers, EDP firms, and other service organizations; the primary emphasis of such reports is an investigation into the internal controls of the service organization. The accountant does not actually audit the service organization; instead, the accountant conducts a specialized study, and produces a report that represents an opinion regarding the internal controls of the service organization, rather than an audit *per se.*

In performing the special study of internal control, the accountant is subject to all of the standards of due care discussed above, and previous chapters. In addition, the accountant is expected to comply with a promulgation aimed directly at this type of project: namely, *Statement on Auditing Standards No. 70, Reports on the Processing of Transactions by Service Organizations.*

SAS No. 70 provides guidance on the factors an independent auditor should consider when auditing the financial statements of an entity that uses a service organization to process certain transactions. The *Statement* also provides guidance for independent auditors who issue reports on the processing of transactions by a service organization for use by other auditors. *SAS No. 70* covers the following topics:

A. The user auditor's consideration of the effect of the service organization on the internal control structure of the user organization and the availability of evidence to--

   - Obtain the necessary understanding of the user organization's internal control structure to plan the audit
   - Assess control risk at the user organization
   - Perform substantive procedures

B. Considerations in using a service auditor's report
C. Responsibilities of service auditors

The proper performance of this type of special engagement, then, calls for compliance with all of the general ethical and technical requirements of GAAP and GAAS, plus *SAS No. 70.*

Fiduciary Accounting Engagements

The establishment of private trusts, pursuant to inter vivos (i.e., during the lifetime of the grantor) trust agreements, increased significantly in the U.S. during the 1980's and 1990's. Revocable living trusts have been used as a estate planning tool that can reduce probate fees, estate and inheritance taxes, and other post-mortem estate settlement costs. In addition, trusts have served as a tool for protecting assets on behalf of children from a remarried grantor's first marriage, disabled beneficiaries, and others in need of specialized estate planning. Accountants have often participated in the estate and financial planning decisions that have led to the establishment of trusts by their clients.

Revocable Living Trust Agreements. A typical revocable living trust arrangement between husband and wife provides for the management of their assets during their joint lifetimes. At the death of either, some assets are often set aside for the children of the couple (and, in appropriate cases, for the children of either, from a previous relationship). The amount set aside is determined by reference to a number of factors, including consideration of the fact that approximately $600,000 of those assets can escape federal estate taxation (and, in many states, state death taxes) because of certain exemption amounts provided by the Internal Revenue Code and state estate and inheritance tax laws.

The assets set aside for the benefit of the children of the decedent are said to have been placed in a "family" trust; the income from the family trust is usually paid to the surviving spouse during his or her remaining lifetime. The surviving spouse is sometimes given a "power of invasion," so that the principal of the family trust can be spent by the surviving spouse if his or her other assets are not sufficient to cover the living expenses of the surviving spouse. All of these provisions, however, are contained in the trust agreement, sometimes called deed of trust or declaration of trust.

Conflict of Interest. The family trust, described above, contains a built-in conflict of interest. That conflict arises upon the death of either the husband or the wife, and stems from the fact that the family trust income is assigned to the wife, while the corpus, or remainder (or "principal"), is held for the benefit of the children. When the surviving spouse dies, the children receive the remainder; until that happens, the surviving spouse enjoys the income from the family trust assets.

The surviving spouse is interested in the yield from the trust assets. Investments of family trust assets that result in an increase in the yield are generally considered favorable to the surviving spouse. High-yield bonds, aggressive income funds, and even "junk bonds" serve to enhance the income of the surviving spouse.

The child, or children, on the other hand, are concerned about the remainder. Investments of family trust assets that serve to protect and secure those assets, and to cause them to grow, are generally considered favorable to the surviving spouse. A blend of government securities, blue-chip growth stocks, and similar investments serve to enhance the value of the remainder to the children.

The conflict of interest described above does not usually result on intra-family problems. Most often, the children are glad to see their surviving parent receive a generous income from their family trust; and the surviving spouse is usually careful to see that the assets are, in fact, invested in a way that will protect the inheritance of his or her children and grandchildren.

But conflicts do occur. Occasionally they are triggered by the remarriage of the surviving spouse, creating unhappiness and resentment on the part of the children. Sometimes a child, enduring a period of financial difficulty, becomes quite concerned about the relief represented by the future inheritance. Once in a while, simple, unadulterated greed takes over.

When conflicts do erupt, they are often fueled by lack of information. The surviving spouse, who is sometimes designated as co-trustee or sole trustee of the family trust after the death of the other spouse, is reluctant to release information to his or her children. And the children, who are then kept in the dark about trust values, trust investments, and the like, are left to their own imaginations. The combination of secretiveness on the part of the parent, and ignorance on the part of the children, can result in a build-up of feelings on the part of both sides of the conflict. When the matter finally explodes, it can often be resolved only in the arena of a courtroom.

Trust "GAAP:" Sorting Out Principal and Income. It is the job of the trustee to balance the interests of the income beneficiary and the remainder beneficiaries. Part of that duty is accomplished by ensuring that a reasonable yield is earned by the trust assets (serving the interests of the income beneficiary), and also that the corpus of the trust is invested with the remainder beneficiaries' concerns about security and growth in mind. This is usually accomplished by diversifying the investments of the family trust assets.

But the definition of "income" (versus "principal") is critical to the calculation of amounts to be paid to the income beneficiary (or retained in the trust on behalf of the remainder beneficiary). For example, if the family trust contains a rental property, is the "income" payable to the surviving spouse net of depreciation? If so, what method of depreciation (straight line, an income tax method, etc.)? Similarly, should capital gains be paid to the income beneficiary, or held in the trust on behalf of the remainder beneficiaries?

To the extent that trust document provides guidance in sorting out income and principal, the trust document is the final authority. In a sense, the trust document defines the accounting principles to be used by the trustee in balancing the interests of the beneficiaries.

Uniform Principal and Income Act.   To the extent that the trust document is silent in regard to allocations between principal and income beneficiaries, the trustee's decisions are governed by state law. State laws, the common law, require that trustees act with prudence in all respects. In addition, most states have statutes prescribing the accounting principles to be applied in the absence of any other directive in a trust document. Most states have enacted either the original (1931) or the (1962) Uniform Principal and Income Act (UPIA); of the 14 states who have not enacted the UPIA, most have their own statutory scheme for resolving questions of allocation between principal and income in situations involving trusts.

Even though the UPIA has specific accounting provisions for such items as depreciation ("GAAP" depreciation is required for capital and business assets[22]), stock dividends (treated as principal[23]), etc., the UPIA gives deference to specific accounting principles prescribed in the trust document.[24] This is the case even if the trust document merely gives the trustee absolute and sole discretion with regard to allocations between principal and income.[25]

What if the trustee, in exercising his or her discretion under the document, clearly favors one type of beneficiary over the other? The statute provides that "if the trust instrument gives the trustee discretion in crediting a receipt or charging an expenditure to income or principal or partly to each, in inference of imprudence or partiality arises from the fact that the trustee has made an allocation contrary to a provision of this Act.[26]

If the trustee, for example, purchases undeveloped real property ("raw land") as a speculative investment, and then sells the land for a significant gain, § 12 of the UPIA requires that a portion of the proceeds from the sale of the land be allocated to the income beneficiary.[27] But if the document gives the trustee discretion in regard to allocations between principal and income, the trustee is authorized to ignore § 12 of the UPIA, and can allocate the gain to the income beneficiary, to the principal beneficiary, or partly to each.

Even though the statute dictates that "no inference of imprudence or partiality" may be inferred from trustee allocations contrary to the UPIA, courts have no been so unequivocal. That is because it is impossible to prevent a judge, in reviewing a trustee's actions, from "thinking" or deliberating about the legislative intent of, and public policies underlying, specific accounting provisions in the UPIA. A judge may take into account all laws, policies, and legislative intents when deliberating the level of prudence exercised by a trustee, and he or she can certainly not be stopped from thinking about (or drawing inferences from) the provisions of the UPIA.

Fiduciary Accounting Standards. There is a solution to the problem of the remainder beneficiary who believes that the income beneficiary is "stealing" the principal. And there is a solution to the problem of the trustee's unenviable position of being caught in the middle between beneficiaries with differing views about the proper allocation of principal and income.

In a word, that solution is: disclosure. Early (in the life of a trust), often (at least annually), and fully. If a beneficiary has a question about an investment, it is better to ask the question before the investment is held by the trustee for a long period of time. And if a beneficiary expresses an objection to an accounting method, it is better to resolve the matter before years of allocations become the subject matter of a lawsuit.

To encourage full and continual disclosure, a Fiduciary Accounting Standards Committee was formed, comprised of members of the American Bar Association's Real Property, Probate and Trust Law sections; the American College of Probate Counsel; the Trust Division of the American Bankers Association; and members of the AICPA. The report issued by the Committee provided for the following accounting standards:

I.   Accounts should be stated in a manner that is understandable by persons who are not familiar with practices and terminology peculiar to the administration of estates and trusts.
II. A fiduciary account shall begin with a concise summary of its purpose and content.
III. Fiduciary account shall contain sufficient information to put the interested parties on notice as to all significant transactions affecting administration during the accounting period.
IV. A fiduciary account shall contain two values, the asset acquisition value or carrying value, and current value.
V.   Gains and losses incurred during the accounting period shall be shown separately in the same schedule.
VI. The account shall show significant transactions that do not affect the amount for which the fiduciary is accountable.[28]

A commentary, with illustrative examples, accompanies the published principles. Model accounts for estates and trusts are also provided.[29]

CONCLUSION

If accountants have a competitive advantage, as business advisors, it is not only because of their specialized skills. It is also because of confidence they engender in their relationships with their clients.

That is the benefit. The "cost" of this benefit is the higher standard of care to which accountants are held. The courts are more than willing to impose liability upon the accountant who breaches that standard, irrespective of the legal theory used to justify that imposition.

To minimize the effect of this cost, the accountant should be aware of the appropriate professional standards, including any specific standards pertaining to each engagement. The recommendations of Rule 201, pertaining to the quality of an accountant's work, are always in order.

Finally, the accountant should appreciate the weight given by courts to the basic values of honesty and loyalty. Seldom will a judgment of negligent misrepresentation, or breach of fiduciary duty, be applied to the accountant who holds dear these basic values.

NOTES

1. See Laurie Cohen, "Party's Over as CPAs Face Tough Times," *Chicago Tribune*, November 25, 1990, Business Section p.1.
2. AICPA, "Statement on Standards for Consulting Services No. 1 (SSCS No. 1), Definitions and Standards," *Journal of Accountancy*, November 1991, p. 164.
3. 744 S.W.2d 170 (Ct. App. Texas, 1987).
4. 744 S.W.2d at 189.
5. Restatement (Second) of Torts § 552(1) (1977); Matter of Hawaii Corp., 567 F.Supp. at 617.
6. Consolidated Gas & Equipment Co. v. Thompson, 405 S.W.2d 333, 336-37 (Tex.1966).
7. Thomson v. Norton, 604 S.W.2d 473, 476 (Tex.Civ.App.--Dallas 1980).
8. Thames v. Johnson, 614 S.W.2d 612, 614 (Tex.Civ.App.--Texarkana 1981).
9. Thigpen v. Locke, 363 S.W.2D 247, 253 (Tex.1963), *citing* Kalb v. Norsworthy, 428 S.W.2d 701, 705 (Tex.Civ.App. 1968).
10. H-B Partnership v. Wimmer, 220 Va. 176, 179, 257 S.E.2d 770, 773 (1979).
11. 60 F.Supp. 627 (D.D.C.1945).
12. *Id.* at 634.
13. *Id.* at 631. *See also* Squyres v. Christian, 242 S.W.2d 786 (Tex.Civ.App.1951); *cf.* Franklin Supply Co. v. Tolman, 454 F.2d 1059 (9th Cir.1971).
14. Frowen v. Blank, 493 Pa. 137, 145, 425 A.2d 412, 416 (1981).
15. Stainton v. Tarantino, 637 F.Supp. 1051, 1066 (E.D.Pa.1986); In re Estate of Scott, 455 Pa. 429, 316 A.2d 883 (1974).
16. In re Estate of Schuyler, 91 Ill.2d 6, 16, 61 Ill.Dec. 540, 434 N.E.2d 1137 (1982).
17. Collins v. Nugent, 110 Ill.App.3d 1026, 1036, 66 Ill.Dec. 594, 443 N.E.2d 277, appeal denied, 93 Ill.2d 541 (Ill. 1st Dist.1982).
18. Owen v. Shelton, 221 Va. 1051, 1054, 277 S.E.2d 189, 191 (1981).
19. 318 S.E.2d 592, 227 Va. 441 (Va. 1984).
20. 756 S.W.2d 788 (App. Texas, 1988).

21.   756 S.W.2d at 792, *citing* Lone Star Ford, Inc. v. McGlashan, 681 S.W.2d 720, 723 (Tex.App.--Houston [1st Dist.] 1984).

22.   § 8, Revised Uniform Principal and Income Act (1962).

23.   § 6, Revised Uniform Principal and Income Act (1962).

24.   § 2, Revised Uniform Principal and Income Act (1962).

25.   *Id.*

26.   *Id.*

27.   §12, Revised Uniform Principal and Income Act (1962).

28.   Report of the Fiduciary Accounting Standards Committee.

29.   *See*, J.G. Denhardt, Jr., "Understanding and Applying Fiduciary Accounting," *Continuing Professional Education Division Course Materials* (New York: AICPA, 1992).

Chapter Eleven

Accountants' Professional Liability Insurance

P rior to the 1980s, litigation or claims brought against accountants was infrequent. But when news of large damage awards against accounting firms became widespread, and as states began to expand access to accountant's liability lawsuits for a widening array of third parties, claims began to increase in logarithmic proportions.

This chapter provides basic information about professional liability products available for the indemnification of accountants.

INSURABLE ACTIONS OR EVENTS

Professional liability insurance generally provides coverage for compensatory damages. Compensatory damages are amounts lost by clients and third parties as the result of an accountant's breach of contract or negligence, as those terms are defined under the common law.

219

Compensatory damages do not include amounts designated by courts as punitive damages, i.e., amounts intended to punish a wrongdoer rather than to reimburse a victim for harm done. Compensatory damages also generally do not include consequential damages, such as recoveries for emotional distress or loss of reputation.

Wrongful Acts. Professional liability insurance policies also do not cover criminal behavior, or actions that are dishonest, fraudulent, or malicious in nature.

An interesting aspect of professional liability insurance is the rare occurrence when both civil suits and criminal prosecutions arise out of the same set of events. Two of the more infamous cases providing such a situation were *Continental Vending* and *Equity Funding*.

It is almost standard practice for professional liability insurance not to provide coverage for any dishonest, fraudulent, criminal or malicious acts or omissions of the insured. One insurer makes this exclusion, which can be found in most policies in one form or another, by inserting the following clause:

> This insurance shall not apply to claims or "costs, charges and expenses" for or arising out of:
>
> acts of dishonest, misrepresentation or fraud if made or committed by the Insured with affirmative dishonesty or actual intent to deceive or defraud.

What is significant about this language is the double implication. First, liability for fraud or deceit is possible, the accountant may become quite anxious to reach a settlement. On the other hand, if affirmative or intentional fraud is established on the part of the accountant, the plaintiff recovers no insurance and is left to his or her own devices to recover directly from the accountant.

Sometimes plaintiffs allege fraud or deceit, and it is unclear whether the insurance carrier has an obligation to assist in the defense of the accountant. In such cases, the carrier can be required to defend the accountant, with the understanding that the carrier reserves the right to be indemnified if the allegations of fraud and deceit are proven.

Extraordinary Services. Accountants purchasing professional liability coverage should carefully read the coverage provisions, as well as the exclusions from coverage.[1] Services that are usually covered by a separate type of policy, such as services as an officer or director, are often not covered by a professional liability policy.[2]

It might be necessary to purchase riders for coverage of such activities as:

- Consulting services
- Computer-related services
- Services involving retirement plans and other programs covered by ERISA
- Services pertaining to securities, limited partnerships, real estate syndications, initial public offerings, etc.
- Estate planning
- Forensic accounting services.

TYPES OF LIABILITY INSURANCE

Occurrence Policy

There are two major forms of professional liability insurance coverage available to the accountant. For many years before the liability explosion, the most common form of coverage was the *occurrence type policy*. This policy provided for an unlimited *tail* or *right to extended discovery*.

The unlimited tail attached to the insurance contract meant that the insured accountant was covered even after termination of the policy for acts, errors, or omissions committed prior to the termination of the policy but not discovered or asserted until after. The policy provides coverage where a negligent act or omission occurs within the policy period, regardless of the date of discovery or the date the claim is made or asserted.[3]

In other words, if an accountant retired or left public accounting for some other area of accounting or changed insurance companies, any service rendered during the period of the policy would be covered even if a claimant discovered the circumstances giving rise to the claim ten years later. This policy also provided coverage for acts, errors, or omissions occurring prior to the effective date of the policy resulting in claims which were *unknown* to the insured accountant subsequent to the effective date.

Claims-Made Policy

An alternative to the occurrence policy is the second type of coverage--the *claims-made policy*. In its unmodified form, coverage is similar to ordinary automobile insurance in that there is no prior acts coverage or tails attached. Coverage extends only to those liabilities incurred and asserted during the policy period. The essence of a claims-made policy is notice to the carrier within the policy period.[4]

A modified form of claims-made coverage is that which provides for prior acts coverage without knowledge, and also an *option* to purchase a tail which is usually limited to two or three years. Such an option might be referred to in the insurance policy as the *right to extended discovery period*.

Alternatives to Traditional Policy Coverage

Going Bare. The cost to the accountant for professional liability insurance has become almost prohibitive for many practioners.[5] Some respond by choosing not to purchase insurance. They believe that they can operate a low-risk accounting practice, render themselves judgment-proof by shifting assets, and rely upon bankruptcy as a last resort.

To the extent that an accountant performs no attestation functions, keeps assets out of his or her name at all times, and is willing to have the few assets that would be left to him or her in the event of a divorce, bankruptcy, or other disaster, this strategy can work. But the accountant should consult with an attorney before relying upon such a strategy.[6]

Other Alternatives. Accounting firms are beginning to consider such alternatives as captive insurers, insurance pools, offshore groups and self-insurance. One-fifth of 500 accounting firms recently surveyed had selected one or more of these alternatives. Again, consultation with an attorney is advised before adopting one of these tactics.[7]

OBTAINING INSURANCE

When an accountant does decides to obtain traditional professional liability insurance, a number of points should be considered in acquiring the coverage that provides the most appropriate protection for the individual's given situation. Certainly, it is not necessary to be an expert on insurance. That monumental task is left to the insurance agent. It is the function of the agent or broker to provide the accountant with all the information and service that is necessary to make an intelligent and informed choice of coverage. However, keeping certain concepts in mind makes the entire process run that much more smoothly. There are few things more efficient and effective than an informed consumer, and the accountant will surely find it worthwhile to be so informed.

Most state societies sponsor group plans for accountants. The American Institute of Certified Public Accountants also sponsors a group plan which is particularly beneficial to those whose states are not covered by other plans.

These societies probably offer the accountant the most convenient source for obtaining insurance. As was mentioned earlier, with the tight liability insurance market that exists today, there are not many sources for such insurance and it is fortunate that the accounting profession is able to sponsor such coverage for its members.

What to Look for in a Policy

It is vitally important for the accountant to thoroughly read and understand the insurance contract, and to be familiar with the terms of the policy no matter how technical the language may seem. This will serve to educate the accountant as to his or her rights, obligations, limitations, and nature and scope of the coverage.

When formulating the nature and scope of the coverage sought, the accountant should consider whether the policy provides for the following items:

1. Determine whether the policy provides *prior acts coverage* for the accountant's entire professional background. This insures the accountant against claims made during the life of the policy for acts, errors, and omissions which occurred prior to the policy taking effect and which was unknown to the accountant.
2. Determine whether the policy provides a tail or option to purchase a tail which extends the period of discovery under the present policy. This insures against existing circumstances which may likely result in a future claim long after the insurance policy has terminated.
3. Determine whether the policy protects and continues to cover an innocent accountant when his partner has voided the policy by some act such as deliberate dishonesty, fraud, or violation of particular policy conditions.
4. Determine what rights of appeal are provided in the event the insurance adjuster concludes that a claim against the accountant involves a non-accounting service and is not covered by the policy.
5. Determine what services are specifically excluded from coverage and what activities in the gray area are covered.
6. Determine whether the policy covers constructive fraud which the courts impose for gross negligence and does not involve actual fraudulent intent, or whether all forms of fraud are excluded from coverage.

7. Determine whether the policy provides for legal defense against any suit or countersuit for dishonesty, intentional misrepresentation (actual fraud), intentional breach of contract, or criminal prosecution up to the time of conviction or being held liable. Remember, although the accountant may not be covered for such liability, the accountant should be defended by the insurer until such liability is legally established by a court of law.
8. Find out who selects counsel, to what extent counsel is paid to investigate and defend a claim, who has a right to settle, who has a right to appeal a court decision, and who pays for appeal bonds in the event a claim goes to court.
9. Determine whether exclusion of SEC registration and prospectus coverage applies to other SEC coverage.
10. Determine whether coverage includes accounting services performed in other positions such as directorships, trustees, administrators, conservators, executors and guardians.
11. Determine whether the coverage includes such services as consulting services, tax services, computer-related services, services involving retirement plans and other programs covered by ERISA, services pertaining to securities (including limited partnerships, real estate syndications, and initial public offerings), estate planning services, and forensic accounting services.
12. Determine whether coverage extends to both accounting and fiduciary liability for client's pension, profit-sharing or employee benefit plans.

Applying for Coverage

With the recent increase in claims, it should not come as a surprise that in state such as those, insurers are beginning to practice careful discretion in insuring accountants against professional liability. This caution manifests itself in the long and comprehensive insurance applications accountants must complete. These applications are then analyzed and from this analytical process many of the applicants will be denied. Some insurance carriers are particularly interested in the following information:

1. Experience of applicant and partners.
2. Whether the nature and scope of "write-up" engagements (compilations), are stipulated in engagement letters; whether distinction is made to client in writing between compiled, reviewed, and audited statements; and whether

disclaimers are issued with such statements.
3. Nature of review before releasing financial statements.
4. Whether some form of calendar or docket system is maintained to ensure timely filing and flow of tax materials.
5. Detailed inquiry into the kind of services performed.

The last item listed may be the most significant information obtained. Accountants' professional liability insurance is not intended to cover non-accounting services. However, some services performed by accountants tend to fall in that grey area between accounting and non-accounting. An insurance company might frown upon these gray areas and require a thorough description of such services. Some of the areas which do not represent popular insurance risks and which are carefully scrutinized include the following:

1. Advice or management of clients' business affairs, money or investments in securities and real estate.
2. SEC or "Blue Sky" work involving federal-state accounting laws or regulations.
3. Publication of tax advice.
4. Non-accounting EDP services.
5. Projections and forecasts.

The applicant might be required to approximate the percentage of his prior year's gross billings derived from the above gray areas in addition to tax work performed, EDP services offered, audit engagements, and write-up services. It is not unusual for specific services to be excluded from coverage.

REPORTING A CLAIM

Insurers should be immediately notified in the event a claim is threatened by a client or third party. This is required in most professional liability policies, and the requirement pertains to any written or verbal intimation that a claim is forthcoming.

Although some accountants would prefer to hesitate before notifying a carrier of a claim, because they fear that premiums will escalate as a result of the notification, it is generally advisable to notify the carrier anyway, for the following reasons:

1. Any delay in notifying the carrier could give the carrier an excuse to deny coverage, based coverage period limitations or on policy language requiring immediate notice.

2. The premium structure of most policies accommodates a few complaints and a few expressions of concern on the part of clients and third parties. That is because most professionals in any field will be able to satisfy most of their clients, but will have the occasional dispute with one or two clients. As long as those disputes do not rise to the level of a lawsuit, and can be settled informally by the accountant, notice to the insurance carrier of such disputes generally does not trigger significant and sudden increases in liability insurance premiums.

3. Many carriers have attorneys and other specialists on hand to help counsel the accountant about a potential claim. They can assist the accountant in attempting to mollify the potential claimant and settle the matter informally, and can often help prevent the claim from being brought into court.[8]

NOTES

1. *See* Jensen v. Snellings, 841 F.2d 600, 613 (5th Cir. 1988) (Professional services normally covered by a policy include services performed in the ordinary course of the practice of [one's] profession, on behalf of another.). *See also* Harad v. Aetna Cas. & Sur. Co., 839 F.2d 979, 984 (3d Cir. 1988) (*citing* Marx v. Hartford Accident & Indem. Co., 183 Neb. 12, 13-14, 157 N.W.2d 870, 871-72 (1968)).

2. *See* Potomac Ins. Co. v. McIntosh, 167 Ariz. 30, 804 P.2d 759, 761 (Ariz. App. 1990), review denied, 812 P.2d 629 (Ariz. 1991).

3. *See* Gulf Ins. v. Dolan, Fertig & Curtis, 433 So.2d 512, 514 (Fla.1983).

4. *Ibid.*

5. *See* Brooks, "Manaaging Your Practice: How the Manage the Risk of Professional Malpractice," *Practical Accountant*, Oct. 1987, p.112.

6. *See* MARK F. MURRAY, MANAGING THE MALPRACTICE MAZE (New York: AICPA, 1992), pp. 42-28.

7. Diane Dimond, "Crunch Time for CPAs; Lawsuits and Liability Insurance," *Insurance Review*, Vol. 51; No. 10; p. 9 (October, 1990).

8. *See* Murray, *supra* note 6, p. 149-150.

Chapter Twelve

Ethical Foundation for Accountants

DEVELOPING A FOUNDATION

A professional accountant is more than a mere technician applying the detailed pronouncements of a rule-making body, such as the FASB or the AICPA, to specific situations. In fact, the legal standard for the proper and careful performance of an accountant's duties is not merely limited to the application of promulgated GAAP and GAAS. Instead, judges and juries expect an accountant to apply his or her own professional judgment to each circumstance and each engagement.

Viewed from the chair of a judge, then, promulgated GAAP and GAAS are not by themselves reliable. Something more must govern the actions of the accountant, or else the courts will hold the accountant liable.

"Judicial GAAP" and "Judicial GAAS". How can an accountant determine when and how to apply his or her judgment in such a manner as to avoid legal liability? Unfortunately, the answer to this question cannot be found in the law books.

Even though an accountant (or his or her attorney) can benefit from an exploration of the various court cases, statutes, regulations, and other sources of law in searching out "judicial standards" for the performance of professional accounting services, the judicial standards cannot themselves be completely ascertained or anticipated. That is because court cases are determined on a case-by-case basis, and despite judicial deference to *stare decisis* (the legal doctrine giving preference to previously established judicial precedence), "new law" (and new judicially-determined accountancy standards) can be formulated when judges determine that older standards have become outdated.

Ethics v. Law. What, then, should govern the actions of an accountant? If promulgated GAAP and GAAS are incomplete, and if judicially ascertained professional standards are dynamic and unpredictable, what behavioral precepts are, in fact, reliable?

The answer is both obvious and enigmatic: in a word, ethics. The answer is obvious, because one's personal morality prescribes that code that one allows (or strives) to govern all of his or her actions.[1] And the answer is enigmatic, because an inquiry into the nature of the person, in an effort to discover one's ultimate responsibilities and the means by which those responsibilities can be fulfilled, is a heady exploration that has occupied and absorbed many great minds over the course of human history.

The study of ethics, and the gleaning of information and ideas from history's great ethicists, do not by themselves accomplish anything. But if an accountant is at least aware of the moral principles governing his or her actions, then it will be easier to measure his or her response to the day-to-day challenges of the accounting profession more readily. It is with this observation in mind that the following summary of ethical systems is briefly *explored*.

Ethical Models

All to often the daily pressures of a career in the field of accountancy govern and control the actions of the accountant. In the parlance of the day, the accountant is so busy "putting out fires" and dealing with "alligators snapping," that principles of right and wrong become blurred in the process. And yet if a mistake is made, or a client (or third party) suffers in some way as a result of one action taken by an accountant, the moral rightness of that action will often determine the legal liability of the accountant. In addition, the individual accountant must deal with the consequences of an unethical action as it affects the accountant's perception of his or her own sense of right or wrong.

If, on the other hand, the accountant occasionally stops and considers the ethics of his or her actions, decisions, and judgments, the likelihood of being snared by an inadvertent but less-than-ethical decision is reduced.

The Utilitarian Approach. One helpful measure of the propriety of one's actions is the assessment of the overall consequence of those actions. An accountant who strives to make decisions that optimize the greatest possible good over bad for the greatest number of people is said to be following the ethical principles of *utilitarianism*.

For example, suppose an auditor must decide whether to disclose a seemingly small (but arguably material) matter, such as a related party lease of property by a corporation to several of its officer/shareholders that includes a rental rate slightly below fair market value rate, on the financial statements of his or her client. If the accountant fails to require disclosure in the footnotes to the financial statements, the officer/shareholders will be pleased. However, other shareholders, especially those who believe the managers of the corporation's affairs are being adequately compensated, would feel betrayed by the nondisclosure.

If, on the other hand, the accountant requires disclosure, the other shareholders (who are not party to the lease) will appreciate the information. Potential investors might also appreciate knowing that the below-market lease represents an untapped opportunity for the corporation. And creditors might favorably look at the lease as an off-balance-sheet "asset," that is, as potential economic advantage. Disclosure, then, would benefit shareholders, potential investors, creditors, and, ultimately, the corporation itself.

The utilitarian ethical analysis of the disclosure decision would lead the accountant to reflect on the fact that the decision to disclose would be in the best interest of the larger number of people.

The utilitarian approach is somewhat inharmonious with the concept of the accountant/client relationship. For this reason, it is helpful only for those accountants who enjoy a strong sense of professionalism and who are willing to withstand resistance by clients.

Pragmatism (Egoism). On the negative side of the above example, an auditor's requirement that the below-market lease be disclosed could result in the auditor's loss of the client as a customer of the auditor's firm.

But nondisclosure also has its risks. Suppose another corporation decides to take over the client, and offers a purchase price based on a formula that "capitalizes" the historical earnings of the client. If the full rental value had been excluded from the calculation of the purchase price (because it was not included in the historical earnings of the client) the selling shareholders would realize a lower price for their shares than would otherwise be the case. If the existence of the below-market lease is discovered after the takeover transaction was closed, the client's former shareholders would have a cause of action against the accountant.

The decision to disclose might still be made by the auditor, therefore, from a purely self-serving standpoint. An accountant who approaches these types of decisions strictly from a "risk management" point of view can be said to be an adherent of *pragmatism*, sometimes called *egoism*. The pragmatist school of ethics leads to decisions that advance one's long-term interests. Pragmatism is, in a sense, similar to utilitarianism because the propriety of an action are measured by the consequences of the action; the propriety, however, is determined by reference to self rather than by reference to the common good.

A purely pragmatic approach to ethics is the most dangerous approach to daily decisions. That is because, like its utilitarian cousin, it is morally neutral. But self-serving decisions are more likely to be morally wrong than decisions made for the common good. Besides, a professional who makes decisions solely on the basis of self will suffer the loss of respect from his or her clients. As John L. Carey, and early leader of the AICPA, wrote in 1947:

> Relationships may shift very rapidly in the business world. A client for whom and accountant tried too assiduously to reduce a tax bill might, as a stockholder, wonder if the same accountant would display similar zeal in the interests of management. Even the beneficiaries of practices bordering on the unethical would be likely to lose their respect for an accountant who forgets his professional responsibilities in the hope for financial rewards.[2]

As will be seen below, a true professional is not generally afforded the luxury of adhering to self-serving moral principles: by definition, a professional is dedicated to the service of the common good rather than to his or her personal interests. The pragmatic, or egoist, approach, then, is not valid for purposes of professional decisions made by an accountant.

The Deontological Approach. What if the accountant's actions themselves, rather than their consequences, become the focus of the ethical inquiry? This approach would apply principles of right and wrong to the actions, without regard to a concern for the short- or long-term effect. An accountant applying this analysis would be considered an adherent of the *deontological* school of ethics.

In the previous example involving the below-market lease of property to owner/shareholders, the decision to disclose would, under the deontological approach, be based on the accountant's own sense of his or her duty. That is, the auditor considers his or her overriding professional duty to ensure that financial statements are a fair representation of the client's economic circumstances. That duty, owed both to users of the financial statements as well as to the public at large (hence, certified "public" accountant), establishes the professionalism of the auditor. The professionalism of the auditor, in turn, is what the client bought when the client engaged the auditor, and that professionalism circumscribes the auditor's duty to the client.

The deontological approach to ethical analysis would lead an auditor to require disclosure, then, if disclosure would serve to fulfill the auditor's duty as a professional. That duty, under this approach, and its fulfillment, overrides the auditor's concern about the consequences of the decision itself.

Religious Influences on Ethics. One's religious views, or lack thereof, can help to define and shape the ethical model, or combination of ethical models, applied by the individual accountant. If a person believes that truth can be discovered by logic (*rationalism*), for example, then secular philosophers such as Descartes, Spinoza, and Leibniz can serve to help that person to define such truth. Similarly, if one believes that truth can be ascertained by experience (*empiricism*), he or she will find affinity in such writers as Locke, Berkely, and Hume.

But many people believe that truth, and the concepts of rightness and wrongness, emanate from an external source, such as God. For the more fundamental or conservative believers, the principles found in sacred books and writings (such as the Bible, the Mishnah Torah, and the Koran), constitute and define principles of right and wrong.

For others, sacred books and writings are not considered to encompass truth so reliably, but principles of right and wrong are nevertheless associated with God or with a similar sense of the supernatural.

For the theist, that is, for the person who believes in God as the source of truth, the utilitarian approach to ethics can be applied in the context of a theological definition of "the common good." The emphasis upon love and concern for one's neighbor would, for example, heighten the believer's awareness of those who would be impacted by a professional decision. In the above example involving a below-market lease, the "good" of the favorable lease rate might be given less weight than the "good" of protecting the potential profits of other shareholders and future investors. The influence of religion would skew the analysis of the relative utility of a decision.

The application of the deontological approach to ethics would similarly, and perhaps more directly, be influenced by religious convictions. Since religious doctrines, such as the Ten Commandments of the Bible tend to prescribe principles of right and wrong, those doctrines are incorporated into the professional's sense of duty under the deontological model. In a decision whether to disclose a matter (such as the below-market lease in the previous examples), the auditor's duty (to ensure the financial statements result in a fair representation) would be influenced, and perhaps expanded, by the auditor's sense of honesty and *integrity*.

Conclusion. Accountants are continually faced with decisions that have moral and ethical connotations. If the accountant is so overworked, or so caught up in his or her daily routine, that decisions are made quickly and without thought, the accountant can easily become ensnared by a decision that is not only technically incorrect: it is morally wrong.

If, on the other hand, consideration is, from time to time (such as at least once a week), given to the larger consequences of small decisions (the utilitarian perspective), and if thought is given to the propriety of actions taken (the deontological perspective), the likelihood of a wrong turn is greatly reduced. For wisdom in both areas, the insights offered by one's religious roots can be of enormous value.

WHAT CONSTITUTES A "PROFESSION"

Thirty years ago Bernard Barber distinguished the concept of a "profession" from other occupations if it was characterized by the following four features:

1. General and systematic knowledge
2. Orientation to community interest

3. Self-monitoring via a code of ethics
4. Recognition of excellent work and technical accomplishments.[3]

Over the years other writers have provided expanded and re-worked versions of this list, but it serves as a good basis for any discussion of *professionalism*.

General and Systematic Knowledge

Accountancy is readily recognized as a rigorous discipline. Business school students who select accounting as their major field of study are often viewed has having selected the most difficult curriculum on campus. Candidates for certification as public accountants in the U.S. endure one of the most demanding licensure examinations in the nation.

And the state of the art continues to develop. Promulgations from the Financial Accounting Standards Board become longer, more technical, and more esoteric each year. Auditing continues to become more sophisticated, as statistical sampling, artificial intelligence, and other new methods and tools are employed.

Fortunately or unfortunately, the public's expectations of the profession also continue to increase. As was observed at the outset of this book, accountants are increasingly seen as the providers of a "clean bill of health" of their audit clients. And when an embezzlement, a clever computer crime, a subtle but significant drop in the market value of an asset category, or some other adverse event slips past the auditor, the public and the courts are unforgiving.

How does the individual accountant survive in such an environment? Several tactics can be employed:

a. Continuing professional education is critical to the accountant's ability to keep up with developments in the field.

b. A commitment to excellence in the work undertaken is essential. In this regard, the general standards of professional accounting services stated at Rule 201 of the Code of Professional Conduct (discussed below) provide guidance:

   i. Professional Competence. Undertake only those professional services that the accountant or the accountant's firm can reasonably expect to be completed with professional competence.[4]

    ii.   Due Professional Care. Exercise due professional care in the performance of professional services.

    iii.   Planning and Supervision. Adequately plan and supervise the performance of professional services.

    iv.   Sufficient Relevant Data. Obtain sufficient relevant data to afford a reasonable basis for conclusions or recommendations in relation to any professional services performed.[5]

c.   Education of the client, as well as creditors and other classes of users of financial statements, as to the tasks undertaken by the auditor is important. Some professionals would prefer to "impress" their clients (or patients or customers) with the mysteries and mystique of their particular discipline. But the professional and the client are both better served if the client fully understands the nature of the engagement, the tasks performed, and the limitations under which the work is accomplished.

d.   The accountant's own integrity, including a readiness to admit mistakes and to, as much as possible, remedy them to the satisfaction of the injured party, is critical. Trial lawyers often admit that two words would greatly reduce their revenues: the two words are "I'm sorry."

Beyond these simple maxims, it is important that the accountant understand the difference between knowledge and good judgment. Anyone with a good memory could, after all, memorize all of the GAAP and GAAS and related promulgations pertaining to the field of accountancy. And anyone with a good sense of numerical algorithms can be taught double entry accounting, from journal entry to financial statements.

But a professional is more than an informed and educated technician. A professional is able to wisely apply that information and that knowledge in an appropriate manner to each situation. In addition, the professional views standards, regulations, rules, and promulgations with a healthy cynicism, and is willing to inject his or her own analysis and judgment in the appropriate circumstance.

It is the willingness to first learn, and then be able to critique and even modify as appropriate, the standards and promulgations of the FASB, the AICPA, the SEC, and other bodies, that elevates each certified public accountant to the level of a true professional.

Orientation to Community Interest

If licensed accountants were to advertise in the manner of some other occupations, they might include in their advertising the phrase "Public is Our Middle Name." Certified public accountants are, in fact, licensed by state boards of accountancy; but then, in many states, so are cosmetologists and dogcatchers.

The civic nature of the accountant's role in the audit process, however, is nearly unique. Only a few other professionals, such as architects and surveyors, assume the responsibility of making a "certification," or authentication, to the general public. The built-in conflict between the need to provide an important service to the client for a fair fee, on the one hand, and the requirement that the general public be properly served and informed, on the other, exists in these types of professions. As one prominent attorney-CPA put it, certified public accountants are expected to "bite the hand that feeds them."

Can an accountant become overly zealous in serving the public, to the detriment of the client? Yes, of course. If an accountant goes far beyond the discipline's generally accepted requirements of conservatism and disclosure, for example, the resultant financial statements and footnotes of that accountant's clients could appear so dismal and dour that the accountant would of necessity become a bankruptcy specialist. No creditors, suppliers, investors, or other potential users of the clients' financial statements would be willing to do business with the accountant's clients. Even the general public is not well served if accountants routinely render clients insolvent by unnecessarily frightening away their clients' creditors, investors, and suppliers.

An accountant is more often tempted in the opposite direction, though. As clients (especially long-term clients who are also good friends of the accountant) come upon hard times, the natural tendency is to attempt to help out. It is the sense of loyalty to one's clients, and the desire to assist during a crisis, the leads the accountant to forego his or her overriding obligation to the general public in favor of a client's immediate need.

As soon as the accountant does anything other than perform his or her duties to the highest degree of excellence, however, the accountant is at risk. The fact that an accountant might have "fudged" the financial statements of a client in order to help the client during a time of crisis will not favorably impress a judge or jury: at best, the client's troubles, and the accountant's proclivity to help a long-time friend and client, will serve as evidence that any problem with the accountant's work was *intentional*. Evidence of intent not only opens the door to additional civil claims (besides professional negligence), but it leaves open the possibility of criminal action against the accountant.

In short, the accountant must strike a balance between the needs of the client and the needs of the public at large. When in doubt (but only when in doubt), the balance must weigh in favor of the public at large.

Orientation to Employer/Firm Interest

The needs of the client and the needs of the public are not the only influences upon an accountant's decisions. At the earliest points in an accountant's career, he or she must also take into consideration the demands and ethos of his or her employer. Retention of an accounting position at a firm, and promotion, are dependant, in part, on the career accountant's ability to confine each of his or her ethical decisions to the range of options favored by his or her employer.

The "ethical culture" of the younger accountant's employer can, therefore, either foster or stymie the individual's development of ethical decision-making skills. Research has shown that the latter is the case more often than not.[6]

PRINCIPLES OF PROFESSIONAL CONDUCT

The Purposes of Codes of Ethics

Barber's third "mark" of a profession is the development of, and adherence to, a professional code of ethics. The purpose for a code of ethics is the establishment of moral norms within which the profession hopes to operate. That is, the code of ethics is less a summary of historical practices than it is an expression of moral standards that are intended to govern the behavior of each member of the profession.

Some codes of ethics, such as those for attorneys and medical doctors, have the force of law. Most, however, have expulsion from a professional organization as their primary enforcement mechanism. The AICPA's Code of Professional Conduct resides in the latter category.

The AICPA Code of Professional Conduct

The AICPA's current Code of Professional Conduct, developed in 1988, is the product of decades of consideration and development. As early as 1907, the organization (then known a the American Association of Public Accountants, or AAPA) adopted ethical rules, including a general prohibition against "acts discreditable."[7]

As stated in the Preamble, the current Code is intended to accomplish the following objectives:

a. Express the profession's recognition of its responsibilities to the public, to clients, and to colleagues; and
b. Guide members in the performance of their professional responsibilities and express the basic tenets of ethical and professional conduct.

The Code contains language that rules out the pragmatist, or egoist, approach to ethical behavior, calling for "an unswerving commitment to honorable behavior, even at the sacrifice of personal advantage."[8]

The current Code was adopted on January 12, 1988, and has undergone relatively few changes since that time. It consists of Principles (general statements of ethical standards) and Rules (specific dictates governing the performance of accountants). In addition, the professional ethics division of the AICPA occasionally publishes Interpretations of the Code (guidelines as to the scope and application of the Rules), and Ethics Rulings (application of the Rules of Conduct and Interpretations to specific factual circumstances.

Membership in the American Institute of Certified Public Accountants is voluntary, but by accepting membership, a certified public accountant agrees to abide by the Code as a condition of continued membership. If a member violates the Code, he or she may be expelled from the organization.

Unlike a breach of the Code itself, violations of an Interpretation (or noncompliance with Ethics Rulings) are not automatically considered grounds for expulsion. Instead, an AICPA member who departs from such guidelines may be required to justify such departure in a disciplinary hearing.[9]

Responsibilities as Professionals

Article I, Responsibilities, of the Principles of the Code of Professional Conduct provides as follows:

In carrying out their responsibilities as professionals, members should exercise sensitive professional and moral judgments in all their activities.

.01 As professionals, certified public accountants perform an essential role in society. Consistent with that role, members of the American Institute of Certified Public Accountants have responsibilities to all those who use their professional services.

Members also have a continuing responsibility to cooperate with each other to improve the art of accounting, maintain the public's confidence, and carry out the profession's special responsibilities for self- governance. The collective efforts of all members are required to maintain and enhance the traditions of the profession.

Article I deals primarily with the accountant's responsibility to *the profession*. The stated responsibility to "improve the art of accounting" is an especially interesting provision, for two reasons. First, it gives recognition the fact that accounting is an art, rather than a science. One of the most difficult concepts for non-accountants (including judges and juries) to grasp is the idea that, for all of their underlying technical jargon and double-entry exactness, financial statements are the product of an art, akin to pictures that have been designed for a "paint-by-numbers" kit.

To "improve the art of accounting," furthermore, is to recognize that the art is dynamic. This argument is often made in court by attorneys defending accountants who may have departed from promulgated GAAP and GAAS. Without constant criticism and improvement, the art of accounting would become static and rigid. By maintaining a willingness to depart from promulgated GAAP and GAAS in the appropriate circumstances (or to create new methods of presenting economic information when current promulgations are inadequate), accountants give life and vitality to the art itself. The worst fate that the profession could suffer would be the intimidation of its practitioners, as a result of litigation, into mindless adherence to GAAP and GAAS decrees as a risk management tactic.

Avoiding Discreditable Acts. To "maintain the public confidence" requires that the accountant avoid discreditable acts. Rule 501 carries forward, from earlier ethics codes, the prohibition against "acts discreditable." Included in this prohibition are the following:

- Retention of a client's records after a demand has been made for same.[10]
- False, misleading or deceptive acts in advertising or solicitation.[11]
- Failure to follow governmental audit standards where applicable.[12]
- Negligence that results in false or misleading entries in a client's books or financial statements.[13]

Confidentiality. The confidentiality of client information is a matter that affects many professionals, including those in the fields of law and medicine. Because the accounting profession is relatively new, compared to law and medicine, however, accountancy does not enjoy some of the common law protection of confidentiality. A few states have statutes providing for an accountant-client confidentiality privilege.

Rule 301 provides that an accountant in public practice "shall not disclose any confidential client information without the specific consent of the client." This Rule does not apply to the following situations:

a. Disclosures on financial statements as required by GAAP.
b. Compliance with a validly issued and enforceable subpoena or summons.
c. Divulgence of client information to "peers" as part of an accountant's participation in a peer review (see below).
d. Disclosures to governmental authorities as part of an investigation or disciplinary proceeding, even if the investigation or proceeding was initiated pursuant to a complaint filed by the accountant.[14]

Serving the Public Interest

Article II of the Principles of Professional Conduct makes the following declarations:

> Members should accept the obligation to act in a way that will serve the public interest, honor the public trust, and demonstrate commitment to professionalism.
>
> .01 A distinguishing mark of a profession is acceptance of its responsibility to the public. The accounting profession's public consists of clients, credit grantors, governments, employers, investors, the business and financial community, and others who rely on the objectivity and integrity of certified public accountants to maintain the orderly functioning of commerce. This reliance imposes a public interest responsibility on certified public accountants. The public interest is defined as the collective well-being of the community of people and institutions the profession serves.
>
> .02 In discharging their professional responsibilities, members may encounter conflicting pressures from among each of those groups. In resolving those conflicts, members should act with integrity, guided by the precept that when members fulfill their responsibility to the public, clients' and employers' interests are best served.
>
> .03 Those who rely on certified public accountants expect them to discharge their responsibilities with integrity, objectivity, due professional care, and a genuine interest in serving the public. They

are expected to provide quality services, enter into fee arrangements, and offer a range of services -- all in a manner that demonstrates a level of professionalism consistent with these Principles of the Code of Professional Conduct.

.04 All who accept membership in the American Institute of Certified Public Accountants commit themselves to honor the public trust. In return for the faith that the public reposes in them, members should seek continually to demonstrate their dedication to professional excellence.

Article II deals primarily with the accountant's responsibility *to society*. It is hard to argue with anything stated in Article II. All if its provisions are admirable, altruistic, and lofty. There are, however, situations when the accountant's duty to the public conflict with his or her duty to a client, or even to the interests of the profession. Article II can be paraphrased, "when in doubt, do what is right by society rather than your client."

Integrity

Principles of Professional Conduct Article III, Integrity, provides:

To maintain and broaden public confidence, members should perform all professional responsibilities with the highest sense of integrity.

.01 Integrity is an element of character fundamental to professional recognition. It is the quality from which the public trust derives and the benchmark against which a member must ultimately test all decisions.

.02 Integrity requires a member to be, among other things, honest and candid within the constraints of client confidentiality. Service and the public trust should not be subordinated to personal gain and advantage. Integrity can accommodate the inadvertent error and the honest difference of opinion; it cannot accommodate deceit or subordination of principle.

.03 Integrity is measured in terms of what is right and just. In the absence of specific rules, standards, or guidance, or in the face of conflicting opinions, a member should test decisions and deeds by asking: Am I doing what a person of integrity would do? Have I retained my integrity? Integrity requires a member to observe both the form and the spirit of technical and ethical standards; circumvention of those standards constitutes subordination of judgment.

.04 Integrity also requires a member to observe the principles of objectivity and independence and of due care.

Articles III, IV and V deal with an accountant's responsibility *to be true to himself or herself*. In the spirit of the deontological school of ethics, Article III places a strong emphasis upon honesty *per se*. That is, no "ends" (including an attempt to "help" a client) would justify the "means" if the means would include, for example, a false or misleading entry in a client's financial statements or records.[15]

Objectivity and Independence

Professional objectivity, and detachment from conflicts of interest, are addressed in Article IV of the Principles of Professional Conduct as follows:

A member should maintain objectivity and be free of conflicts of interest in discharging professional responsibilities. A member in public practice should be independent in fact and appearance when providing auditing and other attestation services.

.01 Objectivity is a state of mind, a quality that lends value to a member's services. It is a distinguishing feature of the profession. The principle of objectivity imposes the obligation to be impartial, intellectually honest, and free of conflicts of interest. Independence precludes relationships that may appear to impair a member's objectivity in rendering attestation services.

.02 Members often serve multiple interests in many different capacities and must demonstrate their objectivity in varying circumstances. Members in public practice render attest, tax, and management advisory services. Other members prepare financial statements in the employment of others, perform internal auditing services, and serve in financial and management capacities in industry, education, and government. They also educate and train those who aspire to admission into the profession. Regardless of service or capacity, members should protect the integrity of their work, maintain objectivity, and avoid any subordination of their judgment.

.03 For a member in public practice, the maintenance of objectivity and independence requires a continuing assessment of client relationships and public responsibility. Such a member who provides auditing and other attestation services should be independent in fact and appearance. In providing all other services, a member should maintain objectivity and avoid conflicts of interest.

.04 Although members not in public practice cannot maintain the appearance of independence, they nevertheless have the responsibility to maintain objectivity in rendering professional services. Members employed by others to prepare financial statements or to perform auditing, tax, or consulting services are charged with the same responsibility for objectivity as members in public practice and must be scrupulous in their application of generally accepted accounting principles and candid in all their dealings with members in public practice.

Article IV asks an accountant to avoid conflicts of interest. A conflict of interest can arise from any number of different circumstances. For example, a conflict can occur if an accountant performs a professional service for a client or employer and the accountant (or his or her firm) has a significant relationship with another person, entity, product, or service that could be viewed as impairing the accountant's objectivity. If this significant relationship is disclosed to and consent is obtained from such client, employer, or other appropriate parties, the matter will have been resolved.[16]

Maintaining Independence from Audit Clients. The concept of independence is more subtle than conflict of interest. Interpretation 101-1 provides that even though an accountant might not have a conflict of interest, he or she would still not be "independent," if any he or she is involved in any of the following transactions, interests, or relationships:

a. During the period of a professional engagement or at the time of expressing an opinion, a member or a member's firm

    i.   Had or was committed to acquire any direct or material indirect financial interest in the enterprise.

    ii. Was a trustee of any trust or executor or administrator of any estate if such trust or estate had or was committed to acquire any direct or material indirect financial interest in the enterprise.[17]

    iii. Had any joint, closely held business investment with the enterprise or with any officer, director, or principal stockholders thereof that was material in relation to the member's net worth or to the net worth of the member's firm.

iv. Had any loan to or from the enterprise or any officer, director, or principal stockholder of the enterprise. This proscription does not apply to the following loans from a financial institution when made under normal lending procedures, terms, and requirements:

(1) Loans obtained by a member or a member's firm that are not material in relation to the net worth of such borrower.
(2) Home mortgages.
(3) Other secured loans, except loans guaranteed by a member's firm which are otherwise unsecured.

b. During the period covered by the financial statements, during the period of the professional engagement, or at the time of expressing an opinion, a member or a member's firm

i. Was connected with the enterprise as a promoter, underwriter or voting trustee, as a director or officer, or in any capacity equivalent to that of a member of management or of an employee.
ii. Was a trustee for any pension or profit-sharing trust of the enterprise.[18]

Other circumstances that could "turn the accountant's head," or at least appear to have a potential influence on an accountant's work, would include:

a. Litigation (or a threatened lawsuit) between client and auditor.[19]
b. The client being audited has hired an accountant formerly associated with the auditing firm, if the auditing firm still has connections with (or financial obligations to) the accountant.[20]
c. An auditing firm and it clients have hired the family members or each other's officers, shareholders, partners, etc.[21]

Auditing the Accountant's Own Accounting Work. If an accounting firm handles all of the everyday accounting for a client, and then audits that client, the accounting firm is, in a sense, auditing itself. From a practical standpoint, it does not make sense for clients, especially smaller businesses, to hire bookkeepers and accounting clerks if it would cost less to have the accounting firm perform these services. This is become more prevalent as clients find that a fully automated accounting firm can often process the recordkeeping and maintain financial records more efficiently (and less expensively) than an in-house accounting staff.

How does the accounting firm deal with the problem of essentially auditing its own work? Interpretation 101-3 makes the following recommendations for accounting firms who audit (and maintain the financial records) smaller businesses:

a. The CPA must not have any relationship or combination of relationships with the client or any conflict of interest that would impair his integrity and objectivity.

b. The client must accept the responsibility for the financial statements as his own. A small client may not have anyone in his employ to maintain accounting records and may rely on the CPA for this purpose. Nevertheless, the client must be sufficiently knowledgeable of the enterprise's activities and financial condition and the applicable accounting principles so that he can reasonably accept such responsibility, including, specifically, fairness of valuation and presentation and adequacy of disclosure. When necessary, the CPA must discuss accounting matters with the client to be sure that the client has the required degree of understanding.

c. The CPA must not assume the role of employee or of management conducting the operations of an enterprise. For example, the CPA shall not consummate transactions, have custody of assets or exercise authority on behalf of the client. The client must prepare the source documents on all transactions in sufficient detail to identify clearly the nature and amount of such transactions and maintain an accounting control over data processed by the CPA such as control totals and document counts. The CPA should not make changes in such basic data without the concurrence of the client.

d. The CPA, in making an examination of financial statements prepared from books and records which he has maintained completely or in part, must conform to generally accepted auditing standards. The fact that he has processed or maintained certain records does not eliminate the need to make sufficient audit tests.

Due Care

The responsibility to perform the tasks of professional accountancy with due care is delineated in Article V of the Principles of Professional of Conduct. Article V states:

A member should observe the profession's technical and ethical standards, strive continually to improve competence and the quality of services, and discharge professional responsibility to the best of the member's ability.

.01 The quest for excellence is the essence of due care. Due care requires a member to discharge professional responsibilities with competence and diligence. It imposes the obligation to perform professional services to the best of a member's ability with concern for the best interest of those for whom the services are performed and consistent with the profession's responsibility to the public.

.02 Competence is derived from a synthesis of education and experience. It begins with a mastery of the common body of knowledge required for designation as a certified public accountant. The maintenance of competence requires a commitment to learning and professional improvement that must continue throughout a member's professional life. It is a member's individual responsibility. In all engagements and in all responsibilities, each member should undertake to achieve a level of competence that will assure that the quality of the member's services meets the high level of professionalism required by these Principles.

.03 Competence represents the attainment and maintenance of a level of understanding and knowledge that enables a member to render services with facility and acumen. It also establishes the limitations of a member's capabilities by dictating that consultation or referral may be required when a professional engagement exceeds the personal competence of a member or a member's firm. Each member is responsible for assessing his or her own competence -- of evaluating whether education, experience, and judgment are adequate for the responsibility to be assumed.

.04 Members should be diligent in discharging responsibilities to clients, employers, and the public. Diligence imposes the responsibility to render services promptly and carefully, to be thorough, and to observe applicable technical and ethical standards. .05 Due care requires a member to plan and supervise adequately any professional activity for which he or she is responsible.

What are "the profession's technical and ethical standards?" Rule 203 of the Code of Professional Conduct explains that an accountant who performs "auditing, review, compilation, management advisory, tax, or other professional services shall comply with standards promulgated by bodies designated by Council."

Departures from Promulgated Standards. One of those standards is Rule 203 of the Code of Professional Conduct, which requires compliance with the "promulgated" standards, for purposes of financial statements:

A[n AICPA] member shall not (1) express an opinion or state affirmatively that the financial statements or other financial data of any entity are presented in conformity with generally accepted accounting principles or (2) state that he or she is not aware of any material modifications that should be made to such statements or data in order for them to be in conformity with generally accepted accounting principles, if such statements or data contain any departure from an accounting principle promulgated by bodies designated by [the AICPA's] Council to establish such principles that has a material effect on the statements or data taken as a whole. If, however, the statements or data contain such a departure and the member can demonstrate that due to unusual circumstances the financial statements or data would otherwise have been misleading, the member can comply with the rule by describing the departure, its approximate effects, if practicable, and the reasons why compliance with the principle would result in a misleading statement.

This Rule, which predates the establishment of the FASB, has probably caused more confusion (and legal fees) than any other pronouncement issued by the AICPA. Part of the problem stems from the fact that many attorneys (and accountants!) read the first sentence of Rule 203, and stop at that point. The first sentence does, in fact, call upon accountants to follow the promulgations of the FASB and other rule-making bodies. But the second sentences explains the standard by which the AICPA would accept a departure from the promulgated standards.

The second sentence of Rule 203, above, contains an "if. . . then" statement:

a. IF there are "unusual circumstances," and
b. IF those unusual circumstances call for a departure from GAAP to avoid a misleading financial statement,
c. THEN a departure, with explanation, is appropriate.

The first "if" condition is not difficult to meet: a survey of the clientele of most accounting firms would lead the surveyor to the conclusion that there are few, if any, "usual" circumstances, as every client has many unusual circumstances.

The second "if" condition is also not an impossible hurdle. An analysis as to whether a departure from GAAP is "misleading" should be made in view of the overall purpose of accounting: the fair presentation of economic data. Perhaps a more precise wording of the second sentence of Rule 203, in view of the overall objectives of accounting, would be as follows:

"If, however, the statements or data contain such a departure and the member determines that due to unusual circumstances the financial statements or data are more fairly presented when incorporating such departure than would otherwise be the case, the member shall comply with the rule by describing the departure, its approximate effects, if practicable, and the reasons the incorporation of the departure results in a more fair presentation than would otherwise be the case."

Judicially Required Departures from Promulgated Standards. This less restrictive form of the second sentence of Rule 203 is consistent with the approach taken by the courts. That is because the courts do not consider promulgated GAAP and GAAS to represent the sum total of the standard of care of accountants. Under the legal standard of care applicable to accountants and others, a professional as a *duty* to depart from the pronouncements of professional and authoritative bodies if the situation calls for such a departure.

In the case of *Maduff Mortgage Corporation v. Deloitte Haskins & Sells*,[22] for example, the plaintiff, who sued the accounting firm for allegedly performing an audit without exercising proper care. The accounting firm contended that the audit was performed within the confines of promulgated GAAS, and that the financial statement complied with promulgated GAAP. One of the arguments made by the plaintiff was that "AICPA standards are only evidentiary."[23] The court agreed. The court ruled that

[AICPA promulgations] are principles and procedures developed by the accounting profession itself, not by the courts or the legislature. They may be useful to a jury in determining the standard of care for an auditor, but they are not controlling. The amount of care, skill and diligence required to be used by defendant in conducting an audit is a question of fact for the jury, just as it is in other fields for other professionals.

And in the case of *Bily v. Arthur Young & Company*,[24] the court made the following comment about AICPA, FASB, and related pronouncements:

Unquestionably [these promulgated] GAAS and GAAP are monumental and commendable codifications of customs and practices within the profession of certified public accountancy. But it is the general rule that adherence to a relevant custom or practice does not necessarily establish the actor has met the standard of care.[25]

In reaching this conclusion, the court in the *Bily* case made the following two observations:

First, neither GAAS nor GAAP is now, or may ever be, so comprehensive as to afford a predictable and repeatable standard of professional responsibility in all conceivable situations. As one commentator has acknowledged: "In situations that are not specifically addressed by the AICPA Professional Standards, a CPA merely has an obligation to use professional care. Although this requires a CPA to comply in good faith with GAAP and GAAS, neither of these concepts have been clearly defined."[26]
Second, in any event so categorical a rule would inappropriately entrust to the accountancy profession itself the balancing of interests implicit in any determination of duty and breach.[27]

Scope and Nature of Services

What kind of services may, or should, a certified public accountant perform? Although the answer to this question seems to continually change as accountants expand and apply their expertise in a wider variety of area, the ethical considerations underlying the decision to perform nontraditional services does not change. Article VI of the Principles of Professional Conduct addresses this issue as follows:

A member in public practice should observe the Principles of the Code of Professional Conduct in determining the scope and nature of services to be provided.

.01 The public interest aspect of certified public accountants' services requires that such services be consistent with acceptable professional behavior for certified public accountants. Integrity requires that service and the public trust not be subordinated to personal gain and advantage. Objectivity and independence require that members be free from conflicts of interest in discharging professional responsibilities. Due care requires that services be provided with competence and diligence.

.02 Each of these Principles should be considered by members in determining whether or not to provide specific services in individual circumstances. In some instances, they may represent an overall constraint on the nonaudit services that might be offered to a specific client. No hard-and-fast rules can be developed to help members reach these judgments, but they must be satisfied that they are meeting the spirit of the Principles in this regard.

.03 In order to accomplish this, members should:

- Practice in firms that have in place internal quality-control procedures to ensure that services are competently delivered and adequately supervised.
- Determine, in their individual judgments, whether the scope and nature of other services provided to an audit client would create a conflict of interest in the performance of the audit function for that client.
- Assess, in their individual judgments, whether an activity is consistent with their role as professionals (for example, Is such activity a reasonable extension or variation of existing services offered by the member or others in the profession?).

Summary: Promulgated Ethics

The AICPA's Code of Professional Conduct is, in many ways, the most important promulgation the organization has published. The Code provides an ethical foundation for the performance of accounting services.

The Code is neither all-inclusive or "perfect." But its continued evolution makes it a viable moral reference point for both AICPA members and non-members. As the Code continues to be modified and improved, it is likely that it will expand it scope into such areas as:

- Continuing professional development.
- Enlargement of knowledge; research; publication.
- *Pro bono* services.
- Nonexploitation of clients, students, and interns.
- Proper treatment of subordinates; encouragement of professional development; giving credit.
- Efforts to reform governmental, educational, and other institutions that bear on the profession.
- Involvement in community activities not related to the profession.[28]

PEER REVIEW AND SELF-REGULATION

Peer review is a process accounting firms audit each other's work to ensure that each firm conforms to professional standards. According to the Securities and Exchange Commission, a peer review must satisfy three objectives to be successful:

First, it must incorporate and apply meaningful standards of quality control to both the work of the reviewer and of the accountant being reviewed. Second, it must be structured in such a manner as to assure independence in fact and promote public confidence in the credibility of the peer review process. Third, the peer review process must be sufficiently open to examination by representatives of the public. . . [29]

Peer reviews evaluate whether an accounting firm's system of quality control is appropriately comprehensive, suitably designed for the firm, and adequately documented. They also ensure that the firm's quality control policies and procedures are adequately communicated to, and complied with by, professional personnel within the firm.[30]

The AICPA formed the Division for CPA Firms in 1977 to accommodate efforts on the part of the profession to exert disciplinary control over member firms. This action by the AICPA has been called "one of the most important steps ever taken by the profession to implement its program of self-regulation."[31]

The AICPA maintains two peer review programs within its Division for CPA Firms. One, administered through the organization's SEC Practice Section, is aimed at accounting firms whose clients include publicly held companies subject to SEC oversight. The other, administered by the Private Companies Practice Section, is designed for accounting firms with closely held business clients.

Peer review as conducted pursuant to AICPA procedures is a two part process, somewhat analogous to an auditor's review of a client's system of internal accounting control. The evaluation is accomplished through:

a. Study and evaluation of a reviewed accountant's policies and procedures that comprise its quality control system; and
b. Review for compliance with a reviewed accountant's quality control policies and procedures by

    i. Review at each organizational or functional level within the organization; and
    ii. Review of selected engagement working paper files and reports.[32]

Reviews are thus conducted at several different levels. The system of quality control itself is reviewed, within the context of the particular firm's professional practice, against the framework established by *SAS No. 25, The Relationship of Generally Accepted Auditing Standards to Quality Control Standards.* The actual conduct of the firm's accounting and auditing practice is measured against:

a. Generally accepted auditing standards (GAAS);
b. The guidelines provided by the authoritative literature under GAAS; and
c. The quality control policies and procedures established by the accounting firm.

The conduct of the accountant's practice is also examined in terms of the judgments made in applying generally accepted accounting principles (GAAP), since engagement reviews include a review of the related financial statements.[33]

Avoiding Direct Government Intervention

Peer review programs serve as an alternative to direct government oversight of the accounting profession. For government agencies that must rely on reports of accounting firms as part of their administrative functions, for example, the quality of the work performed by the accounting firms essential to the efficiency of the agency. Peer review programs allow a government agency to screen the accounting firms it relies upon, rather than establish its own quality review procedures. This cost-effective tactic has been employed by some government agencies, and has been proposed for others.[34]

The most recent example of government reliance upon the peer review process can be found in the Federal Deposit Insurance Corporation Improvement Act of 1991 (FDICIA),[35] discussed in Chapter Six. The FDICIA provides the following requirements for accountants certifying statements with the FDIC ("the Corporation"):

(A) In general. All audit services required by this section shall be performed only by an independent public accountant who--
   (i) has agreed to provide related working papers, policies, and procedures to the Corporation, an appropriate Federal banking agency, and any State bank supervisor, if requested; and
   (ii) has received a peer review that meets guidelines acceptable to the Corporation.
(B) Reports on peer reviews. Reports on peer reviews shall be filed with the Corporation and made available for public inspection.[36]

The above provision goes further than previous efforts to tie government regulation to the attestation functions of accountants. It does this by allowing the FDIC to establish guidelines for peer review, and to impose those guidelines as a condition of an auditor's qualification to provide required audit services.

CONCLUSION

The accounting profession, like any other, will survive within society as a distinct discipline so long as it continues to meet the needs of society as a whole, and to keep those needs foremost among its functions and priorities.

The ethical foundation of the profession is critical to this process. But the ethical foundation of the profession is built upon the moral principles that motivate, and are evidenced in the actions of, each of its members. The level of commitment of each member to high ethical principles, and the willingness of each member to have his or her ethical principles challenged and examined, will determine the likelihood of the profession's success in the twenty-first century.

NOTES

1. *See*, STEVEN M. MINTZ, CASES IN ACCOUNTING ETHICS AND PROFESSIONALISM, 2ND ED. (N.Y.: McGraw Hill, 1992), p.5.
2. Carey, John L., "The Realities of Professional Ethics," *The Accounting Review*, April 1947, 119-123 at p. 120, as quoted in Kultgen, John, *Ethics and Professionalism* (Philadelphia: University of Pennsylvania Press, 1988), p.363.
3. B. Barber, "Some Problems in the Sociology of Professions, *Daedalus*, Vol. 92, P. 672.
4. *See* AICPA, Ethics Interpretation 201-1, Competence, *Code of Professional Conduct.*
5. AICPA, Rule 201 - General Standards, *Code of Professional Conduct.*
6. Lawrence A. Ponemon, "Ethical Reasoning and Selection-Socialization in Accounting," *Accounting, Organizations and Society*, vol. 17, No. 3/4, pp. 239-259 (1992).
7. Edwards, James Don, and Miranti, Paul J., Jr., "Overview: the Past and its Leaders," *Journal of Accountancy*, May 1987, p. 22. *See* AICPA, Rule 501, Acts discreditable, *Code of Professional Conduct.*
8. AICPA, *Principles of Professional Conduct* (Preamble, ¶.02), 1988.
9. AICPA, *Code of Professional Conduct* (Introduction), 1988.
10. AICPA, Ethics Interpretation 501-1, Retention of Client Records.
11. AICPA, Rule 502, Advertising and Other Forms of Solicitation, *and* Ethics Interpretation 502-2, False, Misleading or Deceptive Acts in Advertising or Solicitation, *Code of Professional Conduct.*
12. AICPA, Ethics Interpretation No. 501-3, Failure to Follow Standards and/or Procedures or Other Requirements in Government Audits; *and*, Ethics Interpretation No. 501-5, Failure to Follow Requirements of Governmental Bodies, Commissions, or Other Regulatory Agencies in Performing Attest or Similar Services.
13. AICPA, Ethics Interpretation No. 501-4, Negligence in the Preparation of Financial Statements or Records.
14. AICPA, Rule 301, Confidential Client Information, *Code of Professional Conduct.*
15. *See* Rule 102, *Code of Professional Conduct*, and Interpretation 102-1.
16. *See* Interpretation 102-2: Conflicts of Interest.
17. *See* AICPA, Ethics Interpretation 101-8, Effect on Independence of Financial Interests in Nonclients having Investee Relationships with a Firm's Client.
18. AICPA, Interpretation 101-1.
19. *See* AICPA, Interpretation 101-6, The Effect of Actual or Threatened Litigation on Independence.
20. *See*, AIPCA, Ethics Interpretation 101-2, Former Practitioner and Firm Independence.
21. *See*, AICPA, Ethics Interpretation No. 101-9, The Meaning of Certain Independence Terminology and the Effect of Family Relationships on Independence.
22. 98 Or. App. 497, 779 P.2d 1083 (Ct. App. Ore, 1989).
23. 98 Or. App. at 502, 779 P.2d at 1086.
24. 1 Cal.App. 4th 1263, 230 Cal.App.3d 835, 271 Cal.Rpt.470 (Cal.App.6 Dis., Jul. 20, 1990), *Review Granted and Opinion Superseded by* 274 Cal. Rptr. 371, 798 P.2d 1214 (Cal., Oct. 18, 1990).
25. 1 Cal. App. 4th at 1273, 230 Cal. App. 3d at 845.
26. 1 Cal. App. 4th at 1274, 230 Cal. App. 3d at 847, *quoting* Hagen, Certified Public Accountants' Liability for Malpractice: Effect of Compliance with GAAP and GAAS (1987) 13 J. Contemporary Law 65, 85, 87; *and citing* Cannon, Tax Pressures on Accounting Principles and Accountants' Independence (1952) 27 Accounting Rev. 419, 421, *quoted in* Thor Power Tool Co. v. Commissioner (1979) 439 U.S. 522, 544 fn. 22, 99 S.Ct. 773, 787 fn. 22, 58 L.Ed.2d 785.
27. 1 Cal. App. 4th at 1275, 230 Cal. App. 3d at 847.

28. *See* JOHN KULTGEN, ETHICS AND PROFESSIONALISM (Philadelphia: University of Pennsylvania Press, 1988), p.241.

29. Securities Act Release No. Release No. 33-6695, Release No. 34-24289, Release No. 35-24360, Release No. IC-15655, Release No. IA-1064, 52 FR 11665, 1987 WL 113871 (S.E.C.), [1987] Fed. Sec. L. Rep. (CCH) ¶ 84,122 (Apri. 1, 1989).

30. *Id.*

31. HARRY T. MAGILL & GARY JOHN PREVITS, CPA PROFESSIONAL RESPONSIBILITIES: AN INTRODUCTION (Cincinnati: South-Western Pub. Co., 1991), p.137.

32. *Id.*

33. *Id.*

34. *See, e.g.*, the rules adopted by the Rural Electrification Administration, at 51 F.R. 2788 et seq. (January 21, 1986), and proposed for the SEC, *supra*.

35. Pub. L. 102-242, 105 Stat. 2236-2494 (1991).

36. *Ibid.*

Chapter Thirteen

Confronting Ethical Issues

Issues Addressed by Ethics Rulings
   Responsibilities as Professionals--Confidentiality
   Confidence in the Profession
   Integrity, Objectivity and Independence
   Due Care
Issues Not Addressed by Ethics Rulings
   Serving the Public Interest
Conclusion
Notes

M any of the ethical questions that have confronted accountants over the
years have been addressed by the AICPA's Code of Professional
Conduct, or dealt with in the Interpretations issued by the AICPA ethics
division. Typical fact situations facing accountants have also been presented
in the form of Ethics Rulings. This chapter reviews some of the rulings that
have been issued by the ethics division, and then provides a discussion of
some ethical issues facing accountants but not specifically incorporated into
rulings or other ethics decisions.

ISSUES ADDRESSED BY ETHICS RULINGS

Responsibilities as Professionals--Confidentiality

As noted in the previous chapter, Article I of the Principles section of the
AICPA's Code of Professional Conduct imposes upon accountants the duty
to, among other things, act professionally, and maintain the public
confidence. In part, this is intended to imbue the profession with a sense of
dignity and propriety.

Confidentiality Rulings. An accountant in public practice accumulates very private information about many clients. Some of this information adds to the accountant's general knowledge of business, and enables him or her to serve as a valuable advisor to business enterprises. Other information is industry-specific. But most information pertains to the operations of individual clients.

Often it becomes necessary for accountants to make information available to third parties. Some of that information, of course, is derived from client files and the firm's workpapers. Over the years, it has been necessary for the AICPA's ethics division to examine several dozen situations involving disclosures of some data derived from client files. **Table IV** provides a sampling of a few examples of this type of ethics ruling.

Insider Trading. While not addressed directly in the Code of Professional Responsibility, the problem of insider trading is related to the professional obligation to respect client secrets. When an accountant receives information from (or pertaining to) a publicly held client, the accountant is said to be "entrusted" with that information. That is, the accountant holds the information "in trust," and becomes a fiduciary to the client with regard to that information. As the U.S. Supreme Court pointed out in the case of *Dirks v. S.E.C.*,[1]

> Under certain circumstances, such as where corporate information is revealed legitimately to an underwriter, accountant, lawyer, or consultant working for the corporation, these outsiders may become fiduciaries of the shareholders. The basis for recognizing this fiduciary duty is not simply that such persons acquired nonpublic corporate information, but rather that they have entered into a special confidential relationship in the conduct of the business of the enterprise and are given access to information solely for corporate purposes.[2] When such a person breaches his fiduciary relationship, he may be treated more properly as a tipper than a tippee.[3] For such a duty to be imposed, however, the corporation must expect the outsider to keep the disclosed nonpublic information confidential, and the relationship at least must imply such a duty.[4]

Confidence in the Profession

Professionals benefit when the public holds them in high regard. Some professionals, such as medical doctors, have done a better job of maintaining a good reputation than others, such as attorneys. This does not escape the

Table IV.   Examples of Confidentiality Rulings

No.	Topic of Ruling	OK	Not OK	Comment
1	Using an outside computer firm to process tax returns.	✓		
2	Financial ratio information provided to industry trade groups.	✓		So long as specific client information is not revealed.
3	Information to Successor Accountant about Tax Return Problems	✓		Otherwise clients could CPA-shop as a tax avoidance tactic.
5	Use of a records retention agency to store old CPA workpapers.	✓		Selection of agency should reflect a concern about confidentiality.
7	Revealing names of clients without client permission.	✓		Unless revealing the name implies, e.g., that the client is bankrupt.
15	Use of Results of Earlier MAS Study (for Different Client)	✓		Unless disclosing results alone would reveal confidential information.

notice of professional organizations, who strive to ensure that the profession retains a good public image.

"Dignity" Rulings. Many of the Ethics Rulings issued by the AICPA attempt to limit the mode of advertising, the use of the designation "CPA," the form or content of letterhead, the establishment of franchises, the formation of partnerships between accountants and non-accountants, the conducting of accounting-related businesses (such as actuarial services, computer processing operations, etc.) and other similar matters.[5] Although many of those rulings are issued under the guise of "maintaining the public confidence," their primary objective is the maintenance of a certain level of dignity within the profession.

The FTC Complaint against the AICPA. The public is not always benefitted when professional organizations place restrictions on advertising, commissions, and other similar matters.   The AICPA, in fact, was investigated by the Federal Trade Commission during the late 1980's, and the FTC came to the following conclusions:

- The AICPA is a voluntary association of almost 264,000 CPAs, about three-quarters of the CPAs in the United States. Many AICPA members are in the practice of public accounting and compete among themselves and with other CPAs.
- The AICPA's Code of Professional Conduct was being used to restrain competition among CPAs.
- The AICPA had restricted the methods CPAs could use to set their fees. The AICPA had prohibited CPAs from providing professional services on a contingent fee or commission basis to all persons, including those for whom a CPA is not also performing attest services. An attest service, for purposes of the FTC complaint, meant any of the following: an audit; a review of a financial statement; a compilation of a financial statement when the CPA expects, or reasonably might expect, that a third party would rely on the compilation and the CPA did not disclose a lack of independence; and an examination of prospective financial information.
- AICPA's contingent fee and commission restrictions were harmful to consumers in various ways. For example, the contingent fee rule had prevented CPAs from agreeing to assist State governments to obtain Medicare refunds from the United States Government for no fee if the States receive no refunds. And the AICPA's ban on commissions rule had prevented CPAs from assisting consumers by preparing financial plans for them and then accepting

> payment in the form of commissions only when consumers buy financial products recommended by the CPA.
>
> - The AICPA had restricted CPAs' use of truthful, nondeceptive advertising, including self-laudatory or comparative advertising, testimonial or endorsement advertising, and advertising that AICPA may find not professionally dignified or in good taste. For example, the AICPA's Ethics Interpretations of its advertising rules may have deterred CPAs from advertising that they are "real tax experts," that they offer "the expertise of a large national firm," or that "John Smith says that our firm was particularly responsive to his needs."
> - The AICPA had also restricted CPAs from directly soliciting potential clients and from paying referral fees. These restrictions may have prevented CPAs from soliciting clients by mail and paying marketing firms to refer clients to them.
> - The AICPA had restricted CPAs' use of nondeceptive trade names. For example, AICPA's rules may have prevented CPAs from using trade names such as "Suburban Computer Services" and "Smith and Jones, CPAs, Tax Services" even if such a name truthfully reflects services provided by the CPA.[6]

According to the complaint, the result of these restrictions was a restrained competition among CPAs based on price, quality, and other terms of service; deprivation of consumer information about the availability, price, and quality of CPA services; and deprivation of the benefits of free and open competition among CPAs.

The Consent Agreement. On July 26, 1990, the AICPA and the FTC entered into a Consent Agreement, whereby they agreed that the AICPA, and its members, would cease and desist from:

A. Restricting, regulating, impeding, declaring unethical, advising members against, or interfering with any of the following practices by any CPA:

   1. The offering or rendering of professional services for, or the receipt of, a contingent fee by a CPA, provided that AICPA may prohibit the engaging to render or rendering by a CPA for a contingent fee: (a) of professional services for, or the receipt

of such a fee from, any person for whom the CPA also performs attest services, during the period of the attest services engagement and the period covered by any historical financial statements involved in such attest services; and (b) for the preparation of original or amended tax returns or claims for tax refunds;

2. The offering or rendering of professional services for, or the receipt of, a disclosed commission by a CPA, provided that the engaging to render or rendering of professional services by a CPA for a commission for, or the receipt of a commission from, any person for whom the CPA also performs attest services may be prohibited by the AICPA during the period of the attest services engagement and the period covered by any historical financial statements involved in such attest services;

3. The payment or acceptance of any disclosed referral fee;

4. The solicitation of any potential client by any means, including direct solicitation;

5. Advertising, including, but not limited to:

   a. any self-laudatory or comparative claim;
   b. any testimonial or endorsement; and
   c. any advertisement not considered by AICPA to be professionally dignified or in good taste; and

6. The use of any trade name; PROVIDED THAT

7. Nothing contained in the consent agreement would prohibit AICPA from formulating, adopting, disseminating, and enforcing reasonable ethical guidelines governing the conduct of its members with respect to solicitation, advertising or trade names, including unsubstantiated representations, that AICPA reasonably believes would be false or deceptive within the meaning of Section 5 of the Federal Trade Commission Act;

B. Taking or threatening to take formal or informal disciplinary action, or conducting any investigation or inquiry, applying standards in violation of the consent agreement;

C. Adopting or maintaining any rule, regulation, interpretation, ethical ruling, concept, policy or course of conduct that is in violation of the consent agreement;

D. Inducing, urging, encouraging, or assisting any association of accountants to engage in any act that would violate the consent agreement if done by AICPA provided, however, that nothing in the consent agreement would prohibit AICPA from soliciting action by any federal, state or local governmental entity; and

E. Applying or interpreting any other language contained in the Code of Professional Conduct or its successors in a manner that would violate the consent agreement; PROVIDED THAT

F. The consent agreement does not prohibit the AICPA from:

1. suspending membership in AICPA if:

   a. a member's certificate as a CPA or license or permit to practice as such or to practice public accounting is suspended as a disciplinary measure by any governmental entity;

   b. a member's registration as an investment adviser is suspended by the SEC;

   c. a member's registration as a broker-dealer is suspended by the SEC or by any state agency acting pursuant to any applicable state law or regulation relating to the issuance, registration, purchase or sale of securities; or

   d. a member is suspended from practicing before the IRS, but any such suspension by AICPA shall terminate upon reinstatement of any such certificate, license, permit, registration, or authorization to practice; or

2. terminating membership in AICPA if:

   a. a member's certificate as a CPA or license or permit to practice as such or to practice

public accounting is revoked, withdrawn or
canceled as a disciplinary measure by any
governmental entity;

b. a member's registration as an investment
    adviser is revoked by the SEC;

c. a members's registration as a
    broker-dealer is revoked by the SEC or by
    any state agency acting pursuant to any
    applicable state law or regulation relating
    to the issuance, registration, purchase or
    sale of securities;

d. a member is subject to a final judgment of
    conviction for criminal fraud or for a
    crime punishable by imprisonment for
    more than one year; or

e. a member is disbarred from practicing
    before the IRS.[7]

The Consent Agreement allows the AICPA to continue to monitor and
restrict the activities of its members in three respects:

A. The AICPA can prohibit CPAs from providing audit and
    other attest services for a contingent fee or commission to
    clients for whom they have provided non-attest services.

B. The AICPA can prohibit CPAs from receiving commissions
    from their audit or other attest clients.

C. The AICPA can prohibit CPAs from accepting contingent
    fees for preparing tax returns or tax-refund claims.[8]

Shareholder Disagreement. The FTC acted on behalf of the public in
precluding the prohibition of contingent fees by the accounting profession.
But in a national study of the attitudes of corporate shareholders toward
corporate annual reports and auditors, shareholders were asked their views
toward contingent fees.[9] Shareholders were asked whether "aiding in
acquisition or sale of subsidiaries based on contingent fees if offered to a
client by an accounting firm would cause a conflict of interest that would
compromise the accounting firm's independence and thus should be
prohibited." Nearly two-thirds of the respondents expressed a preference for
the prohibition of contingent fees by auditors. The shareholders voiced clear
disagreement with the position taken by the FTC.[10]

Table V.   Examples of Ethics Rulings on Independence, Integrity, and Objectivity

No.	Topic of Ruling	OK	Not OK	Comment
1	Acceptance of a gift from a client	✓		Unless the gift is more than a token.
2	Membership in an association that is a client	✓		Unless membership is equivalent to "management."
4	Payment of payroll for client, with reimbursement		✓	Ethics Interpretation 101-3 covers this situation.
6	CPA's spouse is client's bookkeeper	✓		Unless spouse is a "manager" at client.
9	Client-debtor asks CPA to serve on creditor's committee.		✓	Cosigning checks, deciding on expenses destroys independence.
10	CPA sits on legislative council of city that is a client.		✓	CPA is overseeing management of city, even if city manager is elected.
11	CPA is named trustee of client's inter vivos trust.	✓		Even if trust holds stock of audited business, trustee role is future.
12	CPA is on board of charity/recipient of client's estate.		✓	Conflict of interest between charity and client's estate.
17	CPA is a "capital account holder" of a country club.	✓		Unless CPA sits on governing board (or manages in some way).
31	CPA audits co-op apartment where he or she lives.		✓	CPA's ownership of a co-op share creates a conflict of interest.
77	CPA is considering employment with audit client.		✓	CPA should formally reject the offer, or else withdraw from the audit.

AICPA Membership Disagreement. Shareholders are not the only persons opposed to the FTC ban on contingent fees. Even though the AICPA has entered into the consent agreement with the FTC, the ruling council of the AICPA has decided to initiate a lobbying campaign to have commissions and contingent fees outlawed by statute at the state level.[11] The consent agreement can be overridden by state law, and the AICPA has set out to accomplish this.

Integrity, Objectivity and Independence

Article III of the Principles section of the AICPA's Code of Professional Conduct calls for the performance of accounting services with the "highest sense of integrity." Article IV, in addition, requires that accountants maintain their objectivity and their independence with regard to their work, especially if the work involves financial audits.

Ethics Rulings. The subjects of independence and objectivity have received a great deal of attention over the years. As accountants have been called upon to provide a variety of ancillary services to their clients, they have had to examine whether a multiple of relationships with the same client would render them (or appear to render them) incapable of giving an objective opinion as to the fairness of the clients' financial statements. **Table V** provides a sampling of the ethics rulings issued by the AICPA in this area. Over fifty such rulings have been issued over the years, and most are still in effect. The AICPA continues to issue several rulings each year on this subject.

Due Care

Article V of the Principles section of the Code of Professional Conduct requires adherence to the profession's technical and ethical standards. In the previous chapter, this requirement was discussed at length.

Ethics Rulings. The AICPA has only issued a handful of ethics rulings on the subject of due care, several of which relate to situations involving an accountant who is not in a position to issue an audit opinion due to a lack of independence. **Table VI** summarizes those opinions that fall outside of the independent/not-independent issue.

Table VI.   **Examples of Ethics Rulings on General and Technical Standards**

No.	Topic of Ruling	OK	Not OK	Comment
4	Audit in 2nd year of engagement: opinion on 2-year statements?	✓		Audit procedures can verify prior year information.
6	Gratis compilation for private club: CPA letterhead?	✓		Better to use club letterhead, show CPA's treasurer status.
7	"CPA" used with signature for non-CPA (business) partnership.	✓		Avoid impression that partnership is a CPA firm.
9	CPA hires technical specialists on MAS engagement.	✓		CPA must be able to evaluate, if not duplicate, specialist services.

ISSUES NOT ADDRESSED BY ETHICS RULINGS

Serving the Public Interest

Noticeably absent from the list of ethics rulings are those that relate to an accountant's duty to the public. Some rulings, such as some of the confidentiality rulings and dignity rulings discussed above, deal with transactions that could conceivably bring injury to a client or other party, such as by disclosing trade secrets or misleading someone with regard to the role of the accountant in a partnership or business venture.

Little guidance, however, is offered to assist the client in sorting out his or her respective responsibilities to the general public, to a client, and to other parties.

Whistle-Blowing. If an accountant discovers a fraud in connection with a client's financial records, what is his or her obligation to disclose that fraud to potential investors, creditors, or other users of the client's financial statements? The answer to this question depends, in part, on whether the client's financial statements have been issued, and whether the accountant has been associated with those financial statements.

If the accountant has not been engaged to issue an audit report, or to make some other attestation in regard to the client's financial statements, the accountant is not under a legal duty to broadcast its finding of fraud. This was pointed out in the case of *Farlow v. Peat, Marwick, Mitchell & Co.*,[12] when the court reviewed the RICO claims and other claims of some investors. The investors sued the accounting firm, in part claiming that the accounting firm had a duty under Section 10(b) of the Securities Exchange Act of 1934,[13] and, in particular, Securities and Exchange Commission Rule 10b-5,[14] to reveal the existence of fraud to anyone who might buy the client's stock.

Section 10(b) of the Securities Exchange Act of 1934, provides that it is unlawful:

> To use or employ, in connection with the purchase or sale of any security. . . any manipulative or deceptive device or contrivance in contravention of such rules and regulations as the Commission may prescribe as necessary or appropriate in the public interest or for the protection of investors.

Rule 10b(5), in turn, covering the "Employment of manipulative and deceptive devices," provides in pertinent part that:

> It shall be unlawful for any person, directly or indirectly, by the use of any means or instrumentality of interstate commerce, or of the mails, or of any facility of any national securities exchange,
>
> A. To employ any device, scheme, or artifice to defraud,
> B. To make any untrue statement of a material fact or to omit to state a material fact necessary in order to make the statements made, in the light of the circumstances under which they were made, not misleading, or
> C. To engage in any act, practice, or course of business which operates or would operate as a fraud or deceit upon any person, in connection with the purchase or sale of any security.

The court in the *Farlow* case concluded that even if the accounting firm know of the existence of fraud, the firm did not automatically have a duty to broadcast that fact to all potential investors. The court observed that the plaintiff/investors' theory of whistleblower liability:

> . . . severs accountants' liability from the making of representations. Under it [the accountants] would be liable to the plaintiffs even if it had never issued an audit report. Rule 10b-5 does not reach frauds that involve no misrepresentations or misleading omissions . . . and the particular theory pressed here has no basis that we know of in the common law. It is not the law that whenever an accountant discovers that his or her client is in financial trouble he must blow the whistle on the client for the protection of investors-- so that (the accountants) should have taken out an advertisement in the *Wall Street Journal* stating that it had just discovered that its client . . . was losing money, rather than waiting to report this in the next audit report. That would be an extreme theory of accountants' liability, and it is one we decline to embrace as an interpretation of the common law of Illinois, having in previous cases specifically rejected it as a possible theory of Rule 10b-5 aider and abettor liability.[15]

In the *Farlow* case, the accounting firm was not associated with the financial statements of the limited partnership into which the plaintiffs had invested. Therefore, the court ruled that the accounting firm did not have a legal duty to disclose fraud, even if the accounting firm had become aware of the fraud. Other courts have also consistently applied this rule to accountants who do not disclose damaging financial information about a client to a potential third party investor or purchaser.[16]

And even if an accountant has been engaged to conduct an audit, he or she is not legally required to announce publicly a client's financial problems as soon as those problems are discovered. The reasoning behind this policy is as follows:

> Such a duty would prevent the client from reposing in the accountant the trust that is essential to an accurate audit. Firms would withhold documents, allow auditors to see but not copy, and otherwise emulate the CIA, if they feared that access might lead to destructive disclosure--for even an honest firm may fear that one of its accountant's many auditors would misunderstand the situation and ring the tocsin needlessly, with great loss to the firm.[17]

Employee-Accountants.   Employee-accountants are apparently not expected by the courts to disclose information pertaining to wrongdoing by their employer.[18]   The case of *Murphy v. American Home Products Corp.*[19] demonstrates this principle. There, the plaintiff, Murphy, was first employed by defendant, American Home Products Corp., in 1957.

He thereafter served in various accounting positions, eventually attaining the office of assistant treasurer, but he never had a formal contract of employment.   On April 18, 1980, when he was 59 years old, he was discharged. The plaintiff claimed that he was fired for two reasons:

> First, because of his disclosure to top management of alleged accounting improprieties on the part of corporate personnel and because of his age. As to this first ground, the plaintiff asserted that his firing was in retaliation for his revelation to officers and directors of defendant corporation that he had uncovered at least $50 million in illegal account manipulations of secret pension reserves which improperly inflated the company's growth in income and allowed high-ranking officers to reap unwarranted bonuses from a management incentive plan, as well as in retaliation for his own refusal to engage in the alleged accounting improprieties. He contended that the company's internal regulations required him to make the disclosure that he did. He also alleged that his termination was carried out in a humiliating manner.
> Second, the plaintiff claims that defendant's top financial officer told him on various occasions that he wished he could fire plaintiff but that, because to do so would be illegal due to plaintiff's age, he would make sure by confining him to routine work that plaintiff did not advance in the company.   Plaintiff also asserts that a contributing factor to his dismissal was that he was over 50 years of age.

The *Murphy* court refused to grant the accountant any relief. The state in which the *Murphy* case arose had no whistleblower statute granting the plaintiff-accountant a cause of action, and the court refused to find a common law cause of action. As a result, the plaintiff received nothing in exchange for his good effort.

SAS 53 and SAS 54. Two AICPA auditing pronouncements have an impact on an accountant's whistle-blowing obligations. *Statement on Auditing Standards (SAS) No. 53, The Auditor's Responsibility to Detect and Report Errors and Irregularities*, provides guidance on the independent auditor's responsibility for the detection of errors and irregularities in an audit of financial statements in accordance with generally accepted auditing standards, as well as for the communication of those errors and irregularities both within and outside the entity whose financial statements are under audit.

The term "irregularities," as used in *SAS 53*, refers to intentional misstatements or omissions of amounts or disclosures in financial statements. Irregularities include fraudulent financial reporting undertaken to render financial statements misleading, sometimes called management fraud, and misappropriation of assets, sometimes called defalcations. Irregularities may involve acts such as the following:

- Manipulation, falsification, or alteration of accounting records or supporting documents from which financial statements are prepared; or
- Misrepresentation or intentional omission of events, transactions, or other significant information; or
- Intentional misapplication of accounting principles relating to amounts, classification, manner of presentation, or disclosure.

Statement on Auditing Standards No. 54, Illegal Acts By Clients, in turn, prescribes the nature and extent of the consideration an independent auditor should give to the possibility of illegal acts by a client in an audit of financial statements in accordance with generally accepted auditing standards, provides guidance on the auditor's responsibilities when a possible illegal act is detected.

Neither *SAS* constitutes a "whistleblowing" directive. In the event a fraudulent transaction or other irregularity is discovered during an audit, *SAS 53* provides for two possible courses of action, depending on the materiality of the irregularity discovered, as follows:

A. If the auditor has determined that an audit adjustment is, or may be, an irregularity, but has also determined that the effect on the financial statements could not be material, the auditor should--

   1. Refer the matter to an appropriate level of management that is at least one level above those involved.
   2. Be satisfied that, in view of the organizational position of the likely perpetrator, implications for other aspects of the audit have been adequately considered.

    a. For example, irregularities involving misappropriation of cash from a small imprest fund would normally be of little significance because both the manner of operating the fund and its size would tend to establish a limit on the amount of loss and the custodianship of such a fund is normally entrusted to a relatively low-level employee.

B. If, on the other hand, the auditor has determined that an audit adjustment is, or may be, an irregularity and has either determined that the effect could be material or has been unable to evaluate potential materiality, the auditor should --

    1. Consider the implications for other aspects of the audit.

    2. Discuss the matter and the approach to further investigation with an appropriate level of management that is at least one level above those involved.

    3. Attempt to obtain sufficient competent evidential matter to determine whether, in fact, material irregularities exist and, if so, their effect.

    4. If appropriate, suggest that the client consult with legal counsel on matters concerning questions of law.[20]

Any fraudulent transaction involving stealing, embezzlement, or the like, is an illegal act. Illegal acts such as embezzlement are covered by *SAS 54* as well as *SAS 53*. But *SAS 54* does not require the auditor to report the matter to the police or other authorities. Instead, *SAS 54* provides as follows:

The auditor should assure himself that the audit committee, or others with equivalent authority and responsibility, is adequately informed with respect to illegal acts that come to the auditor's attention.[21] The auditor need not communicate matters that are clearly inconsequential and may reach agreement in advance with the audit committee on the nature of such matters to be communicated. The communication should describe the act, the circumstances of its occurrence, and the effect on the financial

In today's accounting environment, staying up to date on the latest issues in legal liability is critical to maintaining your edge.

Business One Irwin intends to publish an annual supplement to *The Accountant's Guide to Legal Liability and Ethics* to keep you informed of any developments that may affect your practice.

The paperback supplement will contain the most current information that surrounds legal liability and ethics for the professional accountant.

Please complete this card and mail it to Business One Irwin. When the supplement is published in 1994, you will automatically receive your copy. You will be billed $29.95 plus shipping, handling, and sales taxes upon receipt.

---

business**One**
IRWIN

1818 Ridge Road
Homewood, Illinois 60430-1795

❑ Yes! Please send me the annual supplement to *The Accountant's Guide to Legal Liability and Ethics.* I understand I will be billed $29.95 plus shipping, handling, and sales taxes upon receipt.

Name _____

Title _____

Company _____

Address_____

City, State, Zip _____

Phone (_____) _____

statements. Senior management may wish to have its remedial actions communicated to the audit committee simultaneously. Possible remedial actions include disciplinary action against involved personnel, seeking restitution, adoption of preventive or corrective company policies, and modifications of specific control procedures. If senior management is involved in an illegal act, the auditor should communicate directly with the audit committee. The communication may be oral or written. If the communication is oral, the auditor should document it.[22]

Do *SAS 53* and *SAS 54* serve the public interest? If there is no legal duty to disclose, and no professional duty (according to *SAS 53* and *SAS 54*, does that mean that the accountant is never a whistleblower? The lofty public-service language of the Code of Professional Conduct appears to have no role in this area. However, there will be situations involving the discovery of crimes and other serious problems, and the accountant will not be able to ignore them under the guise of maintaining client confidentiality.

CONCLUSION

Despite the accounting profession's *Code of Professional Conduct*, which places the public's interest ahead of the accountant's interests, the resolution of conflicts between an accountant's client, on the one hand, and the general public, on the other, is usually balanced in favor of the client. The legal system supports this outcome, at least for the time being.

NOTES

1. 463 U.S. 646, 103 S.CT. 3255, 77 L.Ed.2d 911, Fed. Sec. L. Rep.¶ 99,255 (1983).
2. *See* SEC v. Monarch Fund, 608 F.2d 938, 942 (2nd Cir. 1979); In re Investors Management Co., 44 S.E.C. 633, 645 (1971); In re Van Alystne, Noel & Co., 43 S.E.C. 1080, 1084-1085 (1969); In re Merrill Lynch, Pierce, Fenner & Smith, Inc., 43 S.E.C. 933, 937 (1968); Cady, Roberts, 40 S.E.C., at 912.
3. *See* Shapiro v. Merrill Lynch, Pierce, Fenner & Smith, Inc., 495 F.2d 228, 237 (2nd Cir. 1974) (investment banker had access to material information when working on a proposed public offering for the corporation).
4. 463 U.S. at 655, 103 S.Ct. at 3232, n.14.
5. See AICPA, Ethics Rulings issued pursuant to Rule 501 and 502.
6. FTC, Proposed Consent Agreement (Appendix A, Announcement), File No. 851 0020, 54 Fed.Reg. 13529 (April 4, 1989).
7. FTC Consent Agreement, *Journal of Accountancy*, October, 1990, p. 36. *See also* Docket No. C-3297, 55 Fed.Reg. 40944 (October 5, 1990).
8. *Id.*

9. *See* MARC J. EPSTEIN & MOSES I. PAVA, THE SHAREHOLDERS USE OF CORPORATE ANNUAL REPORTS (Greenwich, Ct: JAI Press, Inc., 1992).

10. *Ibid.*

11. *See* Lee Berton, "Accountants Aim to Uphold Commission Bar," *Wall Street Journal*, October 28, 1991, p.A16.

12. 956 F.2d 982 (10th Cir. 1992).

13. 15 U.S.C.S. 78j(b) (1992).

14. 17 C.F.R. 240-10b-5.

15. *Citing* Barker v. Henderson, Franklin, Starnes & Holt, 797 F.2d 490, 496 (7th Cir.1986) *and* LHLC Corp. v. Cluett, Peabody & Co., 842 F.2d 928, 932-33 (7th Cir. 1988). "When the problem consists in keeping silence while the primary violator carries out the fraud, the plaintiff must show that the silent person had a legal duty to speak" LHLC Corp. v. Cluett, Peabody & Co., Inc., *supra*, 842 F.2d at 932.

16. *See, e.g.*, Schatz v. Rosenberg, 943 F.2D 485 (4th Cir. 1991); DiLeo v. Ernst & Young, 901 F.2d 624 (7th Cir.) (accountant under no legal duty to blow the whistle on client upon discovery that client in financial trouble), cert. denied, --- U.S. ----, 111 S.Ct. 347, 112 L.Ed.2d 312 (1990); Latigo Ventures v. Laventhol & Horwath, 876 F.2d 1322, 1327 (7th Cir.1989) (accountant has no duty to blow the whistle on client in order to protect investors); LHLC Corp. v. Cluett, Peabody & Co., 842 F.2d 928, 933 (7th Cir.) (accountant under no duty to disclose client's fraud to potential investor), cert. denied, 488 U.S. 926, 109 S.Ct. 311, 102 L.Ed.2d 329 (1988); Windon Third Oil & Gas Drilling Partnership v. Federal Deposit Ins. Corp., 805 F.2d 342, 347 (10th Cir.1986) (absent fiduciary relationship, accountant had no duty to disclose information about corporation's financial condition during discussions with potential investor), cert. denied, 480 U.S. 947, 107 S.Ct. 1605, 94 L.Ed.2d 791 (1987); Leoni v. Rogers, 719 F.Supp. 555, 566 (E.D.Mich.1989) (accounting firm owed no duty of disclosure to potential investor of client as long as accountant had no fiduciary relationship with investor); Hudson v. Capital Management Int'l, Inc., 565 F. Supp. 615, 623 (N.D. Cal. 1983) (The professional and underwriting defendants who may have known, or were reckless in not knowing, of certain aspects of the fraud did not aid and abet it by failing to disclose this information to the investing public, since they did not owe plaintiffs a duty to disclose any knowledge of the fraud and therefore they cannot be liable for mere failure to 'whistleblow.').

17. DiLeo v. Ernst & Young, 901 F.2d 624, 629 (7th Cir.), cert. denied, --- U.S. ----, 111 S.Ct. 347, 112 L.Ed.2d 312 (1990) (Accountant under no legal duty to blow whistle on client upon discovery that client was in financial trouble).

18. *See* G.H. Lander, Michael T. Cronin, & Alan Reinstein, Reduced Liability for the Management Accountant, 68 U.Det. Mercy L. Rev. 1 (1990).

19. 58 N.Y.2D 293, 461 N.Y.S.2D 232, 448 N.E.2D 86 (Ct. App. N.Y., 1983).

20. AICPA, *Statement on Auditing Standards No. 53, The Auditor's Responsibility to Detect and Report Errors and Irregularities.*

21. For entities that do not have audit committees, the phrase "others with equivalent authority and responsibility" may include the board of directors, the board of trustees, or the owner in owner-managed entities.

22. AICPA, *Statement on Auditing Standards No. 54, Illegal Acts by Clients.*

A New Direction

H ow can an accountant provide valuable services to a client without becoming an easy target for a lawsuit filed by the client (or any number of possible third parties)? This chapter suggests some approaches to this intractable problem.

THE BUSINESS PLAN

The first question that could be asked is, "What kind of business am I in?" Accountants accustomed to providing business planning assistance to clients will be familiar with the importance of this question.

But just as the proverbial cobbler's children often go barefoot, the accountant has often not given sufficient thought to business planning.

Some might answer the above question in terms of "national firm" versus regional or local firm. Others might look to the revenues earned in such traditional functions as auditing, tax services, and consulting.

But the question asks for more than an analysis of one's place in the industry, or the functions performed. It asks for an assessment of the type of professional one seeks to be, and the level of professionalism that one strives toward.

Responding to Price Pressures. The printing industry operates by an old saying that states, "We can provide: (a) low price; (b) speed (or convenience); and (c) high quality. Pick two."

Accountants face a similar dilemma. Some accountants strive to provide excellent professional service in a timely manner. To accomplish this, they must carry a large staff of employees, and must be able to continually win large projects that utilize their staff throughout the year. But this requires a fee structure that will accommodate a large, well-managed organization.

Other accountants provide excellent service, and do so with relatively low overhead. Partners in their firm are adept at a variety of functions, and staff are also trained to serve clients in various ways. But with a lower cost operation comes a drawback: clients who can wait, are served well; those clients who are in a hurry for the accountant's work product are not well satisfied.

A third type of operation provides quick service at a low fee. But this type of accounting practice cannot (or should not) accommodate audit engagements, sophisticated tax consulting engagements, or complex consulting engagements. Instead, the operation must focus primarily on compilation services and tax compliance services.

Toward professionalism. The third type of accounting practice, described above, generally does not respond to the demands of today's legal and regulatory system, for the following reasons:

1. GAAP and GAAS, even for a "write-up" practice, are becoming more complex. As discussed at Chapter Two, courts are not accepting an accountant's broad disclaimer of disclosure, even in the case of a compilation. Many firms have developed plans of work that cover the simplest accounting project. These procedures might seem cumbersome, but they constitute the most inexpensive and most efficient form of risk management for those firms.
2. If a client, creditor or other party relies upon the accountant's work product (including a compilation), courts will not excuse the accountant for failing to disclose a problem about which the accountant knew or should have known, even if GAAP and GAAS do not require the disclosure. The accountant is not afforded the luxury of "quick and dirty" compilations, as discussed in Chapter Two.
3. The increasing number and types of preparer penalties imposed by the IRS on accountants are designed to require preparers to be more careful. Again, tax returns assembled with minimal thought about required disclosure, or with

minimal concern about the prevailing laws pertaining to the items on the returns, are no longer safe.

Raising fees. If an emphasis on quality, as exemplified by the first and second types of accounting operations described above, is required by today's legal and regulatory environment, does that emphasis translate directly into a higher fees structure for clients of accounting firms? Probably.

The cost of the litigation described in must be born by someone. If the profession is to be saddled with the kinds of lawsuits and damage awards described at the outset of this work, then those costs must be reflected in higher malpractice insurance premiums, and/or higher standards of performance.

Professionalism, as defined in terms of excellence, does not always accommodate a low-cost, high volume operation. It is true that a well managed practice can result in competitive pricing. But the efficiencies obtained by computerization, management proficiency, and similar endeavors must always accommodate the standards established by the profession and the courts.

Clients will ultimately choose between the (more expensive) higher quality of services provided by accountants who strive to meet the higher standards of performance imposed by the profession and by the courts, or the (less expensive) below-standard services of those who do not. But accountants, especially certified public accountants, who attempt to remain in the latter group will not necessarily be immune from damage awards by a judicial system insistent upon imposing its expectations upon all professional accountants.

For those accountants who choose to provide services at the level of excellence prescribed by GAAS and GAAP, and by the courts, it will be necessary to "sell" higher quality (and higher priced) services to clients. To succeed, the advantages to the client must be considered and promoted.

THE CLIENT

Of course, it is not only the client who chooses. The accountant must also target and select its clientele.

Before the accountant accepts an engagement, he or she should ascertain by one means or another the reputation, and financial stability of the client. This is one way to exercise preventive litigation. A client may be suspect from the very beginning, and a bad situation could be avoided by the accountant not accepting the engagement.

The *Codification of Statements on Auditing Standards* provides the following considerations as to the accountant's quality control policies and procedures pertaining to clients:

> .19 *Acceptance and Continuance of Clients. Policies and procedures should be established for deciding whether to accept or continue a client in order to minimize the likelihood of association with a client whose management lacks integrity.* Suggesting that there should be procedures for this purpose does not imply that an auditor vouches for the integrity or reliability of a client, nor does it imply that an auditor has a duty to anyone but himself with respect to the acceptance, rejection, or retention of clients. However, prudence suggests that an auditor be selective in determining his professional relationships. [Emphasis in original.]
>
> .20 *Examples of policies and procedure.* In pursuing its quality control objectives with respect to the acceptance and continuance of clients, a firm may use policies and procedures such as reviewing financial statements of a proposed client; inquiring of third parties, such as the proposed client's previous auditors, its banks, legal counsel, and investment bankers, and others in the financial and business community as to the reputation of the proposed client; evaluating its ability to service the client properly... with particular reference to industry expertise, size of engagement, and manpower available to staff the engagement; and periodically reevaluating clients for continuance.

Even after the accountant has been engaged, he or she may find that the client's methods, practices, and internal control (if performing an audit) create a substantially high risk of potential problems for the accountant. By terminating such a relationship, the accountant might be losing a client, but avoiding legal complications.

Engagement Contracts

Accountants who perform services for clients without written agreements specifying in detail the terms of the engagement are gambling. The minimization of one's liability is accomplished minimizing one's exposure to liability. Engagement contracts are primary to minimizing exposure to liability by defining the scope, nature, and limits of the services to be performed. For example, a client may have orally employed an accountant to do write-up work which was performed with great care. Months later, a court may find that the services performed by the accountant were adequate for write-up work, but that the engagement called for an audit which was performed negligently or not at all.

The engagement contract also serves another purpose. It gives the accountant an opportunity to analyze whether he or she definitely possesses the skills called upon to perform the services delineated in the agreement. It is true that certification of a public accountant indicates the attainment of a certain level of proficiency. And it is also true that a system of continuing education is directed toward maintaining that proficiency. However, an accountant should realize that in order to keep his or her skills sharp, they must be practiced. And with the broad range of possible accounting services offered by the profession, the accountant might find that his or her practice does not even begin to involve the same broad range of services. An accountant who directs most of his or her practice toward tax work might not possess the same level of proficiency in performing an occasional audit if he or she is not up to date on current applications of statistical sampling and electronic data processing, and vice versa. For example, the first general standard of auditing states that "[t]he examination is to be performed by a person or persons having adequate technical training and proficiency as an auditor."

Only the accountant can accurately judge the level of his or her own proficiency. He or she should not be misled by the credentials he or she holds. Such credentials will not relieve the accountant of moral and legal responsibilities. He or she will be held accountable to perform up to a requisite level of proficiency regardless of what level he or she actually possesses.

There is another aspect which should be considered in formulating the engagement contract. All too often, such agreements specify the services to be performed, but do not explain what will not be performed. This may lead to the potentially adverse result of the client thinking he or she is receiving more than will actually be received. Probably the most common example of this situation is when a client engages an accountant to perform an audit and expects any fraud or defalcation to be discovered. Though such detection is not the purpose of an ordinary audit, it is the client's expectations with which the accountant must contend. It is such expectations, whether or not justified, that give rise to litigation by the client and, in some cases, by third parties. An effective engagement contract should not leave anything to the imagination, and indicating significant limitations on the services to be performed helps to do just that.

Documentary Evidence

When an accountant is named as the defendant in a liability suit in the performance of an audit, all that he or she has to fall back on in the way of evidence are audit working papers.

They represent the only substantial documentary evidence as to what he or she did, how it was done, and when it was done. Working papers should be so complete and organized that a judge or members of a jury can trace the accountant's steps from beginning to end and be left with no doubt as to the quality and scope of the work performed which led to the conclusions reached. There is probably no other way to prove that an examination of the client's financial statements was made in accordance with generally accepted auditing standards. And, of course, the weaker the audit papers, the weaker ultimately is the accountant's defense. The following guidelines for quantity, types, and content of working papers are recommended by the *Codification of Statements on Auditing Standards*:

a. Data sufficient to demonstrate that the financial statements or other information upon which the auditor is reporting were in agreement with (or reconciled with) the client's records.

b. That the engagement had been planned, such as by use of work programs, and that the work of any assistants had been supervised and reviewed, indicating observance of the first standard of field work.

c. That the client's system of internal control had been reviewed and evaluated in determining the extent of the tests to which auditing procedures were restricted, indicating observance of the second standard of field work.

d. The auditing procedures followed and testing performed in obtaining evidential matter, indicating observance of the third standard of field work. The record in these respects may take various forms, including memoranda, check lists, work programs, and schedules, and would generally permit reasonable identification of the work done by the auditor.

e. How exceptions and unusual matters, if any, disclosed by the independent auditor's procedures were resolved or treated.

f. Appropriate commentaries prepared by the auditor indicating his or her conclusions concerning significant aspects of the engagement.

Almost equally important is the preparation of an effective audit program. From an audit point of view, it serves as a valuable planning device. From a legal point of view, it serves a very persuasive evidentiary purpose. Whether the audit program is developed from a standard program or is completely developed from new, the audit program affords the trier of fact the opportunity to examine the procedures utilized based on the particular situation involved.

WHEN A PROBLEM FIRST ARISES

The best intentions, and even the highest standards of excellence, will not keep every client happy at all times. And clients usually telegraph their unhappiness by refusing to timely pay an invoice.

When the accountant performs work for a client and that client refuses to pay the accountant's fee, the first inclination will probably be to sue the client. Certainly it is every citizen's right to seek legal redress when that citizen has been wronged. And, of course, a public accountant has the right to expect nothing else.

However, the accountant should be aware of the possible ramifications to be incurred for following such a course of action. When an accountant sues a client for his or her fee, the accountant can often expect the client to turn around and sue him or her for negligence. Almost all of these counterclaims turn out to be annoyance suits and are ultimately either settled or lost by the client in court, but at a great expense to the accountant or his or her insurer, not to mention the adverse effect on the accountant's professional reputation. Insurance companies report that a significant number of claims against accountants are of this type.

Does this mean that the accountant should do nothing if the client refuses to pay? The answer might be yes, depending upon the locality, if the engagement involves tax services and the client uses the unauthorized-practice-of-law defense. Otherwise, the answer will be a definite "maybe" or an "it depends." The accountant is the only one who can weigh the advantages and the disadvantages (i.e., the size of the fee versus the expense, the time, and the aggravation of possible litigation brought by the accountant, assuming of course that the client's claim is not legitimate; if the client's claim is valid, then that presents an entirely different matter, one in which the accountant should have no difficulty deciding what to do about his or her fee).

Fortunately, the failure to pay the accountant's fee can often be traced to a sincere misunderstanding between the parties. For example, the accountant may have performed services that the client did not ask for and therefore does not feel he or she should be charged. Or the client may have intended to pay the accountant in stock rather than money. What this all adds up to is the need for an effective engagement contract. It has been stated before in this chapter, but it bears repeating. Regardless with whom you are dealing, nothing should be performed until there is a concise and clear agreement in writing which defines the scope of the services to be performed and is signed by both parties.

In any event, the accountant should always do everything possible to ascertain the reason for non-payment, and then attempt to come to some mutually acceptable agreement.

COMMON FACTORS THAT LEAD TO LAWSUITS

It may or may not have become apparent that the outcome of legal cases involving accountant liability are not very predictable. However, there are least some common factors in the long line of cases which seem to occur repeatedly. Two such factors are client insolvency and the client's internal control.

Insolvency. Many of the reported cases have been the result of litigation initiated, especially by third parties, after the client became bankrupt or insolvent. In other words, such parties as banks, creditors and investors incurred significant losses because the accountant's client was unable to continue as a going concern and thereby meet its financial obligations.

When a client has been operating at a loss the last few years, or is need of outside capital through loans or other sources, a red warning light should go on for the accountant. What if such financing is unavailable? What if the client continues to operate at a loss? What if the client ultimately becomes insolvent? Is the accountant taking on a lawsuit?

The accountant should keep in mind that his or her primary obligation is to ensure full and complete disclosures in order to avoid misleading the public. Thus, if a client's financial condition seems to be questionable, the accountant cannot afford to overlook this and should consider rendering a qualified opinion.

Internal Control. Many of the reported cases have made reference to the absence of a study and evaluation of internal control in compliance with generally accepted auditing standards. The internal control primarily refers to accounting control. Such study and evaluation is intended to establish a basis for reliance on the internal control in order to determine the nature, extent, and timing of substantive audit tests to be applied in the examination of the financial statements.

There is no requirement that the auditor must rely upon the client's internal control. In fact, sometimes the internal control is so weak that very little reliance can be made on the client's results. Or maybe the auditor might determine that the effort to test compliance will exceed the reduction in substantive testing effort resulting from such reliance. Of course, if internal control is too weak, the auditor may be unable to express a favorable opinion. However, there must be a review of the client's system of internal control unless there is a 100 percent verification of transactions.

The review of the client's system of internal control involves obtaining information about the client's prescribed procedures and methods. Various means of obtaining such information include discussions with personnel of the client, observation, and examination of such documentation as flow charts, organization charts with job descriptions, and procedure manuals. All information obtained should be recorded by the auditor in some manner. It may be in the form of narrative memoranda, flow charts, or answers to internal control questionnaires. The questionnaire can be a very effective tool for the auditor. Not only is it useful in reviewing the client's system, but is also of value in testing for compliance that the prescribed procedures are actually in use and are satisfactorily obtaining the planned results.

As previously mentioned, tests for compliance are not necessary unless the prescribed procedures are being relied upon to reduce the substantive audit work. If relied upon, compliance testing is intended to provide a reasonable assurance that the procedures are in use and are being applied as prescribed. From such tests, the auditor determines the nature, timing or extent of the substantive tests to be utilized in completing the audit.

One of the most common weaknesses in internal control is the failure to provide segregation of responsibilities. Many cases of employee embezzlement and defalcations have resulted, and continued undetected because one individual performed significantly all phases of a single transaction. Such a situation affords the employee an opportunity to perpetrate the fraud and then to conceal it. This is a definite legal liability area for the accountant, especially in small business where employees frequently handle more than one responsibility. Failure to discover this high relative risk area because of an inadequate review of internal control has dangerous possibilities for the accountant.

A NEW DIRECTION

The courts have expressed a variety of views regarding the standards to be used in measuring the accountant's exercise of reasonable care: the *Continental Vending* case--compliance with generally accepted accounting principles is not a conclusive defense to criminal fraud; the *Herzfeld* case-- compliance with generally accepted accounting principles does not conclusively shield the accountant in civil cases; the *Bloch* case--AICPA standards fix the existing and accepted standards of the profession; the *BarChris* case--accountants should not be held to a higher standard of care than that recognized in the profession.

If it were possible to reconcile these statements into one single thought, it would go something like this:

Compliance with generally accepted accounting procedures and generally accepted auditing standards will not *conclusively* shield the accountant from legal liability; rather they are a starting point, a

minimum level of acceptable performance to be applied with good judgment and due diligence so as to avoid misleading the public. Nothing so vital to the protection of society can ever be *conclusive*, meaning uncontestable, indisputable and absolute. Justice cannot permit it, not when the needs and expectations of society are continually changing.

However, if the public accountant is genuinely satisfied that he or she has complied with the standards established by his or her profession as the minimum level of care and has made adequate disclosures necessary to inform the public, then, at least for as long as the profession itself continues to be responsive to public needs, the accountant should be able to carry on a practice with a manageable exposure to legal liability.

Accountants do not live in a world apart from their clients. If an accountant who reads this book concludes that the legal system is needlessly questioning the profession, then that accountant should read this book once again.

There are, in fact, problems to be addressed. Some solutions are practice-oriented, and others are personal and ethical, as described above. Others pertain to the profession as a whole, or our legal system as a whole.

Before the profession can move in a new direction, and away from the clutches of an adversarial legal system, professionals must change. But the members of the profession must also ensure that the profession as a whole participates in the process of change.

Toward this end, the following are recommended:

1. **Get involved.** The AICPA is the primary organization of the U.S. accounting profession. Join it and work for change within. Also, join the appropriate state society or association, and become active.

2. **Push for excellence in the profession.** There is a need to upgrade the standards of the profession, including the ethical standards and audit practices. Changes in the way such organizations as the FASB and the SEC operate with respect to standards should also be sought. And the profession needs to look at new ways of providing financial statement users with that information that would be helpful for credit and investment decision-making. Many suggestions for such changes are included in this book. Others will be raised by accounting professionals throughout the U.S. These suggestions should be given serious consideration by the appropriate organizations and rulemaking bodies.

3. **Educate.** Judges, lawyers, and jury members have reflected an ignorance of the work of the accounting profession. Their misconceptions translate into damage award dollars. The profession must do a better job of defining itself to laypersons.

4. **Fight the good fight.** If a client or third party sues an accountant, there is tremendous pressure to settle the case. Sometimes the malpractice insurance carrier is the source of the pressure. Sometimes the pocketbook of the accountant is. In any event, if the accountant has performed to the high standards of the profession (and the individual professional), it is important to establish precedents that will prevent future lawsuits. Find out if there is a possibility that attorneys' fees and court costs can be covered by malpractice insurance, by a professional organization, by a "frivolous lawsuit" ruling in the case at hand, or from some other source. If so, invest in the profession and carry on the litigation.

To the extent that the profession does a better job of convincing the general public of its standards of excellence, efforts at tort reform will be more successful. It is true that tort reform, including limitations on joint and several liability, and the establishment and use of limited liability corporations, will not save the profession.[1] But these legal changes will be an important step in giving the profession "breathing room" to develop and to achieve higher standards of excellence.

The Accountant's Ethics. Finally, ask the question, "How do I resolve ethical dilemmas?" As discussed in Chapters Twelve and Chapter Thirteen, accountants are constantly faced with ethical issues. And the professional accountant must decide whether to resolve ethical issues in favor of:

1. Firefighter Approach: the immediate needs (or demands) of the client at the time.
2. Client/Pragmatic Approach: the long-term benefit to the client.
3. Egoist/Pragmatic Approach: the long-term benefit to the accountant.
4. Utilitarian Approach: the long-term benefit to society.
5. Deontological Approach: enduring principles of right and wrong.
6. Situation Ethics Approach: some combination of the above, depending upon the circumstances.

Sometimes the benefits to one of the above categories necessarily benefits the others. But the decision is often quite difficult.

Who is the Client? The accountant often must consider who the client is. Is it corporate management? Is it the corporate shareholders? Is it a lender, or the general public, or other constituent that might rely on the work product of the accountant for investment or other decision-making?

Sometimes the "client" (or, at least in some jurisdictions, the plaintiff) is a supplier who might furnish resources, or a lender who might provide capital, or even an employee who might contribute human resources.

Many users rely on the accountant's expertise, and in this era of "customer satisfaction" the accountant must become more user driven. The professional accountant must strive to supply various users with the information they need for decision-making.

Quality First. In many cases, becoming user driven requires an increase in the quantity and the quality of corporate financial disclosures. In many cases, it also requires an increase in the amount of verification that auditors perform.

If an auditor wants to decrease exposure to legal liability, for example, he or she must examine what work needs to be completed so that management's representations to users can be verified. An increase in audit quantity and quality, and a corresponding increase in fees, may be required.

A Profession of Excellence. The profession also needs to work for changes in the FASB, the SEC, the AICPA and the legislative and judicial branches of government. In part, these changes should include efforts at reconciling the conflicts between the various parties, and efforts at arriving at a modicum of consistency in the expectations that each party or group holds for the accounting profession.

And the profession must continually strive to upgrade the quality of its work product, and the standards of the profession.

As noted earlier, pushing for tort reform would help: but it is not the complete answer. A profession cannot achieve its highest aspirations if its strength and value are derived from the political arena.

Primarily accountants and auditors must reexamine the foundations of their professions and determine how they can best satisfy user needs. Then they need to determine to whom they are responsible.

Restoring the Foundations. As we have seen, reliance on GAAP and GAAS (and especially, reliance on FASB and AICPA pronouncements) is important, but not necessarily adequate.

The accountant must also look to professional codes of conduct, societal expectations (and codes of conduct), and personal codes of conduct.

And the accountant must determine that the information with which he or she is associated (including financial statements, projections, testimony in court, or other information) is accurate, verifiable, and a fair representation of the facts at hand. The accountant must also consider whether the financial information reflects economic reality and, if not, whether users will be misled to their detriment.

Whether a user has been misled or not is often a fact question decided by a judge or jury. And so the accountant could ask himself or herself, "Would a judge or jury agree that someone could have been misled by this information?" The test is not whether someone with an accountant's background and skills has been misled. The test is whether a user (including a nonaccountant investor or lender) could reasonably have been misled.

The courts have been prodding the accounting profession generally, and individual accountants specifically, to make the determination as to whether the information being presented by management, and verified by auditors, presents the information users need in a language that they can understand. If not, and if investors and other users believe that they have been misled, they are likely to commence litigation.

Though tort reform is probably desirable, a reevaluation of the quantity and quality of disclosure and verification of information with which accountants are associated is probably necessary for both the profession as a whole as well as for each individual accountant. If the reevaluation takes place within a consistent set of ethical and professional principles, the accounting profession has a very bright future.

NOTE

1. Some proposals for limitations have been developed by the Washington D.C.-based American Tort Reform Association; others have been introduced by the Coalition to Eliminate Abusive Securities Suits, a multi-industry coalition supported by the "Big Six" largest accounting. *See* Stewart Yerton, "Federal Help To Fight Off Fraud Suits," *American Lawyer*, October 1992, p. 40 (Inside Moves).

Index